The
Reign of
Botnets

The
Reign of Botnets

Defending Against Abuses, Bots and Fraud on the Internet

David Sénécal

Published by John Wiley & Sons, Inc., Hoboken, New Jersey.
Published simultaneously in Canada and the United Kingdom.

ISBNs: 9781394262410 (Paperback), 9781394262427 (ePDF), 9781394262434 (ePub)

For general information on our other products and services, please contact our Customer Care Department within the United States at (800) 762- 2974, outside the United States at (317) 572- 3993. For product technical support, you can find answers to frequently asked questions or reach us via live chat at https://support.wiley.com.

If you believe you've found a mistake in this book, please bring it to our attention by emailing our reader support team at wileysupport@wiley.com with the subject line "Possible Book Errata Submission."

Wiley also publishes its books in a variety of electronic formats. Some content that appears in print may not be available in electronic formats. For more information about Wiley products, visit our web site at www.wiley.com.

Library of Congress Control Number: 2024936163

Cover image: © CSA-Printstock/Getty Images
Cover design: Wiley

SKY10076001_053124

For Dana, Daphne, Dawson, and, of course, Mr. Dean!

About the Author

David Sénécal grew up in France, lived in Germany and England, and immigrated to the United States in 2005. He lives with his family in the San Francisco Bay Area, California, and works for Akamai Technologies as a principal product architect. He brings 25+ years of experience working with web performance, security, and enterprise networking technologies through various roles (support, integration, consulting, development, product management, architecture, and research). He started working on bot detection concepts for Akamai in 2010, which became the very successful Bot Manager product, consistently recognized as a market leader by Forrester. He helped define the concept of *bot management* in the early 2010s, which combines bot detection, classification, visibility, and response strategy. The competition and the industry later adopted this term. In his current role, David leads a team of researchers, developers, and architects to keep up with the evolution of attacks and define the next generation of bot and fraud detection products.

Follow David on LinkedIn at www.linkedin.com/in/davidsenecal.

About the Technical Editor

Tyson Thomas has been a researcher in application security for eight years, focusing on bot detection algorithms leveraging behavioral biometric, device telemetry, and network data from web and mobile clients. Originally part of Akamai's acquisition of Cyberfend in 2017, he now leads the data science team at Akamai for the Bot Manager Premier security product. Prior to entering cybersecurity, he worked on developing pattern recognition and anomaly detection algorithms for drug discovery, manufacturing, automotive, retail, and military hyperspectral imaging applications. Before entering the private sector, Tyson worked at the NASA Jet Propulsion Laboratory researching neural network and evolvable hardware while completing a PhD in electrical engineering at the University of Southern California. He has a bachelor's degree in physics and economics.

About the Technical Editor

Acknowledgments

It takes a village to raise a child, and this is also true when writing a book. Many talented researchers, data scientists, developers, and business leaders have indirectly contributed to this book while working with me on building the Bot Manager product I have been responsible for the last 10 years. Their input and feedback have been invaluable in shaping the direction of the product and furthering my understanding of the bot and fraud problem.

I want to acknowledge my mentors throughout the years who helped me in my journey as a professional: Patrice Boffa, who allowed me to build the very first prototype of Bot Manager more than 10 years ago; John Dilley, who recruited me as a product architect and trusted me to build Akamai's Bot Manager product; and finally Sreenath Kurupati, who helped me appreciate and understand the world of machine learning and artificial intelligence. I'm grateful for their trust in my instincts, for giving me guidance and support to solve difficult problems, and for allowing me to experiment and develop a fantastic product that protects thousands of websites around the world.

From the research and development team, I'd like to call out in no particular order key people who helped me throughout the years execute and deliver my vision: Spandan Brahmbhatt, Luke Stork, Chunliang Wu, Pujan Motiwala, Yossef Daya, Ory Segal, Nils Rehm, Nikolai Tschacher, Idan Pinto, Michael Bergmann, Harish Somaraddi, Prajaka Bhurke, Tu Vuong, Sai Modalavalasa, and more.

From the product management team, I'd like to acknowledge my partners in crime for many years, Pawan Bajaj and Maik Maurer.

A special thank you to my technical editor, Tyson Thomas, a cybersecurity veteran and lead data scientist who peer-reviewed this work and provided valuable feedback to improve the quality of this book. Finally, a shout-out to a rising artist, my niece Julie Sénécal, who designed the robot illustrations and icons, adding character to the book.

All traffic graphs come from the Akamai Control Center with authorization from Akamai Technologies.

I'll always be grateful to be surrounded by such talented people.

—*David Sénécal*

Contents

Introduction

I've been interested in technology since a very young age with a particular attraction to computers, even if in the late 1980s and 1990s their capabilities were limited compared to what we have today. When I finished high school, the Internet existed but was not widely available. When it came time for me to choose a major for my college application, I looked for something that would allow me to learn and work with this emerging technology. I graduated from the Paul Sabatier University in Toulouse in the South of France in 1998 with a major in electrical engineering with a specialty in computer networking and telecommunications. Armed with this unusual high-tech degree and my knowledge of network protocols and computer programming, I started my career as a network administrator for a major insurance company (Les Mutuelles du Mans Assurances – MMA) in France, overseeing and enhancing the headquarters' network, supporting more than 5,000 users. After a few years, with my solid understanding of networks and telecommunication, I felt I needed an extra challenge. I moved to England to work as a multilingual technical support engineer for Azlan, a company later acquired by Tech Data, specializing in distributing networking equipment. Remotely helping customers configure and install their switches, routers, and firewalls was occasionally challenging. Doing so in French, English, and German and dealing with multiple regional accents made things even more interesting. Not only did I have to learn several products, but I also sometimes helped customers configure them in unexpected ways.

Several years later, I felt like introducing a change in my life again, and I moved to the United States, where I started working for Akamai Technologies. There, I became more familiar with the intricacies of the Internet. My focus was initially on helping companies accelerate their websites. I worked with the top brands on the Internet from various industries, including e-commerce, travel and hospitality, media, social media, healthcare, and banking. It quickly evolved to help secure their websites as well. What became rapidly apparent to me was that most of the traffic on any website came from bots, causing stability issues. The tools available at the time to defend against such activity (mainly web application firewalls) were only partially effective. New tools needed to be developed to deal with the problem more effectively. So, once more, I decided to get out of my comfort zone and started building a product focusing mostly on bot detection. After all, how hard could it be? This started a new phase of my career as a product architect. At the time, I thought I'd work on solving this problem for a couple of years and then move on to the next challenge. I certainly managed to solve the original threat, but I did not anticipate how it would evolve then. More than 10 years later, I am still working on bot management.

Bot management products evolved rapidly and grew in complexity while becoming a must-have product for protecting life online. However, existing knowledge on bot and fraud detection is fragmented, surrounded by many misconceptions fueled by marketing pitches, myths, and sometimes outdated best practices. This makes the subject much more confusing and frustrating for web security professionals and website owners to understand. The lack of understanding of the problem prevents them from dealing with it effectively, ultimately benefiting fraudsters.

While building bot management products, educating security professionals became a big part of my mission. My peers, the sales force, the product support staff, and, more importantly, customers looking to use my products to protect their online business needed to be trained. Good content that goes to the heart of the problem in simple terms is hard to find and mostly nonexistent. So, I thought: maybe I should write a book! Because, after all, how hard could it be? It turns out it's not easy but somewhat easier and less time-consuming than building a bot management product! I persevered and wrote this book to cover the knowledge gap on the threat landscape and defense strategies. I want to unveil the mystery, clear up some misconceptions, clarify best practices, and make bots and fraud detection more accessible. This book focuses on the bot management concepts and applies to any product, whether from a vendor or homegrown.

This book aims to provide a comprehensive overview of the threat landscape and defense strategies. It provides some insight into the evolution of attacks and defense strategies over time, the motivation of attackers, how detection methods work, and how to analyze the traffic to assess accuracy and decide on the most appropriate response strategy. The knowledge acquired from this book will help security teams regain their advantage over attackers.

Who Should Read This Book

The target audience for this book includes web security professionals, website administrators, and anyone interested in or wanting to learn more about web security and, more specifically, bot management and automated fraud detection. No specific prior knowledge or experience is required to understand the content of this book.

Beginners will learn the basics of the Internet and web security while progressively diving deeper into bots, fraud, and abuse detection and mitigation. *Web security practitioners* with intermediate or advanced knowledge will better understand the threat evolution and the methods and best practices to mitigate attacks consistently and successfully. *Executives and decision-makers* reading this book will better appreciate the topic without the common vendor buzzwords or marketing bias, which will help them ask the right questions and make informed buy or build decisions. *Technology managers* (product managers) and *implementers* (security architects, developers, solution architects) will better understand the context of the bot problem and the best practices to integrate and use bot management technology to drive the most optimal outcome. *Data scientists, data analysts, and security operation support staff* monitoring and evaluating the activity detected will be able to interpret the data with a full understanding of the problem and help make data- and context-driven decisions to support the needs of their organization. *Students* in the field of computer science who are attracted to the cybersecurity space will gain a general understanding of the most critical security issues that affect online businesses today.

Any online business that generates significant revenue is at risk of fraudsters attacking their website using botnets to steal information, take over their users' identity, and make off with any assets included in the accounts. E-commerce sites (Amazon, Nike, Macy's), social media and dating sites (Facebook, LinkedIn, Match.com), fintech/banking sites (Bank of America, U.S. Bank, Wells Fargo), digital media (Netflix, Hulu, NBC), and gaming websites (Roblox, Electronic Arts, Epic Games) are all targets of bot and fraud attacks abusing the resources available on the website.

1 | A Short History of the Internet

Our journey begins with a description of the evolution of the Internet and the emergence of a new type of fraud and abuse that leverages botnets.

From ARPANET to the Metaverse

The Internet is so ingrained in our day-to-day life that it seems as though it's always been around. However, the Internet is a relatively new invention—and it keeps evolving. The precursor of the Internet, called the Advanced Research Projects Agency Network (ARPANET), was invented in the 1960s, in the middle of the Cold War, to ensure continuity of availability of the network and computing resources even after a portion of it is removed or destroyed. Government researchers could also share information quickly without requiring them to travel to another location. ARPANET was a closed system using proprietary protocols, and only explicitly authorized people could access it. The idea of a network where one could share information and computing resources sparked the interest of academics, and the need for standardized communication protocols arose. Various communication protocols, including Transmission Control Protocol/Internet Protocol (TCP/IP), Hypertext Transfer Protocol (HTTP), and Domain Name System (DNS), were developed in the 1980s, marking the birth of the Internet as we know it today. TCP/IP defines how information is exchanged between two machines on the Internet. DNS, the equivalent of the phone book, transforms a hostname into the IP address where the service can be found. HTTP defines how web content is to be requested and shared between the browser running on the client and the web server. These protocols enable communication between systems from different vendors and connect them. Secure Sockets Layer (SSL) and, later, the Transport Layer Security (TLS) protocols add a layer of security and safety to the HTTP protocol. Newer languages like HyperText Markup Language (HTML) and JavaScript were invented to help develop websites and make content available in a structured and dynamic way.

Initially, the Internet was reserved for the technical elite who knew the protocols, had the right equipment, understood how to connect to the network, and knew how to query it to retrieve information. The development of web browser software in the 1990s, like Netscape and Internet Explorer, compatible with all of the aforementioned protocols and languages, made the Internet accessible to all. Web search engines such as AltaVista, Yahoo! Search, and Google Search also made it easier to query and find information online. When I was a college student in the 1990s, the Internet was in its infancy. All you could do was visit various websites to find information. Most news outlets would have a website with the latest sports results or events of the world. Major retailers started to create websites to showcase their products, and airlines advertised their flights. But e-commerce wasn't quite a thing just yet, and we still had to go to a brick-and-mortar shop to buy products or to a travel agency to book a flight.

Rapid technological advancement, including faster modems and expansion of the network infrastructure, supported the growth of the Internet. As the Internet grew more popular, investors started pouring money into a multitude of Internet companies with the hope of turning a profit one day. These companies' valuations, which were purely based on speculative future earnings and profits, surged in the late 1990s with record-breaking initial public offerings (IPOs) that saw their stock triple within a day. These events fueled an irrational investment strategy from venture capital firms to companies that sometimes did not have a strong business plan or viable products for fear of missing out. In March 2000, large stock sell orders from leading high-tech companies like Cisco or Dell caused a panic sale and marked the beginning of the decline of the "Internet bubble." Investors became more rational, and capital became harder to find for startups that were not profitable. Many of these cash-strapped startups disappeared rapidly. Companies that reorganized and refocused their effort on developing valuable services and products survived, and some, like Akamai Technologies, Google, Amazon, and Apple, became very successful and key players in the development of the Internet.

When the bubble burst, it felt like a setback, but eventually, the Internet not only survived but started to thrive. As the quality of the Internet network improved, so did the content. The classic dial-up modem connection that had a maximum speed of 56Kbps was soon replaced by a more advanced and reliable network and telecom infrastructure. Integrated Services Digital Network (ISDN) offered speeds of up to 128Kbps, more than double what a dial-up modem could achieve. At the turn of the century, digital subscriber lines (DSLs), which offered high-speed Internet, became more widely available through conventional telephone networks, cable, and fiber optics. Today, Internet service providers offer connections as fast as 10Gbps, which is 178,571 times faster than the fastest dial-up modem. Advancements in mobile telecommunication and the emergence of smartphones meant that consumers could access the Internet from anywhere at any time for the first time. Mobile network expansion also helped expand the reach of the Internet to rural areas. Today, one can even browse the Internet while on a plane or cruising on the ocean, thanks to satellite networks.

As more and more people were drawn to the Internet, the distribution of rich content became a real issue. The networks that carried the Internet traffic did not always have the adequate capacity to handle the demand. Telecom operators would do their best to route the traffic, but frequent congestion and often long distances between the client and the server led to slow page load or stream buffering for Internet users, especially during popular events. Content Delivery Network (CDN) companies like Akamai Technologies, Fastly, and Cloudflare, to name a few, became the backbone of the Internet. CDNs helped fix the problem by avoiding transporting the content long distances and bringing it closer to the user. CDNs helped make the Internet faster and more reliable. I've worked on and off for the biggest CDN company in the world, Akamai Technologies, since 2006 and saw the Internet evolve from a front-row seat.

Let's look at different types of websites and services that became available on the Internet and how they managed to turn their online presence into a revenue stream.

Social Media   The first decade of the 21st century saw the emergence of social networks with Myspace, Hi5, Friendster, Tagged, Bebo, Pinterest, Instagram, Facebook, Twitter (now X), Google+, YouTube, and LinkedIn. Storing and delivering user-generated content (photos, videos, articles) to someone's restricted circle was challenging and costly. CDN providers like Akamai had to adapt to the new trend and develop a multi-tier caching strategy to store and deliver content efficiently. Many of the early social media companies did not survive, mainly because they could not figure out how to monetize their content. Facebook, Instagram, X, YouTube, and LinkedIn fared the best and remain the biggest social networks in America and Europe. But these established platforms are getting some competitive pressure from new entrants like TikTok, favored by younger crowds. The primary source of revenue for social media companies comes from online advertisements or premium membership.

Dating Websites   Dating sites such as Match, eharmony, and Tinder piggybacked on the social networking model. The business model and monetization aspects were much more straightforward for them. Instead of flooding their users with ads, they would charge a monthly subscription fee to give them access to millions of profiles and connect them with compatible people who share their interests.

Media Websites   Websites belonging to the largest broadcasters, like NBC, first published news articles or content about shows on their site. Then, progressively, they started streaming their programs online or making them available on demand. It took broadcasters a while to find a way to monetize the Internet, but, in the end, the solution to monetize free content consisted of building technology to interrupt playback or a live stream with commercials. Later, media sites also introduced online subscriptions or pay-per-view for premium content. What was challenging initially for broadcasters was the need to support multiple proprietary formats such as QuickTime from Apple, Windows Media, and Adobe Flash. It was also a significant headache for CDN companies, as they had to maintain several networks to support all these formats. Standardization of protocols like HTTP Live Streaming (HLS) or WebRTC normalized the streaming methods. What made things even more challenging was that the screens that users used to watch the content became bigger and bigger with the introduction of smart TVs. Media websites wanted to offer the same quality of picture whether the user watched through traditional cable or satellite services or online. The image quality also had to be the same whether the user watched from a phone connected to a mobile network, a tablet connected to a medium-speed residential Internet service provider (ISP), or a large-screen TV connected to a high-speed Internet connection. This required CDN companies to support different bitrates and ever-increasing standards, starting with standard resolution, followed by High Definition (HD), Ultraviolet, 4K, and Over-the-Top (OTT).

Retailers   The Internet allowed retailers to have a point of sale open 24/7. The consumer could browse products and shop from the comfort of their home any time of the day or night, and the product would be delivered a few days later. It required retailers to open new procurement centers to fulfill the orders, but this proved a very lucrative business, generating millions of dollars daily. It took a few more years for grocery stores to offer an online shopping experience with a delivery service since dealing with fresh produce is more complex. E-commerce transformed how retailers interacted with customers and opened new opportunities to expand their brand outside their traditional audience or borders. I've seen many well-known brands offer international shipping over time, turning their website into a global store overnight.

Gaming   In the early days of the Internet, the gaming industry used the Web to advertise its products, which were available only as physical media to run on a personal computer or game console. In the past, if someone wanted to play video games with their friends, they first needed a game that supported multiplayer capability and a game console and they needed to go to their friend's house. Little by little, consoles could connect to the Internet. New games were developed to support playing online with other people. At the same time, gaming applications for mobile devices that offered an online experience by default emerged. An avatar represents each player, and a player can even buy digital content to outfit their avatar and interact with others who may live on the other side of the planet. While before the main revenue stream for video game studios was only selling the game, online gaming opened up new opportunities to sell additional packages or extensions to enhance the playing experience. For the increasing number of free games available on the Apple App Store or Google Play, the in-game purchase option that generally opens a more exciting or interactive experience becomes the only source of revenue for the publisher.

Banks and Financial Institutions   Banks and financial institutions adopted the Web and offered online services in the mid-1990s. However, because the industry is more regulated and due to the nature of their business, this led to a more conservative attitude toward adopting CDN technologies to accelerate and secure the user's transaction. Their main hesitation was allowing the CDN service to handle their certificates. The reluctance was understandable, considering the risk associated with the transactions and content they were dealing with. They needed to ensure their user identity and life savings would stay safe and secure.

Healthcare Providers   Like the banking industry, healthcare providers were conservative in adopting the Web to ensure they could stay compliant with regulations such as the Health Insurance Portability and Accountability Act (HIPAA) and not inadvertently leak their patients' medical records.

Looking back over the last 20 years, the Internet has changed everything: it has altered the way we shop, bank, interact with our healthcare providers, interact with each other, book our vacations, explore the world, and even work! In the past, someone starting a new business was required to open a physical location. It was only possible to sell products with points of sale at various strategic locations that consumers visited. Now, one can quickly open an online shop and make their product available worldwide. A company doesn't even need to have physical offices anymore. With collaboration tools like Zoom, Webex, Teams, and Skype, meeting virtually from anywhere and running a business is easier. This has been a lifesaver and allowed businesses to survive during the COVID-19 pandemic. The rare few companies that did not have a solid online strategy struggled or disappeared.

Now that the Internet is very well established, we have started to hear about the Metaverse. But what is the Metaverse? The Metaverse is a vision of what the Internet and the online experience may become in the future. But not everyone has the same idea of what that looks like. Some say virtual reality (VR) or augmented reality (AR) technology is key to the Metaverse. The experience will be similar to playing games through an Oculus device. The Metaverse may include some existing components, such as cryptocurrency, that would represent the main means of buying goods or services. But what would those goods be? Are we talking about real products that will be delivered to our doorstep or a virtual shirt and hat to dress an avatar? Maybe all of the above? What about people? Will we interact with real people or AI entities trained to converse on various topics? During the pandemic, I participated as a speaker and attendee in virtual trade shows and security conferences where one could attend pre-recorded or live presentations and ask questions to the presenter through a chat application. One could also visit virtual booths on the virtual show floor to discuss with a sales representative about products solving various security problems. The experience was a mix of video games, social media, video streaming, Zoom meetings, and a good dose of awkwardness. One could navigate the various areas of the conference and join group activities, presentations, and chatrooms to meet other professionals and discuss topics or even join a virtual happy hour to sip wine sent by mail by the event sponsor. The experience was so different from an in-person conference that it fits what the Metaverse means to me. Now, one could argue that none of this is it since all I described already exists. It's always difficult to envision the technology of the future, as we can only imagine it based on what we know is possible today. What the Metaverse will be also depends on what technology or experience users will be the most comfortable with and adopt. Further technological advancement in computing will also be required to support the complex and rich interactions. If we look at how our parents' generation envisioned the future 30 years ago, they got a few things right but also many things wrong. For example, I remember seeing a documentary about the house of the future when I was a kid, and it featured a device that looked like a tablet where one could read the news. That part became a reality with tablets and smartphones, which is how most people consume news today. That same documentary also described something like virtual reality. However, they made it sound like holograms would be common by now, and no one ever talked about wearing those bulky goggles. What things did they get wrong? Well, nothing to do with the Internet, but where's my hoverboard, and what about flying cars? It's probably a good thing they got those concepts wrong!

The Different Layers of the Web

The Web is not uniform, and not all content is readily visible and accessible by all. Figure 1.1 presents the different layers of the Web as an iceberg.

The visible and easy-to-access part is known as the *surface web*. Its content is discovered, indexed, and found through web search engines. It comprises all e-commerce, travel, news, social media, gaming websites, and more. The content can be accessed freely. This part of the Web represents only about 4% of the Web.

Next comes the *deep web*. Access to the content and resources is generally restricted behind authentication mechanisms and may contain private information. Most industries are represented in this part of the Web. For example, in the case of e-commerce, the deep web corresponds to the user's purchase history, shopping reward, or tailored services. For social media, it consists of posts and pictures that users publish and share only with their network. This corresponds to an account holder's bank statement in banking or a patient's medical records for healthcare. The deep web represents about 90% of the Web and is legitimate. Access to the

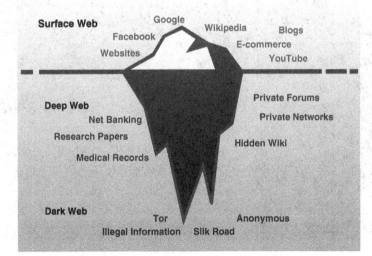

Figure 1.1 The different layers of the Web

content of resources is restricted to the population subscribing to specific services, and web search engines cannot discover and index the content.

Finally comes the mysterious *dark web*, often associated with criminal and illegal activity. This is true but somewhat of a misconception since the dark web was initially designed to provide Internet users with anonymity. For example, the infamous The Onion Router (TOR) network was initially invented to protect American intelligence online communication. The code was released in 2004 under a free license and later launched as a free service to all Internet users who wanted to browse without being tracked. Anonymity is, of course, what criminals and hackers look for so that they can carry out their schemes without being disturbed or traced. The dark web is where one can find marketplaces to acquire stolen data from various security breaches, accounts harvested through credential stuffing attacks, or stolen credit cards. You'll also find forums for hackers who exchange methods and best practices to carry out various fraud schemes without being detected or caught. The dark web accounts for about 6% of the Internet. Sellers offer multiple categories of products or services on the dark web. Figure 1.2 shows the now-defunct AlphaBay marketplace that once offered various categories of products, including fraud, hacking and spam, malware, drugs, and illegal chemicals. The FBI announced the takedown of AlphaBay in 2017.

Figure 1.2   The AlphaBay marketplace on the dark web

The Emergence of New Types of Abuses

When companies develop a website, they usually focus on specific use cases. For example, suppose a retailer makes its inventory available online. In that case, its focus is on showcasing its products, giving its users the best possible experience, and making the shopping experience as easy as possible to increase its revenue. Security is not part of their core business, and they would not necessarily think about how someone with not-so-good intentions could exploit their site to defraud them and their users. The expansion of commerce on the Internet provided many opportunities for new abuses. In retrospect, it's easy to criticize past design choices made by software companies or website developers when new vulnerabilities that seem evident and outrageous today are found, especially when one realizes that the vulnerability existed for years. However, as a longtime product and software designer, I can attest to the difficulty of anticipating how a feature or workflow could be misused and exploited to commit fraud or abuse a resource. Some hackers specialize in developing viruses that exploit vulnerabilities in the operating system or browser running on the user's machine. Computer viruses have been omnipresent for years, and the ever-increasing ease of exchanging information through a growing number of communication channels has made their spread easier. Viruses can serve multiple purposes, including spying on the user's activity and collecting information like credentials or credit card numbers by logging key presses, stealing or encrypting the content of a disk (ransomware), or serving as a relay in a botnet. Antivirus is part of the enterprise security strategy and is beyond the scope of this book. Other hackers choose to exploit public website's resources and application programming interfaces (APIs) to collect information and defraud users. Protecting against such attacks is within the realm of application security, which we'll discuss further in the following chapters.

As product architects and developers, we follow certain design principles to achieve a specific goal, and overall, we want to keep things as simple as possible to make a product as easy as possible to use and maintain. Thankfully, the software development community has learned about common exploits and past mistakes over time. Most developers also go through yearly secure coding training. Security awareness has improved along with coding practices, but all this knowledge is relatively new and did not exist when the first e-commerce sites started to appear.

How attacks were classified changed over time based on the improved collective understanding of the attacker's motivations. The 2000s saw the rise of what is now known as *application-layer attacks*. SQL injection, cross-site scripting (XSS), command injection, and cross-site request forgery (CSRF) are commonly used to exploit vulnerabilities on a site to steal information or money or sometimes deface a website. The Open Worldwide Application Security Project (OWASP), MITRE's Common Vulnerabilities and Exposures (CVE) Program, and other organizations have been vital in spreading awareness of new vulnerabilities, providing guidance on how to solve them, and encouraging better coding practices. The development of open-source web application firewalls (WAFs) such as ModSecurity or equivalent commercial offerings has also been vital in proactively preventing such exploits even when vulnerabilities exist on the site.

By the early 2010s, there was much talk about denial-of-service (DoS) attacks—or their distributed denial-of-service (DDoS) variant. DoS/DDoS attacks come in two primary flavors. First, there are activist attacks, like the infamous Anonymous group that targeted companies or organizations because of their position on specific issues. I'm not going to debate whether Anonymous' motivations were right or wrong, but they were undoubtedly disruptive when they managed to rally a large crowd to their cause. Those with experience dealing with them probably remember the infamous Low Orbit Ion Cannon (LOIC) or the High Orbit Ion Cannon (HOIC) DoS tools, both point-and-shoot attack tools that offered various options. Sites that were not well protected would soon get overwhelmed by the load and essentially be taken offline, which sometimes led to me having to do an emergency integration of the web security product from the company I was working for at the time to protect a site. It often happened on a Friday evening. (Come on, guys, have some compassion for the hard-working web security community here!) A well-executed DDoS attack against a retailer on a critical day like Black Friday can lead to millions of dollars in losses. When these attacks became more common, web security companies extended their WAF, offering DoS/DDoS protection. This mainly consisted of rate-limiting features, IP reputation, and a set of rules designed to detect known attack tool signatures like LOIC or HOIC, most of the time also coupled with a dedicated security analyst who could craft new rules to deal with more recent attack signatures or so-called zero-day attacks.

Beyond the activist attacks, a lot of what is perceived as a DDoS is, sometimes, overzealous botnet traffic scraping a site to collect product descriptions, pricing, and inventory, running a credential stuffing attack to test if a username/password combination is valid, or other types of attacks we'll discuss in detail in Chapter 2, "The Most Common Attacks Using Botnets." In the early 2010s, no one talked much about bot attacks. But I saw firsthand that a lot of the traffic causing site availability issues was poorly calibrated bot activity. Now, you must remember that in the case of content scraping or a credential stuffing attack, an attacker who takes the site offline is making their attack less effective since it will increase the time it takes to complete the task and, ultimately, their cost. So, a denial of service caused by a botnet is an unintended consequence since their intent is not to take the site down but rather exploit it. Botnet operators quickly learned how to work around the DDoS detection in place, making them ineffective.

At first glance, excessive activity on the login API, for example, can prevent real users from logging in and purchasing products. This can be perceived as a DDoS attack from an activist group wanting to impact the revenue of the targeted company. When looking closer into the

In contrast, Figure 1.5 shows the traffic distribution for a retailer selling auto parts online with a mild bot problem. In this case, just over 15% of the traffic comes from bots, two-thirds of which comes from good bots.

Figure 1.6 shows another example from a home improvement company catering to the U.S. market, where the distribution between scraper, human, and good bots is more evenly distributed. Yet, the overall bot activity accounts for 60% of the total traffic to the product pages.

Looking at all the sampled websites, the average bot-to-human traffic ratio is about 70/30 (see Figure 1.7). The sample used for the study is not large enough to conclude that 70% of the Internet is bot traffic, but we can safely conclude that the great majority of the traffic on the Internet originates from bots.

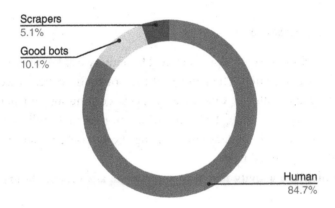

Figure 1.5 Traffic distribution for an auto part retailer in the United States

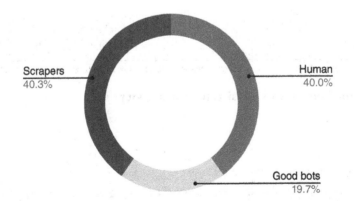

Figure 1.6 Traffic distribution for a home improvement company in the United States

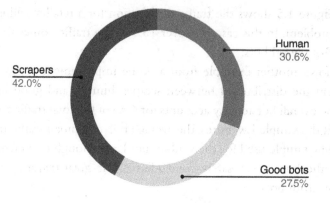
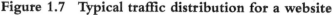

Figure 1.7   Typical traffic distribution for a website

Botnets Are Unpredictable

Botnet activity on a website is very unpredictable. The activity can be intense for a few days and disappear as quickly as it appeared. The pattern of the bot traffic varies as well. Here are a few examples of botnet traffic patterns. One often expects continuous and persistent activity, as shown in Figure 1.8. In this example, the botnet made more than 4 million daily requests using various randomization methods, such as randomizing the User-Agent and HTTP headers and leveraging 100,000 unique IP addresses.

With some botnets, the activity may stop and resume after several hours or days, as shown in Figure 1.9.

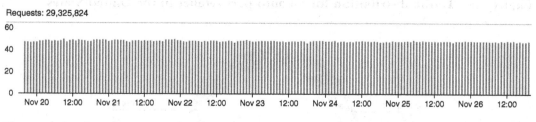
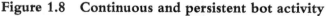

Figure 1.8   Continuous and persistent bot activity

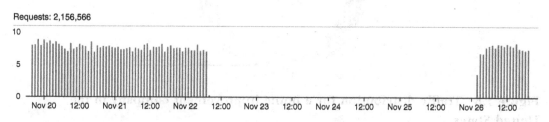

Figure 1.9   Persistent bot with long periods of inactivity

But sometimes, the activity is more punctual, as shown in Figure 1.10. The activity may start and stop at specific times, and the same content may be consistently requested daily from the same set of IP addresses.

One-off activities, as shown in Figure 1.11, may also occur where the botnet will get the information it's looking for, never to return.

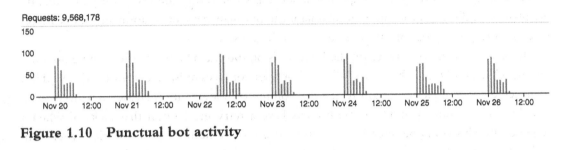

Figure 1.10   Punctual bot activity

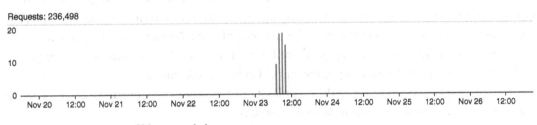

Figure 1.11   One-off bot activity

How botnets behave depends on the needs of the entity or operator that controls them. The quality of the detection and mitigation strategy plays a significant role in the botnet behavior. Mitigating the activity (for example, deny) will force the bot operator to take action. I remember one of my first fights against a botnet back in the days when the tool of choice for such occasions was a simple WAF. After analyzing the traffic, I found that the bot traffic was coming from a very specific network that belonged to a cloud provider. I could also confirm that no legitimate traffic was coming from that same network. Content with that finding, I updated the WAF policy to block the traffic coming from that network. Happy to have come up with a quick solution, I confirmed that the activity was getting blocked once the new policy was deployed. A few minutes later, the bot activity that I had identified with my detection seemed to stop. As part of the resolution, I expected the overall traffic volume to drop. Strangely, though, it remained the same.

After some more digging, I found that the bot traffic had "migrated" to a different cloud provider and had resumed after a short interruption. It took a few more iterations to come up with a more clever signature to block it once and for all. With a strong detection strategy that includes multiple detection methods looking at the traffic from different angles, bot operators have far fewer opportunities to evade detection. They ultimately stop their activity and go after an easier target whenever possible. Seeing the bot activity disappear doesn't mean it is gone forever, though. Motivated and skilled bot operators will try various methods to defeat the detection to get access to the content they are after. It's common to see small bursts of activity that sometimes last only a few seconds. This is usually the sign of bot operators trying a new attack strategy and cutting their experiment short as soon as they are still getting blocked. It's essential, even during "peacetime," to maintain the bot management solution and adopt newer detections to prevent opportunistic returns from botnets.

It's hard to say if bot activity on the Internet is on the rise. The bot traffic volume does not represent the number of adversaries. When a bot operator faces resistance from an advanced bot management system, it's common to see the volume of bot activity increase, sometimes even doubling. The reason is simple: some botnets have a retry mechanism that kicks in when a request fails. This could be interpreted as an increase in the number of adversaries, whereas in reality, this is still the same botnet that is retrying some failing requests. Looking at the volume of bot requests matters since excessive activity can overwhelm a website and take it offline, but what matters the most is understanding the number of botnet-sending requests. Each botnet corresponds to an adversary. Having good visibility on the number of botnets attacking a site will provide a better understanding of the threat landscape affecting it.

In later chapters, you'll discover the complexity of bot attacks and how to build an effective bot management solution to defeat them consistently.

Bot Activity and Law Enforcement

Vendors selling bot management solutions often use terms like *criminals* or *criminal organizations* when talking about the adversary (the bot operator). Bot activity other than that coming from good bots is a nuisance and violates most websites' acceptable use policies. Undoubtedly, the adversary has strong intentions for some types of attacks and aims to defraud or take advantage of others for their benefit. This is the case, for example, for account takeover and carding attacks, which I'll discuss in more detail in Chapter 2. That something is considered criminal, however, assumes that laws are in place to deal with these situations. Unfortunately, few legal regulations exist regarding the usage of bots on the Internet.

The Better Online Ticket Sales Act, also known as the BOTS Act, was introduced into law in the United States in 2016. This act prohibits individual organizations from buying tickets using bot technology and reselling them at a profit. This activity, known as *ticket scalping*, has plagued ticketing companies like Ticketmaster and ultimately artificially inflated the price of concert tickets for legitimate users. The fine for a convicted bot operator is $16,000. This law is a step in the right direction. It was enforced in 2021 against Just In Time Tickets, Inc. and

Concert Specials, Inc. which were found guilty of purchasing tickets from Ticketmaster using a botnet and reselling them on their website at a premium. But this law seems to do little to discourage thousands of scalpers from buying and reselling tickets online, as seen regularly when tickets for famous pop stars go on sale. It is extremely difficult for legitimate fans to purchase tickets due to the excessive usage of botnets that grab up the inventory as soon as they are released. This situation led to a controversy in November 2022 when tickets for Taylor Swift's Eras Tour went on sale on Ticketmaster. The demand was such that the website struggled to keep up, but it also appeared that scalpers purchased many tickets.

Enforcing the BOTS Act—or any regulation around bot activity on the Internet—is difficult. Although the bot activity can be detected, bot operators are masters at hiding their tracks, making it challenging to attribute the activity to any particular person or entity for prosecution. Additionally, the bot activity may come from different countries (or even U.S. states) with different regulations from those where the site is hosted. This leads to difficulties enforcing acceptable use policies or determining what legal regulation applies.

Law enforcement is not powerless and scores some victories by taking down botnets regularly. However, as will be discussed in Chapter 3, "The Evolution of Botnet Attacks," bot operators are nimble. Shutting down a botnet doesn't always translate to a permanent operation shutdown. A botnet is just code that is waiting to be deployed on servers. The logistics involved in reactivating the botnet are relatively trivial. Thousands of companies offer cloud services from which a bot operator can choose. Most of these providers do their due diligence to prevent botnets from running from their servers since it could tarnish their reputation. When they find bot activity originating from their servers, they may shut down the activity and close the associated account. However, a provider with a self-service offering may apply less scrutiny to vet their customers or the services they are running from their servers. Considering this, companies with a major presence on the Internet must arm themselves with bot and fraud detection products to defend their website, prevent abuses of their resources and intellectual properties, and protect their users.

Summary

This chapter provided a brief history of the Internet, described the bot problem, and identified the main types of attacks that use them. It also looked at how prevalent bot activity is on the Internet and its typical behavior. There is little to no law at this time that can help website owners fight the initiator. But even if there were, attributing the activity to a particular person, group, or entity is always challenging. Now that you have a high-level understanding of bot attacks, the next chapter dissects how the various attacks work.

2 | The Most Common Attacks Using Botnets

This chapter takes a deep dive into the most common attacks leveraging bots against websites, how they are carried out, and their role in broader fraud schemes that lead to revenue generation. You'll learn about account takeover, scraping, scalping, account opening abuse, inventory hoarding, and more.

Account Takeover

Account takeover attacks (ATOs) emerged around 2008 and have become increasingly prevalent ever since. Despite some efforts to introduce alternate password-less authentication methods such as biometrics (fingerprints) or one-time tokens sent over SMS or email, the good old username and password combination is still the primary method today to identify and authenticate users on the Internet. Account takeover is such a problem that it ranked seventh in the 2021 OWASP top 10 security vulnerability as "Identification and authentication failure" (OWASP, 2021). Over the years, our understanding of the attack has evolved. This section describes it in detail and exposes some nuances based on the targeted site's industry. As shown in Figure 2.1, a successful ATO generally consists of three steps.

Data harvesting The data may consist of credentials, a set of usernames and passwords, and personal data such as home addresses, phone numbers, government ID numbers, etc. To get the data, attackers use a combination of application layer attacks like local file inclusion (LFI), SQL injection (SQLI), or command injection (CMDI). They may also attempt to get the data by exploiting known software vulnerabilities on the web server, misconfiguration, or other security flaws. The data may be directly exploited by the same fraudster and/or sold on the dark web. When sold on the dark web, the data may be repackaged for specific purposes. For example, a username and password combo list will attract fraudsters specializing in credential stuffing, whereas other personal data like home addresses and phone numbers would attract fraudsters looking to craft more targeted attacks.

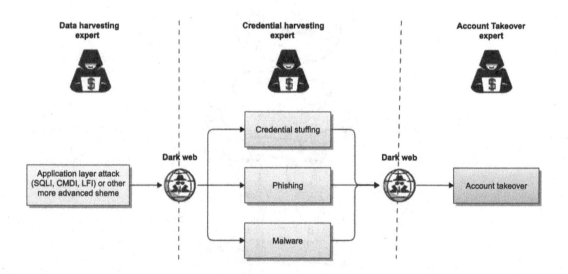

Figure 2.1   The three steps of account takeover

Credential Harvesting   One way to harvest valid accounts for a given website is by replaying combo lists against the login API. This step of the attack is known as *credential stuffing*. Fraudsters take advantage of users who commonly reuse the same credentials on multiple websites. Another way to harvest accounts is by crafting a phishing campaign by sending personalized messages and enticing users to visit a fake site. Attackers may also craft viruses or malware designed to log keystrokes when the user interacts with a login page. These techniques aim to get the same results and get a list of valid credentials on a given website. The list may be directly exploited by the same fraudster or, more likely, put up for sale on the dark web.

Account Takeover   A fraudster will acquire the harvested list of accounts from the previous step and exploit it to carry out various forms of fraud depending on the services provided by the targeted website and the assets available in the compromised accounts.

An ATO involves multiple actors, each with a specialty and role in this ecosystem. The following sections describe the various steps of account takeover attacks, the economics surrounding them, and the nuance of the attacks in different industries.

Data Harvesting

Data harvesting represents the raw material used in any ATO attacks. Even if the data doesn't come from the company the fraudster is targeting, it can still be exploited to derive useful information. Let's take a look at published data breaches and the methods used.

Vulnerability Exploit   We often hear about large data breaches exploiting a company's web or network security vulnerabilities. Attackers leverage penetration testing (pen-testing) methods to learn about the system and software in place. Pen-testing is an art that consists of testing a site for vulnerability and working around complex defenses. This term typically refers to security consultants tasked to look for vulnerabilities in an infrastructure. Pen-testers are considered *white hat* hackers; they try to discover and exploit vulnerabilities without ill intent. When such activity is performed with ill intent, they are called *black hat* hackers. By sending malformed requests, the targeted web system may leak information about the software it's running and its version. With this information, the attacker can look for known vulnerabilities in the software version and build an attack that exploits them. Also, through trial and error and overall knowledge of how web application firewalls (WAFs) work, the attacker can look for weaknesses in the defense. For example, website owners may have a WAF configured to protect their website against SQLI, CMDI, and LFI. But sometimes, the firewall is configured only to monitor potentially malicious activity without proactively mitigating it.

New vulnerabilities are revealed weekly, and website owners don't always patch their systems immediately. Even vulnerabilities that have been known for years are not always taken care of.

Attackers will exploit the security team's lack of resources or discipline and exploit such weaknesses to carry out their attacks. Smaller companies are potentially easier targets for attackers as the site owner may not have the means or knowledge to secure their network correctly. However, breaches from large companies make the news front pages and fuel the so-called combo lists that are available on the dark web. Here are a few examples of significant data breaches of high-profile companies:

- In December 2009, *TechCrunch* reported that RockYou.com, a company that developed applications for social media sites, was the victim of a credential leak consisting of 32 million usernames and passwords that were stored unencrypted (Cubrilovic, 2009). The attacker reportedly extracted the information through a trivial SQL injection attack.
- In April 2011, *The Guardian* reported that the PlayStation Network, a major gaming and entertainment platform, announced that up to 77 million user accounts were compromised (The Guardian, 2011).
- In October 2013, the *BBC* reported that Adobe, a software company, revealed that 38 million user records, including usernames and encrypted passwords, were stolen (BBC, 2013). After Adobe found out about the breach, it updated all user settings to force users to reset their passwords.
- In October 2017, the *New York Times* reported that in 2013, Yahoo!, a major Internet portal, lost 3 billion accounts in an attack (Perlroth, 2017). This represents all the accounts ever created on the platform. The breach included usernames and encrypted passwords and was reported years after it happened. The encryption scheme used for the password was reportedly outdated compared to today's standards and easy to crack.
- In March 2018, the *Washington Post* reported that Under Armour, an apparel company, suffered a data breach of more than 150 million MyFitnessPal accounts (Shaban, 2018). The breach included usernames, email addresses, and hash passwords. Following the discovery of the incident, users were forced to reset their passwords.
- In December 2018, *CBS News* reported that Quora, a social media platform, was affected by a data breach that impacted 100 million users (Reals and Picchi, 2018).
- In July 2019, *CNN Business* reported that Capital One, a major bank, suffered a breach that affected 100 million accounts and credit card applications (McLean, 2019). The hacker was identified as a former Amazon employee and was arrested. She exploited a common application layer attack and took advantage of a misconfigured web application firewall protecting the site.
- In September 2019, *Norton*, a security company famous for its antivirus and anti-malware software, revealed the compromise of 172 million accounts on the gaming platform Zynga (Norton, 2019). The stolen data included usernames, email addresses, and hash and salted passwords.

- In April 2020, *Forbes* revealed that Zoom, a major online collaboration and video conferencing platform that helped the corporate world continue to function during the pandemic, had 500 million of its user credentials for sale on the dark web (Winder, 2020).
- In July 2020, *Dark Reading* revealed that 130 accounts of prominent U.S. politicians, celebrities, and high-profile personalities were stolen from a major social media network (Vijayan, 2020). The number in this case is not impressive, but considering the people it affected, the effect could be significant if the stolen data is exploited.

The list goes on and on, and new announcements are made regularly. Based on the preceding events, the total number of accounts breached is more than 4.1 billion. It fuels the combo and personal data lists found on various marketplaces on the dark web or some hacker forums on the surface web. These lists are continuously used to carry out credential stuffing, phishing, and malware attacks against multiple websites on the Internet.

If you want to know if your account has been compromised by one of those breaches, check out Troy Hunt's site (Figure 2.2), Have I Been Pwned. In March 2024, the site reported nearly 13 billion breached accounts from more than 600 websites. I recently verified that two

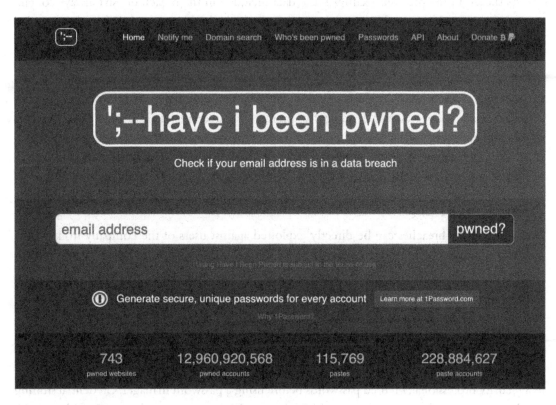

Figure 2.2 The haveibeenpwned.com portal

of my email addresses had been part of multiple breaches. One of them was used in an attempt against me in an extortion fraud scheme.

What Happens to the Harvested Data   Beyond street credentials, bragging rights, and the thrill of completing an attack, attackers generally seek ways to monetize the data. Large-scale attacks may be discovered and disclosed by the victim only days or months after they happen. In the case of the Yahoo! breach, it took years. During that time, the data may be sold to a limited number of attackers at a high price. Once the data leak becomes public knowledge, more attackers may want to acquire the list and try it against multiple targets. At the same time, the compromised site owner may proactively lock the impacted accounts and force users to update their password the next time they log in. Users may update their password on the compromised site, but most don't have the discipline to do the same on all the sites where they use the same credentials. Therefore, long after the data breach has been made public, attackers may still purchase the original list to carry out their credential stuffing or phishing attacks against various targets, resulting in hundreds of copies of the original list being sold over several months, translating to significant revenue for the attacker.

As shown in the previous examples, the data included in the breach doesn't always contain clear-text passwords. Most of the time, the password is hashed, salted, or both. When the password list is only hashed, hackers may be able to "guess" the clear-text password using a rainbow table attack. A rainbow table is a precomputed table for caching the output of a cryptographic hash function. By comparing the hash password in the stolen database to the rainbow table, hackers can derive clear-text values. Adding a random salt when hashing the clear-text value helps protect against a rainbow table attack and better protects the credential database in case of a breach. Even if the passwords are almost impossible to decrypt when salted, it still represents a major incident since usernames and maybe other personal data are still exposed and can significantly tarnish the company's reputation as a victim of the breach or be used against the site's users.

Credential Harvesting

Data from major breaches can be directly exploited against users of the company from which the data was harvested. However, the data can also be further exploited against any website through other intermediate attack methods. Let's look at how these attacks work, the tools available, and the potential financial gain for the attacker.

Credential Stuffing   The credentials from the previously discussed data leaks have high value for attackers specializing in credential stuffing. More than half of Internet users admit to using the same username and password combination everywhere, making it easier to remember. Even as a security professional, I reused passwords before using a password manager. Credential stuffing involves replaying a large set of credentials against multiple targeted websites. Considering the password reuse problem, I wanted to simulate the chances of an attacker finding a valid account when replaying the list based on the industry and the quality of the combo list used. It is challenging to get accurate data on the success rate of credential-stuffing attacks. Therefore, the assumptions taken in this simulation and compiled in the following table are based on anecdotal observations. Yet, I believe it provides an interesting perspective and represents a realistic enough view of the potential benefits for the fraudster.

Industry	Expected Credential Stuffing Hit Rate
E-commerce, social media	Consumers who regularly shop on multiple e-commerce sites or interact with friends and family on various social media sites are more likely to reuse the same username and password, just for convenience. Based on this assumption, the estimated hit rate during a credential stuffing attack is expected to be about 15%.
Fintech and banking	Fintech and banking websites don't always leverage the email address as the identifier, which will have an impact on the hit rate. However, even if the site doesn't accept emails, users may decide to use their email address handle for convenience. For example, if John Smith's email address is `john_smith1234@mydomain.com`, he may use `john_smith1234` as his identifier with his bank. So even if combo lists with identifiers other than the email address are less common, they are still usable. Users may, however, be a bit more mindful of not reusing a set of credentials they use on other sites for their bank login. Hence, a 10% hit rate is expected.
Gaming	For gaming sites, we differentiate between two types of accounts: • The first type, *premium accounts*, are considered high value because they provide valuable assets to a player to progress in the game, such as powerful weapons, credits, a large fleet of sports cars, etc. These accounts can have a very high resale value on the dark web. • In contrast, lower-value accounts are sold in *bulk*. They are considered lower value because the assets associated with them are unknown or limited. Because gaming websites have a large community of young users, their credentials are less likely to have been part of a data breach from other major e-commerce or social media sites, in which case we expect the hit rate for bulk accounts to be no more than 5%. Lastly, the chances of premium accounts being harvested from the credential stuffing attack are considerably lower and should not exceed 0.0075%.

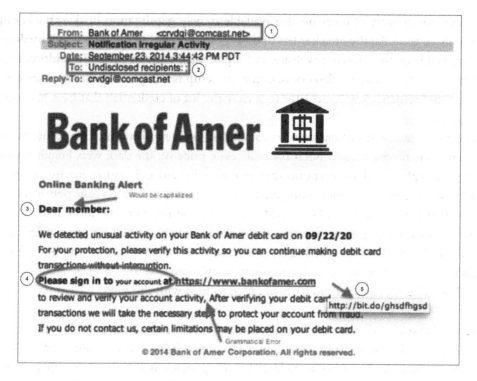

Figure 2.4   Phishing attack against a bank

Trained security professionals will spot the trap quickly, but what about less computer-savvy people? Clicking the link will send you to a login page that looks exactly like the original. Most embedded content (images, JavaScript, and style sheets) will come from the real site. After submitting your credentials to the fake website impersonating your bank, your credentials are logged into a database, and you may be redirected to the real website's login page. This unusual experience will come across as a glitch to most users, or they may think they entered an incorrect password. They will promptly re-attempt to log in, this time successfully.

Malware Campaigns   A phishing or vishing campaign can be the conduit to malware getting installed on the victim's computer. The password extracted from the data breach may be hashed and salted, but the email addresses can be used as an initial source of information for potential victims. A personalized message containing a link is sent to the email address list. Some messages can be very convincing to entice the user to click a link, triggering a silent malware install. Most of these emails go to my junk folder, but some occasionally go through.

Vishing attacks are somewhat similar, except the attack is done over the phone instead of email. Have you ever received a call that warned you that malware had been detected on your Windows system? Isn't it also entertaining when the person posing as a technical support agent insists that you download software that will supposedly cure the problem free of charge, wherein, in reality, you work on a system running macOS or Linux? It happened to me once. I always wonder if these pressure methods really work, but I suppose if some poor souls do this, it's probably because they manage to convince people occasionally and extract some value from this scheme. Once more, someone less savvy with computers from my parent's generation would most likely gratefully follow the instructions and download the malware.

What Happens to the Refined List of Credentials   As you've seen earlier, credential harvesting can yield several thousands of credentials per site. Once enough are collected, they are sold on the dark web marketplace. An account's price depends on a website's popularity and industry. Based on dark web data, accounts from well-known e-commerce brands may yield 8 cents per account. Assuming an attacker can verify 150,000 accounts and sell two-thirds of the inventory, this can translate to revenue of $8,000. Social media accounts are generally offered for 10 cents, and fintech/bank accounts for 40 cents. But the real money is in gaming accounts, which are offered for more than $1 per account.

The following table breaks down potential revenue from selling stolen credentials by industry. Gaming accounts are the most lucrative, followed by fintech accounts. The average revenue per credential is based on the asking price advertised on dark web marketplaces or specialized forums.

Industry	Average Revenue/Credential	Potential Revenue per 100,000 Sold
E-commerce	$0.08	$8,000
Social media	$0.10	$10,000
Fintech/bank	$0.40	$40,000
Gaming (bulk)	$1.70	$170,000

Account Takeover

Lastly, a fraudster will acquire the list of verified accounts. These accounts may be sold separately, but they are more commonly sold in bundles depending on what access, data, or potential monetary value is attached to them. Figure 2.5 shows the different ways the account can be exploited after it's taken over, depending on the industry.

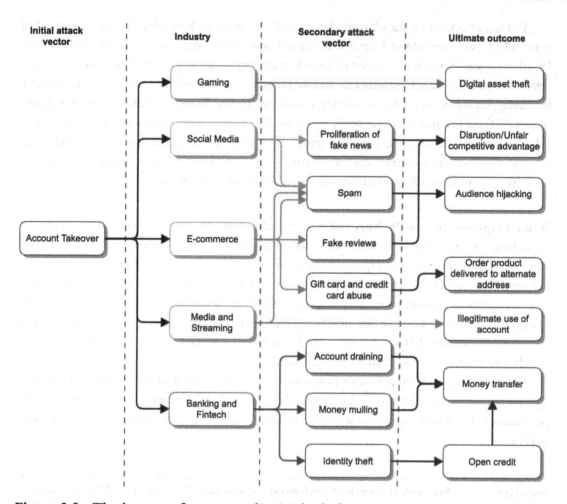

Figure 2.5   The impact of account takeover by industry

Gaming   After the account is taken over, the fraudster may use it for two different schemes: digital assets theft and spamming. Once the fraudster can successfully log in to the account, he checks available assets. A subscription may be associated with the account providing premium content access. A credit card would typically be on file, allowing the fraudster to purchase new content. The account may also give access to premium digital assets. For example, in the case of my son, who likes car racing games, this translates to a virtual garage full of Lamborghinis, Ferraris, and Bugattis. Some games allow digital assets to be sold to other players through an auction system. The fraudster may then put some of the premium content (for example, a Bugatti Veyron) up for sale at a short auction for a low price. The assets are then purchased from another account he controls, which is how the digital assets get transferred. Avid gamers buy these accounts on the dark web for an average price of $670, representing a massive profit for fraudsters.

Also, many games have a "social media" aspect for people to play together. Those accounts that have been taken over can be used to spam other players and entice them to visit websites with potentially inappropriate content.

Social Media   The accounts that have been taken over can be used for two different schemes: spam and potentially fake news proliferation. In the case of spamming, the motivation is like the gaming use case, enticing users who already follow the account that has been taken over to visit a specific website. This could be a typical campaign that attempts to lure people to sites selling porn or drugs or lead people to some news site jammed with ads to boost their revenue.

The fake news/disinformation aspect is more subtle. In this case, the attacker is taking advantage of the trust one's network may have in the account owner that has been taken over to influence their opinion by posting targeted content that may or may not be accurate. The attacker aims to disrupt and gain a competitive advantage.

E-commerce   Stolen accounts are primarily exploited to buy products with credit cards, gift cards, or loyalty points linked to the account and have them delivered to alternate addresses the fraudster controls. This is the most lucrative way for the attacker to generate revenue from the whole scheme.

All commerce websites have a social media aspect through the "review" section, where consumers can share their opinions on products. Instead of fake news, e-commerce sites need to worry about spam, including fake reviews that would attempt to hijack the audience to lead them to an alternate website selling similar products at a lower price.

Media and Streaming   Some media and streaming websites also have a social media aspect where people can leave comments to share their opinions on the content offered by the site. Like what has already been discussed for social media and e-commerce verticals, the same risks apply with the risk of spam, fake news, or audience hijacking.

Streaming services struggle with legitimate user accounts that have been taken over and sold on the dark web. As subscription prices have increased over the years, more and more accounts from premium streaming services are found on the dark web at a fraction of the monthly subscription cost. Instead of paying $15 for a monthly subscription to access content, one may prefer to buy an account for a one-time fee of $5 on the dark web. This represents a significant potential revenue loss for streaming platforms.

Banking/Fintech Beyond the username and password, there are several obstacles a fraudster needs to deal with before being able to take over an account. Banks usually track the legitimate user's device fingerprint and location. Someone logging in from a different location and/or device will generally trigger an alert. At the minimum, the legitimate user will receive an email asking him to confirm he initiated the login request to authorize it. Usually, the user will be requested to verify their identity through an email or SMS one-time token authentication process. The system will use the information on record to challenge the user. Unless the attacker also controls the phone and/or email address, attackers will be blocked from taking over the account. Advanced attackers who can overcome the step-up authentication challenge would then have access to the user's account, and as a next step, they may do the following:

- Issue a full or partial transfer of the money available to an account fully controlled by the attacker.
- Use the account as an intermediary to redistribute money from multiple accounts (known as *money mulling*). This could be part of a money laundering scheme and make the origin and destination of the stolen or ill-gained money difficult to track by a single institution.
- Use the account as part of identity theft and as collateral to open credit in another financial institution.

Targeted ATO Attacks

In general, ATO attacks are not personal. Fraudsters simply exploit the data they bought on the dark web but do not target anyone in particular. Instead, they target everyone except, in some scenarios. As seen from the *Dark Reading* report from July 2020, 130 accounts from US politicians, celebrities, and high-level personalities were stolen from a major social media site (Vijayan, 2020). In this case, attackers go for quality, not quantity, and such high-profile accounts can yield more benefits than thousands of accounts from random people. These accounts can be used for extortion, embarrassing the victim, influencing the victim's followers on certain social and political issues, spreading fake news, or, as some say, alternate reality. The technique needed for a successful attack may differ significantly from those discussed so far. Credential stuffing would only work through sheer luck; the credentials of famous people would need to be present in the list and valid on sites like social media. Vishing and phishing are unlikely to succeed. An alternate approach is to collect information about the victim, for example, the name of their kids, wife, birthday, place of birth, place of residence, favorite vacation spot, or anything else personal that can be used by the victim as an easy-to-remember password. The goal is to come up with a word list that can be used as a basis to craft possible password combinations. This is a form of targeted dictionary attack. Once the password list is generated, a botnet is used to replay it against social media sites or email services to take over the account.

Network Administrator Accounts   Most networking equipment comes with default admin usernames and passwords. Unfortunately, not everyone is careful enough to change it to a strong one or set up a RADIUS server linked to a corporate authentication system to manage the account. Doing a quick search on Google gives you several links to pages that list the default credentials of various vendors' networking equipment. These are typically published to raise awareness and help network administrators build a script to detect vulnerable access points automatically. Unfortunately, attackers also use this wise advice. If an attacker can access a router, they may be able to reroute the traffic of a web server to an alternate location. Or they may shut down access to the network and deny access to all users. This type of attack would significantly impact the site's reputation.

System Administrator Accounts   Cloud services don't generally have a default password. Site administrators for small to medium-sized businesses may not always be well-versed in security best practices and only rely on password-based authentication methods. Most people, even security professionals, may sometimes use easy-to-remember passwords. Often, the password consists of a word available in the dictionary, a combination of words with some letters swapped with numbers, or an easy-to-execute keyword sequence like "qwerty." A quick Google search lists the most common passwords, which can be used to build a word list. The list can then be utilized in a brute-force attack to take over the targeted account. Social engineering may also be an option where the fraudster pretends to be calling from cloud service support to address some issues with the account. Once the account is compromised and, depending on the access rights associated with it, the attacker may be able to do all sorts of damage, including denying access, defacing the website, or exfiltrating data.

Specific Individual Accounts   Celebrities' social media accounts are regular targets of attacks. Some attackers may hold a grudge against someone and decide to embarrass or discredit them by taking over their social media accounts. Again, a dictionary attack would be a logical step in the process. If that fails, they may try to guess the password by collecting personal information about the targeted person, for example, the name of their kids, birthday, or place of birth, and craft possible passwords.

A Credential Stuffing Attack Example

Figure 2.6 shows an example of a credential stuffing attack on a popular e-commerce website that generated millions of requests within a few days. The whole campaign lasted about a week and consisted of four rounds.

The attack shows a significant traffic spike with a sustained high request rate between 850 and 1,050 requests per second on December 16. The attack lasted only three hours, and more than 5.8 million requests were blocked.

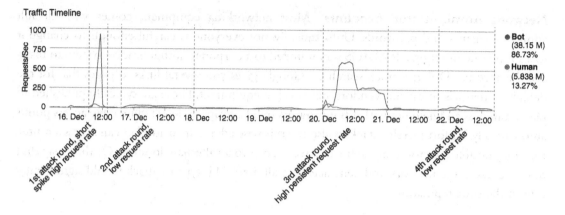

Figure 2.6   A credential stuffing attack against an e-commerce website

The attack pauses for several hours, during which time the attacker likely worked on adjusting their script to improve the attack success rate. The second round of attack starts 8 hours later. It is much lower in intensity, between 30 and 40 requests per second, likely due to the lesson the attacker learned from the earlier attack failure. Indeed, attacks of high intensity are generally easier to detect and mitigate by web security products. In this second round, the attacker hopes a lower request rate will increase the success rate. The second round of attack turned into a failure. More than 2.8 million requests were denied, and this second round eventually subsided within 24 hours.

The attack resumed at a much higher intensity two days later, varying between 200 and 600 requests per second, and persisted for 24 hours. More than 26 million requests were blocked during this third round.

The attack paused again for about 20 hours and resumed one last time with a request rate of around 60 requests per second sustained for nearly 24 hours, during which more than 4.2 million requests were blocked.

Overall, the attack campaign for this single actor consisted of more than 37 million requests.

Figure 2.7 shows that the attack originated from five countries, with the United States leading in terms of volume, followed by Turkey, Germany, the Netherlands, and the United Kingdom. During the week-long attack campaign, the botnet leveraged a total of 87,723 unique IP addresses distributed in 4,320 networks.

There may be several botnet campaigns active at any given time. Botnets can be identified by their header signatures. (Chapter 5, "Assessing Detection Accuracy," discusses how to define a botnet signature or botnet ID.) Figure 2.8 shows two attack campaigns at play. The first row represents the week-long attack campaign discussed earlier, consisting of 14,170 unique IP addresses sending more than 37 million requests. The other row corresponds to a minor attack consisting of a smaller set of botnets that seem active around the same time. Note, however, that the scale is much larger in terms of IP distribution compared to the number of requests sent.

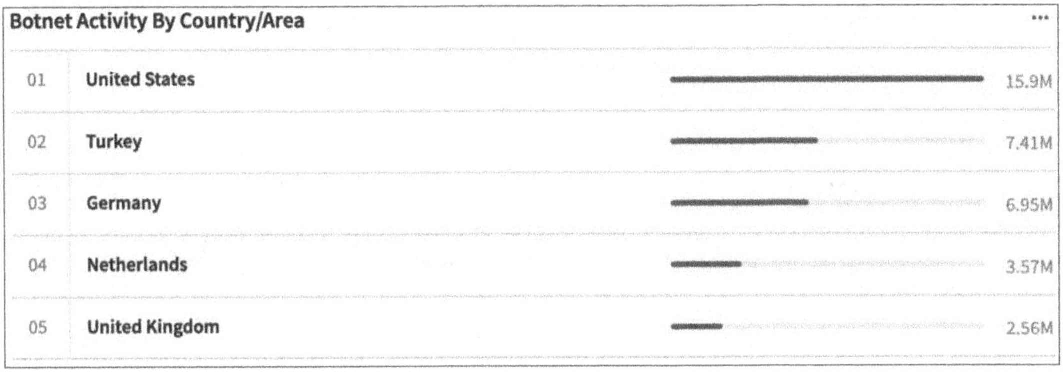

Botnet Activity By Country/Area		...
01	United States	15.9M
02	Turkey	7.41M
03	Germany	6.95M
04	Netherlands	3.57M
05	United Kingdom	2.56M

Figure 2.7 Attack distribution by country of origin

Botnet ID	Number of IPs	Total
Bot_44DEDE6B7B331670546753FA686B5B54	14.17 K	37.4 M
Bot_CE90C2C50B91B1DEFDB046194B960A72	16.29 K	179.8 K
Bot_D6EA5D22585BDBB476B837B86B98A914	32.68 K	140.6 K
Bot_40696F8AEC016F4CEB252975282FB393	10.31 K	85.48 K
Bot_73BA882094C3D1AB0EB8CE410FC18151	2,272	56.85 K
Bot_08B6C15A0B6FF82CFE8084DB17A022A7	14.37 K	53.87 K
Bot_1B79119D067613B87ECB581ADA3EAD83	13.07 K	41.73 K
Bot_C55B4AC0CDAD7573F5B567FF9E4A1A1C	2,073	29.22 K
Bot_29A044680D61F8B4B735C11CAB53CB40	2,553	14.45 K
Bot_E144E77341F78B8AB4603583245BF0FB	2,641	11.78 K

Figure 2.8 Attack distribution by botnet

Some attackers are more advanced than others. In Figure 2.9, the attacker mainly focused on adapting their request rate and adjusted their HTTP header signature to look like what is expected of a legitimate web browser.

These attack campaigns were easily detected because the attacker was unaware that the bot management service was protecting the site and did not send the fingerprint and telemetry the security product was expected to receive from the client. The lack of telemetry and fingerprints, combined with the excessive request rate, make for easy detection. As will be discussed in Chapter 3, however, advanced and financially motivated attackers can be much more sophisticated and adapt their attack strategy to defeat the detection in place. Not all sites have the same

HOST:	▓▓▓▓▓▓▓▓
CONTENT-LENGTH:	919
SEC-CH-UA:	"Google Chrome";v="107", "Chromium";v="107", "Not=A?Brand";v="24"
SEC-CH-UA-MOBILE:	?0
SEC-CH-UA-PLATFORM:	"Windows"
UPGRADE-INSECURE-REQUESTS:	1
ORIGIN:	https://▓▓▓▓▓▓▓▓
CONTENT-TYPE:	application/x-www-form-urlencoded
USER-AGENT:	Mozilla/5.0 (Windows NT 10.0; Win64; x64) AppleWebKit/537.36 (KHTML, like Gecko) Chrome/107.0.0.0 Safari/537.36
ACCEPT:	text/html,application/xhtml+xml,application/xml;q=0.9,image/avif,image/webp,image/apng,*/*;q=0.8,application/signed-exchange;v=b3;q=0.9
SEC-FETCH-SITE:	same-origin
SEC-FETCH-MODE:	navigate
SEC-FETCH-USER:	?1
SEC-FETCH-DEST:	document
REFERER:	https://▓▓▓▓▓▓▓▓/identity/login?signin=c69290e4ae59fb7fabe677580e93eecc
ACCEPT-ENCODING:	gzip, deflate, br
ACCEPT-LANGUAGE:	en-US,en;q=0.9,nl;q=0.8,it;q=0.7,pl;q=0.6,zh-TW;q=0.5,zh;q=0.4

Figure 2.9   An example of an HTTP header signature during an attack

level of protection against ATO attacks. Considering the constant evolution of attack methods, an efficient detection strategy requires continuous maintenance of the security posture to maintain a good level of security.

Account Opening Abuse

Completing a transaction on most websites, whether in retail, travel, or especially banking, requires creating a new account first. Various sites have different standards of security. Retail, travel, and hospitality sites mostly require a first and last name and an email address. Sites that offer subscription-based services such as streaming, news articles, or cloud services would also need a credit card number and a billing address. Financial services are generally the strictest and may also require the user to provide more personal information such as government ID, proof of residence, and a phone number. The verification level of the information provided before the account is created also varies. In banking, all personal data will be validated through know your customer (KYC) services. The user will be asked to verify their email address or phone number with a one-time password, and they may also be asked to set up multifactor authentication (MFA). MFA is a multistep account login process that requires the user to authenticate with two factors, which can be something they know (most commonly a password), something they are (a fingerprint), or something they have, which can be a variety of things, including a token generator, an email address, a phone number, or a private key. If this practice is becoming more common in the financial and banking industry, its adoption is still limited in the retail/e-commerce industry, where the focus is mainly on avoiding adding friction to the process as much as possible to attract more customers and sometimes cater to an older audience that may not be as comfortable with web technologies.

　　The most popular sites are plagued by fraudsters who open large numbers of accounts. This type of attack is known in the industry as *account opening abuse* or *new account fraud*. The question is why this happens and what attackers do with these accounts. This section answers these questions and gives some insight into how fraud rings are organized.

The Tree Hiding the Forest

The mass creation of accounts observed on popular websites is just a symptom of a broader attack scheme. As shown in Figure 2.10, the fraud scheme leveraging fake accounts varies

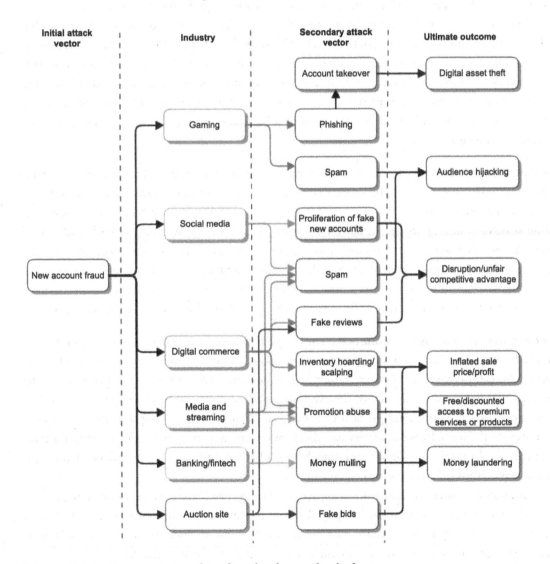

Figure 2.10 Account opening fraud scheme by industry

depending on the industry, attackers' interests, and the incentives companies offer to attract new customers. Even though the fraud scheme varies, financial and personal gain are the common denominators that motivate attackers. The following is a nonexhaustive breakdown by industry of the most common attack schemes that require fake accounts.

Gaming   Many games, like esports, have a social media side to them. A superstar gamer is expected to have many fans, and the number of followers matters for credibility. Bots may control fake accounts to post comments, cheering for the star player while bashing on the opponents, giving the "star player" an unfair psychological advantage in the competition.

Fake accounts may also be an instrument for a phishing attack as an intermediate step for taking over accounts or stealing digital assets. The digital assets may include better weapons, a garage full of exotic cars, or special powers. The fraudster controlling the fake account may befriend other players and entice them to give them their usernames and passwords. Once they get the credentials, the fraudster will connect to the victim's account and check their digital assets. As seen in the ATO use case, the assets may be stolen through an auction using the fake account as a proxy.

Social Media   One may leverage fake accounts to increase their popularity on the platform. One with more followers will be more visible, appear more credible, draw more "real" followers, and give the company or individual who owns the account a competitive advantage. In a large-scale operation, bots would comment or like a post and grow their network with "real" users. Some of these posts may include fake news that may alter the population's perception of specific political issues or personalities, which could destabilize a country in the worst-case scenario. Beyond simply making a post more visible, fake accounts may also post spam to direct users to unrelated content, hijack the audience, or even draw them to malicious content.

E-commerce   Premium e-commerce sites regularly have hype sales events on popular or limited-edition items, such as concert tickets, sneakers, or other products from luxury brands. Such sales can draw a sizable virtual crowd where bots are commonly used to get a chance to buy the coveted item. In advance of the event (it could be hours, but preferably days or weeks), bot operators will create multiple accounts that will then be used during the sale event to try to purchase the item. Bots can access and check out items as soon as the event starts, faster than a human could ever react. These items may be resold at a premium on a secondary market like auction sites, thus inflating legitimate consumers' prices.

E-commerce sites also allow users to give reviews on products. Fake accounts may be used to write fake positive reviews on less popular/low-quality items while providing bad reviews on more popular high-quality items. The comments may also include spam to steer the user to alternate content. In both schemes, the goal is to hijack part of the audience.

Fake accounts may also be created to take advantage of coupons or discounts awarded to new users on their first purchase.

Media and Streaming   Access to premium content usually requires a monthly fee. However, most platforms will offer promotions where the service is free for some time (generally a month). The new subscriber is allowed to cancel the new account at any time. Fraudsters who want to access the service without paying may keep opening and closing new accounts once the trial period expires. Fake accounts may also be created using fake credit cards and sold for a fraction of the monthly subscription cost on the dark web.

Also, some news media platforms allow users to view a limited number of articles for free before requiring the user to pay to see more. Creating multiple accounts is a way to access more content without paying. The social media aspect of the site also opens the door to spam abuse or the proliferation of fake news.

Financial Services   New neo-banks operating exclusively online look to challenge traditional institutions. To attract customers from traditional banks, they commonly offer a cash bonus to anyone opening an account, setting up a direct deposit, and maintaining a certain sum of money for some time. The attacker will use a synthetic identity crafted with stolen personal information and an email address to open the account. Once the account is opened successfully, the direct deposit is set up, and the minimum amount of funds is transferred to get the cash bonus. Once the reward is received, the attacker will move their money out of the account, including the cash reward.

Fake accounts may also be used for money mulling, to transit cash from one institution to another, making it more difficult for anyone to trace or retrieve the stolen money in a money laundering scheme.

Auction Sites   Sellers on auction sites may create fake accounts that will be used during an auction to bid on the item for sale. If the item is popular, fake bids may be generated by bots using the fake account to inflate the item's price, which starts a bidding war.

The reputation of a seller is essential on an auction site. Fake accounts may be used to leave fake comments to artificially increase his reputation.

Fraud Ring

As discussed in the previous section, creating new accounts is just a step of a broader fraud scheme. The complexity of completing the initial account creation step depends on the type of validation a site applies when receiving a request. Some want to avoid friction as much as possible and will not validate anything other than that the username selected doesn't already exist in the database. Most sites will validate at least the email address provided, and banks and fintech will also validate the personal information supplied to open the account. This section describes the various scenarios.

Sites Without Email Verification   In the simplest use case (Figure 2.11), someone may be able to open an account, with very little validation beyond verifying if the same username exists already on the site before the account is created. In this situation, the attacker doesn't need valid inboxes, and they can create random accounts on the site at will.

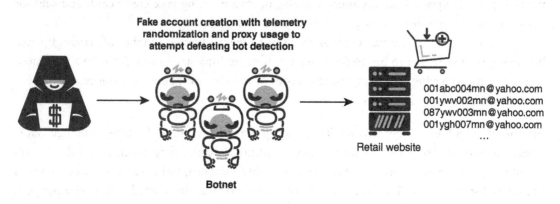

Figure 2.11 caption (within image):
Fake account creation with telemetry randomization and proxy usage to attempt defeating bot detection

001abc004mn@yahoo.com
001ywv002mn@yahoo.com
087ywv003mn@yahoo.com
001ygh007mn@yahoo.com
...

Retail website

Botnet

Figure 2.11   A fraudster uses invalid email addresses when the site doesn't enforce email validation.

Sites with Email Verification   When email verification is enforced, the attacker needs to supply a valid email address that they control to handle the verification step. Harvesting valid inboxes on legitimate email systems and harvesting fake accounts on various websites is too much for one actor. That's where the "ring" comes into play, as represented in Figure 2.12.

In the fraud world, like in the legitimate world, each has their specialty and sells the product of their labor (credentials) to others. A "new account fraudsters" category specializes in harvesting inboxes on legitimate email platforms that are then sold in bulk on the dark web marketplace (steps 1 and 2). An example of such a provider is the now-defunct `Hotmailbox.me` (Figure 2.13), a subsidiary of `1stcaptcha.com` based in Vietnam. They specialized in harvesting email accounts on platforms like Outlook, Hotmail, or `Live.com`. At the time of the attack, Microsoft protected its email service with CAPTCHA technology. CAPTCHA stands for Completely Automated Public Turing Test to Tell Computers and Humans Apart. I'll describe detection based on this technology further in Chapter 4, "Detection Strategy." `Hotmailbox.me` used their CAPTCHA-solving technology to harvest new accounts.

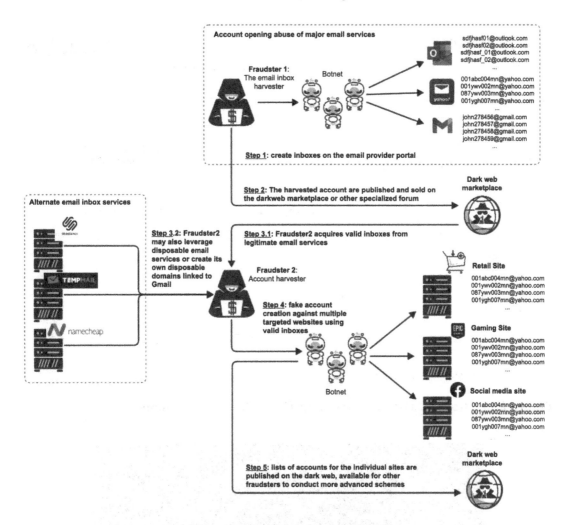

Figure 2.12 Account opening abuse with email validation

Fraudsters interested in creating fake accounts on various sites will acquire these inboxes (step 3.1) and use them as part of their account creation process.

Alternatively, an attacker may procure disposable inboxes (Figure 2.14) through sites like `Temp-Mail.org` (step 3.2) or hundreds of similar services. The primary purpose of disposable or temporary email services is to help legitimate users preserve their privacy when creating a new account online. Still, like many privacy-oriented services, they are also commonly used by fraudsters.

Another technique is creating disposable domains registered with low-cost registrars like Namecheap or Squarespace, which are among the most used. Information about the

Recognizing unusual traffic patterns in the various email domains is key to helping identify account opening abuses. Figure 2.16 shows the distribution of account creation using email addresses from a major email service (Gmail.com) over seven days. We see a regular circadian pattern (traffic that peaks during the day and decreases at night), which is the expected traffic pattern from legitimate user activity.

In contrast, Figure 2.17 shows account creation with emails from the icloud.com domain. The circadian pattern is somewhat visible but dwarfed by occasional sharp traffic spikes, reflecting short attacks using addresses from the popular email services. By using email addresses from a well-known email service, the attacker aims to make it harder for the defender to identify the fake accounts.

The pattern of account opening with emails from uncommon domains looks drastically different. Figure 2.18 and Figure 2.19 show activity with uncommon email domains like cantuenzal.com or cpzmars.com, with short activity spikes. Both domains are registered with Squarespace.

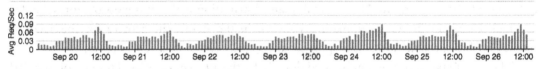

Figure 2.16   Account creation pattern with emails from the domain Gmail.com

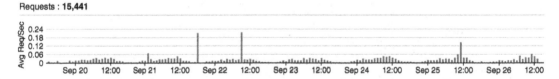

Figure 2.17   Account creation pattern with emails from the domain iCloud.com

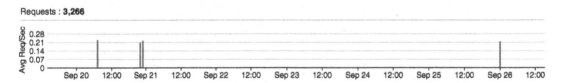

Figure 2.18   An account creation pattern with emails from the domain cantuenzal.com

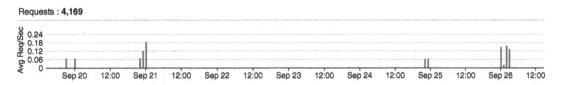

Figure 2.19 An account creation pattern with emails from the domain
`cpzmars.com`

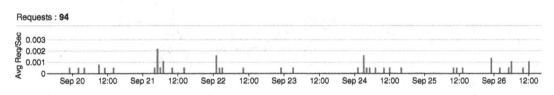

Figure 2.20 Account creation pattern with emails from the domain `yahoo.gr`

In contrast, traffic with uncommon but legitimate email domains like `yahoo.gr` is expected and acceptable at low volume, as shown in Figure 2.20. However, seeing thousands of new accounts created with uncommon email domains within a short period is highly suspicious.

Sites with Email and Advanced User Input Verification   With financial, banking, or insurance company websites, users must provide more information about their identity, including home addresses, government-issued IDs, and phone numbers. The site will verify the email address and all the other information with some level of scrutiny. Fraudsters who want to create new bank accounts will need reasonably valid data that can be verified. The attacker will likely use something other than disposable emails as they would be too obvious an anomaly for the bank security team to catch.

As shown in Figure 2.21, the attacker is more likely to use regular email services like Google's Gmail or Microsoft Outlook. In this scenario, two different fraudsters may supply information upstream.

- One will supply valid inboxes (steps 1 and 2).
- The other will supply personal information that may have been harvested through major data leaks (step 3).

Fraudsters wanting to open a bank account and take advantage of the promotional offers will acquire both data sets from the dark web and combine them to create synthetic identities (step 4).

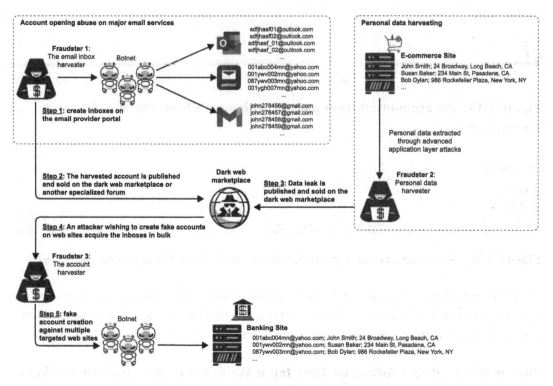

Figure 2.21 Account opening abuse ring with advanced data input validation

The fraudster would generally provide a disposable mobile phone number for websites requiring phone verification to open an account. The more advanced verification step may be done through human labor.

Web Scraping

Web scraping is the process of extracting data from websites. Information is collected using automated software applications (bots) and structured into a usable form. Web scraping is also known as *data scraping, data extraction, data crawling, web crawling, web harvesting,* or *screen scraping.* When the data collected are prices or product inventory information, it may also be referred to as *price scraping* and *inventory scraping,* respectively. In this section, we'll focus on the data extraction activity, which generates a lot of traffic on websites. As described in Chapter 1, "A Short History of the Internet," scraping activity can account for 50% to 90% of the overall traffic in the worst-case scenario for some websites. The sheer volume of traffic can be challenging for website owners to deal with, as it may cause occasional site stability and availability issues. It also increases the cost of content distribution, storage, and computing to process the extra load. Web scraping also has some impact on the business as the extra load significantly skews key metrics such as conversion rate, which measures the ratio of users visiting the site to complete a purchase. Marketing teams rely on this metric and others to measure the success of their product positioning strategy or advertising campaigns. Let's review the intent behind scraping and how it impacts various industries.

The Intent Behind Scraping by Industry

When a botnet scrapes a website, it harvests publicly available information. Despite the problems it may cause, there is little that a website owner can do legally to prevent the activity. The botnet operators regularly trigger their scraping activity to collect the necessary information, including product details, pricing, and inventory. Within the scraping category, there are different use cases; not all are bad, depending on the context. E-commerce, travel, hospitality, and media are the most affected. Figure 2.22 shows the consequences of scraping based on the industry and the intent.

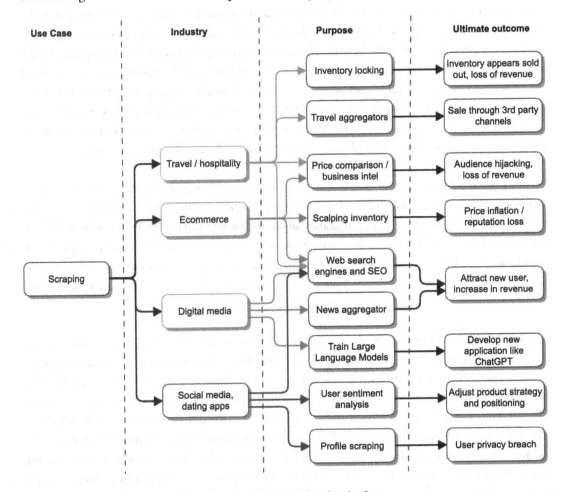

Figure 2.22 The outcome of scraping activity by industry

All industries have in common the need to serve their content to what is commonly referred to as *known bots* or *good bots*, which include web search engines, bots that support SEO services, or social media bots. These categories of good bots help make the content more visible on the Internet and attract potential customers. Site monitoring services also regularly pull content from the site to evaluate the response time and availability from various parts of the globe. Traffic coming from these so-called known bots, like Googlebot or Bingbot, must be accurately identified to prevent serving content to impersonators.

Travel/Hospitality   Travel aggregators or booking engines scrape travel and hospitality websites. These sites allow travelers to quickly find flights, hotel rooms, car rentals, and even entertainment at their destination. Booking engines may sell their own products or services on top of the airfare or accommodation. This is a very convenient way for consumers to book a vacation or a business trip. To make the content readily available to the account aggregator, the airline or hotel may make the data available through APIs or allow the aggregator to scrape their site. There is typically a mutually beneficial agreement in place between the two parties. However, aggregators sometimes scrape the site directly, advertise, and resell the airfares or hotel rooms without consent, which goes against the site's acceptable usage policy. Some airlines or hotel brands may only want to be associated with specific booking engines they partner with.

Depending on the website's architecture, the scraping activity may cause the airfare or room inventory to be locked for a few minutes, making it unavailable to legitimate users.

E-commerce   Most website owners would like to avoid scraping activity that is hard to attribute to any specific entity as much as possible. E-commerce sites receive significant activity from bot operators scraping a site in search of items for sale during an event. This activity is commonly referred to as *scalping*. It is usually punctual and sporadic. The scraping activity that causes the most traffic usually comes from entities harvesting data to extract business intelligence. This can be initiated by well-funded companies specializing in data extraction or individual companies wanting to monitor their competition.

Digital Media   Websites want to attract as many users as possible who may be interested in the content they produce. News outlets generally welcome scraping activity from new aggregators or larger news organizations to get a chance to have their content referenced and increase their visibility. More readers or viewers translate to more subscriptions, ad impressions, and revenue. The content may only be available to subscribers for premium media services like the *Wall Street Journal*. Although it's essential that web search engines or social media bots can index and reference the content behind a paywall, it's also essential that these scrapers are identified to ensure the entire content is not made available to a scraper attempting to impersonate legitimate bots like Googlebot and facebookexternalhit (Facebook bot).

With the rise of generative artificial intelligence (GenAI) powered by large language models (LLM) and exposed to the public as services like ChatGPT, there is also a need to scrape reliable sources of information to train the models, ensure the service provides accurate answers, and avoid inadvertently spreading fake or inaccurate information. A crowdsourced knowledge base like Wikipedia, known for its relative accuracy, can be used as a point of reference. Major and reputable news outlets like *Le Monde* in France, the *BBC* in the UK, or the *Washington Post* in the United States are known to verify their sources and provide fair and accurate information. They, too, could be used as reliable data sources to train these models. The topic, however, remains controversial at this time since the issues around intellectual property do not seem to be solved.

Social Media   Since consumers have been using social media like X (formerly Twitter), Instagram, TikTok, or Facebook to discuss and provide their opinions on various matters, these platforms have become a considerable source of information that marketers can use to infer user sentiment toward a product, company, or even social issues. Companies specializing in business intelligence and product marketing also scrape social media sites to collect data and process it through complex machine learning algorithms like natural language processing (NLP) to extract valuable insight, which can then be used to adjust a product strategy. Social media sites may sell that data and may restrict the scraping activity.

Social media and dating sites hold a trove of personal data on individual users. User profile scraping represents a privacy concern. A company searching on LinkedIn for professionals suitable for a role in their organizations is entirely acceptable and in line with the site's purpose. Still, it is unacceptable for a company or individual to scrape all profiles to build a personal information database that could later be sold for profit.

Good Bot Scraping

Good bots refer to automated traffic that is beneficial for the smooth operation of a website (site performance and availability monitoring services, for example), makes its content easily accessible to potential customers through search engines, or improves the positioning and ranking of the site content on the Internet (search engine optimization, online advertising). It also includes other use cases where the bot operator has positive intents, and the activity will not cause any negative impact on the site performance or availability. It may also not have any undesirable effect on the reputation or revenue of the company that owns the site.

As described in Chapter 1, good bot traffic generally represents around 27% of all scraping activity. Of course, this ratio may vary depending on the value of the content and the company's position in the market. In the top position, we usually find web search engines, SEO bots, social media, and site monitor tools across all websites. Figure 2.23 illustrates the "good" bot trend traffic on a retailer's website. SEO bot traffic represents the majority of the activity on this site, with more than 89 million requests during the period observed, and is represented by this large circadian pattern peaking above all traffic. Web search engine activity is the category of good bots that represents the second highest volume with more than 71 million requests, followed by social media bots with more than 44 million requests, represented by that seemingly straight line.

Scraping activity from web search engines is broadly accepted and critical to an e-commerce site's success. Some website owners can have specific preferences regarding the web search engine they would allow. Indeed, most broadly accept Googlebot, Bingbot, and Baidu. However, other regional web search engines, such as the Russian Yandex and the Chinese 360Spider, are not always readily accepted in North America or Western Europe. Ultimately, it all comes down to user preferences. Some users (and potential customers) are wary of the effect that web search engines operated by large corporations can have on their privacy on the Internet and may prefer alternatives like DuckDuckGo. Limiting which web search engine can scrape a website may limit its audience and opportunity to attract new customers. Figures 2.24 to 2.27 show the activity from the most popular web search engine on a popular e-commerce site. As you can see, the volume of activity and the botnet's behavior may vary depending on the search engine.

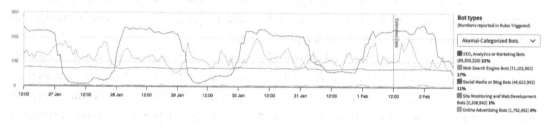

Figure 2.23   Good bot traffic distribution on a retailer site

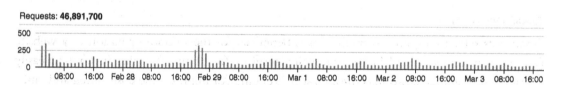

Figure 2.24   Scraping activity from Googlebot

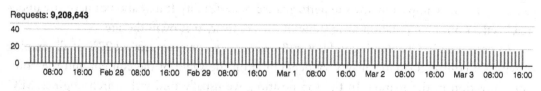

Figure 2.25   Scraping activity from Bingbot

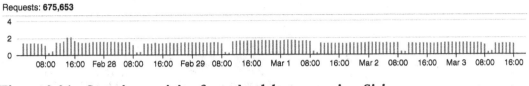

Figure 2.26 **Scraping activity from Applebot powering Siri**

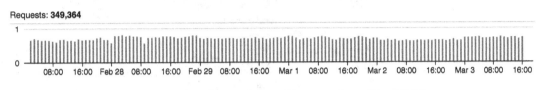

Figure 2.27 **Scraping activity from OpenAI powering ChatGPT**

Inventory Hoarding

Scalpers or inventory hoarders scrape websites searching for popular discounted items or items in low supply. For example, when the supply chain was disturbed during the pandemic, there was a shortage of GPUs. Scalpers search the Internet to find inventory and automatically acquire it when found. Since price is driven by supply and demand, scalpers can profit by reselling the items on marketplaces like Amazon or eBay. A similar phenomenon happens with hype events when a shoe company releases a limited edition pair of sneakers or a ticket company releases seats for a world-famous pop star. Scalpers will either design and build their scraper or use one of the many open-source or subscription-based scraping services available on the market. The sophistication of the botnet will depend on the skill set of the developer or operator.

Figure 2.28 describes the different steps of the process and how scraping helps in the overall scheme:

1. The scalper develops a botnet targeting various popular e-commerce sites. Sites can be scraped as often as once a day.
2. The data collected is analyzed based on specific criteria. The analysis will provide a potential shopping list of products on sale when resold at a regular price, which could yield a good margin.
3. The scalper reviews the list and buys the discounted products on the relevant site. This step may be automated or performed manually.
4. The scalper will also put the product up for sale with a markup on a marketplace like Amazon.
5. Once the product is sold, the scalper pockets the difference.

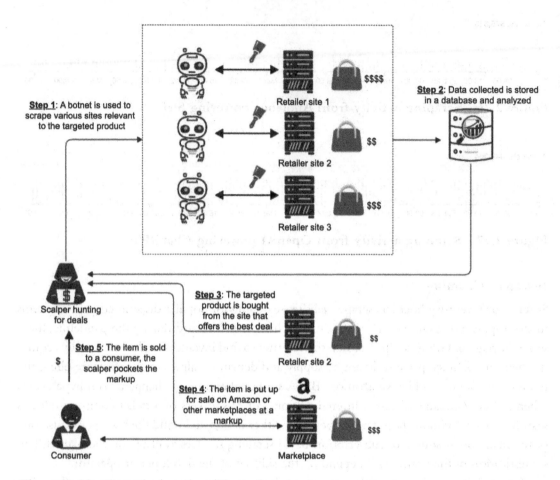

Figure 2.28 Bargain hunting life cycle

Figure 2.29 shows an example of a product (premium dog food) found on eBay at twice the price compared to an e-commerce site specializing in pet products. This example is not proof that the product was initially sourced from the site, which shows a discount, but it is highly possible and certainly shows that the practice can yield significant revenue.

Scalpers have done this with big-box stores for a long time. The Internet and e-commerce have allowed them to automate and optimize their operations and run more efficient businesses. For the websites where the products are sourced from, the scraping activity will be most visible to them, is a significant source of nuisance, and could cause site availability issues if it is too aggressive. When one of the bargain products is checked out, this will just come across as a regular order.

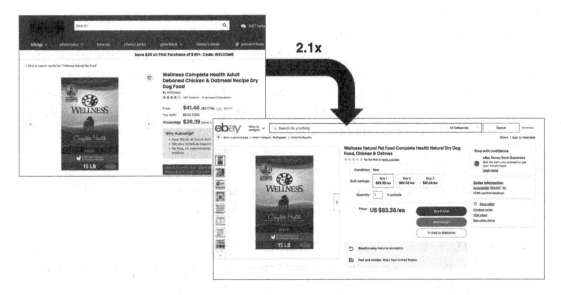

Figure 2.29   Example of product resale on the marketplace at a premium

Business Intelligence

Retail or travel companies like to monitor their competition to understand how their product positioning and pricing strategy compare. Before the Internet, it required someone to go to the competing store, check their catalogs, product positioning, and pricing, and then return with the intel to adjust their product strategy as necessary to attempt to keep the advantage and attract more customers.

When companies want to understand consumer sentiment and preferences, they turn to comments left on product review boards or social media like X, Facebook, or Instagram.

The Internet has allowed competitors to automate and accelerate this process, making the market more competitive and dynamic. Collecting and analyzing the data manually would not be feasible. Scraping botnets are the ideal tools for the job. Extracting business intelligence or customer sentiment can be complex, but the evolution of machine learning algorithms has made the process easier and more accessible.

Companies can build their own business intelligence systems. However, this requires a team of expert developers and data scientists to build a scraper that can defeat bot management solutions protecting the targeted site and building a parser to extract and structure the data in a usable way to be consumed by machine learning algorithms and derive valuable intelligence. The process can be very complicated and time-consuming, and the team may need to update their software constantly to adapt to the bot management solution, protecting the targeted site and adapting to the layout and structure of the site, which may change over time. The task is made even more difficult if the task involves scraping several websites that may have different levels of protection and different structures. Scrapers in this category are generally less sophisti-cated and easier to detect and ultimately defeat.

Alternatively, companies can turn to data extraction service providers. There is such a signifi-cant demand for online data that a whole industry is dedicated to harvesting it and extracting competitive intelligence for e-commerce sites. Dozens of data extraction services providers offer services to provide business intelligence. These well-funded companies are staffed with engineers responsible for building an advanced network of proxies and a scalable botnet infrastructure. Their data scientist team is dedicated to structuring the data collected and extracting actionable intelligence. They use web scrapers to extract the data they need from the Internet. Considering the staff skill set of these companies, the botnets are more sophisticated, more challenging to detect, and more persistent. Here are a few examples of companies offering such services:

- **ScrapeHero:** Based in the United States, ScrapeHero offers services for price monitor-ing, web crawling, sales intelligence, and brand monitoring. They claim to have Fortune 500 companies and the top five global retailers among their customers.
- **Zyte:** Based in the United States and Ireland, Zyte offers scraping and data extraction services. One can simply take advantage of their scraping services with anti-bot detec-tion technology. Or one can buy the data they already scrape regularly for a monthly fee.
- **Outsource Bigdata:** Based in the United States, Canada, India, and Australia, Out-source BigData offers web scraping and data labeling services.
- **Bright Data:** Based in Israel and the United States, Bright Data offers scraping and data extraction but also operates a vast network of proxy servers to facilitate scraping operations.

From the web security point of view, we always like to portray the parties we try to defend against as the "bad guys." In this case, it would be the party initiating the scraping activity. The aforementioned companies don't fit the typical "bad guys" profile. Scraping is the means that allows the collection of necessary data that they process through complex models to extract valu-able business intelligence. Everyone wants data from others, but one may not always be willing to share theirs. So, third-party data extraction companies fulfill the need, and web security com-panies offering bot management products are here to prevent the activity as much as possible. As both these opposite markets evolve, this promises an intensive fight between the two parties. Figure 2.30 shows the business intelligence life cycle when a data extraction company is used:

1. A company—for example, a retailer—defines the scope of the analysis, the type of data, and the targeted competition with the data mining company.
2. The data extraction company will configure its botnet to scrape relevant websites. The scraper may also target social media to collect consumer comments and opinions on various products or the company itself.

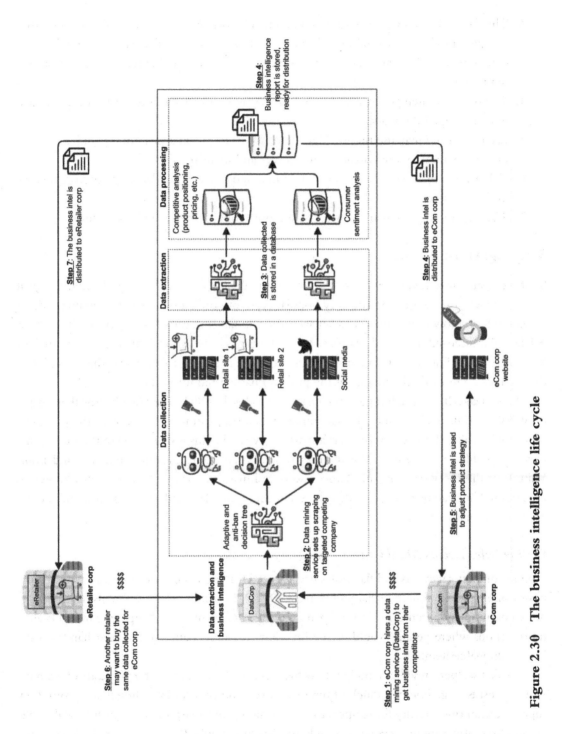

Figure 2.30 The business intelligence life cycle

3. The data collected will be structured in a usable format, stored, and analyzed through complex machine-learning models. The data from online retailers will be used for competitive analysis, and the data from social media will provide insight into consumer sentiment.

4. The business intelligence will be stored and ready for distribution to the company that initially scoped the work.

5. Each company may use the intelligence to adjust its product positioning and/or pricing to attract more customers to the site and increase sales.

6. Other e-commerce companies may be interested in the same data and purchase a copy of the intelligence.

7. The data mining company distributes a report copy to the second customer.

Scalping: Hype Events

Scalping is similar to inventory hoarding, which was already discussed in this chapter, except it mostly happens during specific and very popular types of product sales. The two main products attracting flash crowds are concert ticket sales for popular pop stars like Taylor Swift, BTS, or Adele and limited-edition sneaker drops. We've all heard about the Ticketmaster fiasco for Taylor Swift's 2023 Eras Tour ticket sales, where scalpers managed to purchase the majority of tickets. This event made the news, but the problem has existed for years.

Also, sneakerheads (including my teenage son) closely follow the weekly "sneaker drops" from Nike and its retailers and get disappointed when they cannot secure one of the pairs. I've supported sneaker drop events for years as part of my work. This is by far one of the most complex bot problems to solve on the Internet today. Other companies like luxury brand Louis Vuitton or the footwear company Crocs also occasionally run these flash sales, also known as *hype events*. They can be so popular that the event sometimes lasts only a few minutes before the entire inventory is sold out.

Online Sales Events Mania and Scalping

Online commercial events and flash sales have existed for years. Still, with more and more businesses taking place online, especially since the COVID-19 pandemic, those events have become more common and intense. Five to ten years ago, big sales events were happening in brick-and-mortar shops where people would queue for hours to get a chance to lay their hands on the latest fashionable item.

Sneaker scalpers/resellers closely follow hype events. They have mastered the art of scalping, which consists of grabbing as much of the inventory as possible and reselling it at a profit. Low supplies are an opportunity for scalpers to score a high profit margin. These professional resellers continuously monitor evolving trends to determine which items are in high demand, monitor product resupplies on retailer sites, buy the stock when available, and resell them on popular marketplaces like Amazon or eBay (Figure 2.31).

This practice, which involves bots to scale the operation, raises concerns about consumer fairness. Because of the intense competition that legitimate consumers face against scalpers, they sometimes resort to using bots themselves to increase their chances of buying the product. The problem was so severe with ticket scalpers that the Better Online Ticket Sales Act (a.k.a. BOTS Act) was signed into federal law in the United States in 2016 to thwart the attempts by individuals or organizations to automate the process of buying tickets en masse using bots. However, this law has done little to solve the problem and doesn't extend to the sneaker problem. This activity can significantly impact the price of goods and the retailer's reputation, which e-commerce sites need to protect against.

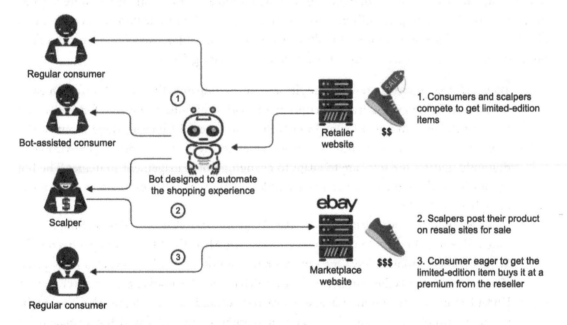

Figure 2.31   Scalping with hype events

The Retailer Botnet Market

This dramatic change in market dynamics significantly increases the competition where legitimate consumers compete with scalpers. Crafty software developers found a new opportunity within this new dynamic by offering bot software to help scalpers and legitimate consumers alike acquire their products and even out the competition. This section describes the bot market, what these sales events look like, and what it takes to prepare for a successful event.

Bot software developers who traditionally focused on a handful of sneaker retailers have branched out to offer their services to support other fashion brands, electronic retailers, and even home improvement stores. Several bot vendors on the market readily sell bots designed to look for specific items on various websites, add them to a cart, and automatically go through the entire checkout process, as highlighted in Figure 2.32.

There are dozens of bot products designed for scalpers and hype sales events on the market. Like any software, each product has strengths and weaknesses and offers various features to defeat bot and fraud detection products. Like any legitimate business, most bot vendors advertise their ability to handle multiple websites and use cases. However, the reality is that their performance largely depends on the sophistication of the web security product and the team defending the targeted website, as well as the ability of the bot developer to adapt their product to defeat the defense. Some are designed to support multiple websites; others are more tailored to specific use cases. The price of bot software may vary based on their known success rate in checking out products and support of multiple use cases or sites. Here are a few examples of top bot performers against sneaker drops at the time of this writing (2024).

- *Wrath AIO bot* supports sites like Shopify and shoe companies like Nike. It offers an easy-to-use interface, allowing users to configure it within minutes to prepare for a release. It will cost the user an initial fee of $350 with a $50 renewal fee every three months. The subscription-based model ensures a steady revenue stream to the developer, who continuously updates the software to adapt to changing bot management strategies. The bot creator limits the number of licenses available for sale, which drives its aftermarket resale price beyond $5,000.
- *Kodai bot* supports several sites like Adidas, Amazon, Nike, ASOS, Rakuten, Shopify and more. The initial cost is lower than that of Wrath AIO Bot. One can buy a license for $75 with a $50 monthly fee. One can also rent the bot for $110 per event, a hefty price. Kodai Bot also limits the number of licenses, driving its aftermarket price to over $6,000. Kodai has an easy-to-use interface, supports proxies, and can be integrated with captcha solvers to handle more complex checkout workflows and advanced bot management solutions. This bot is favored by scalpers. The bot's website shows examples of the scalpers' success and their profit margin reaching over $1,000

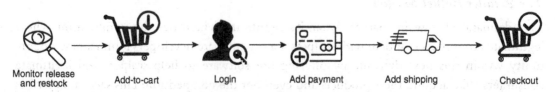

Monitor release   Add-to-cart   Login   Add payment   Add shipping   Checkout
and restock

Figure 2.32 The checkout process supported by most botnets used for scalping

  – *uSNKRS* exclusively focuses on Nike releases. Slightly cheaper than the one described above, a license (when available) costs $90 for two months. The *utools.store* site where the bot can be purchased claims over 500k pairs bought by its users. The site offers regular updates to keep up with Nike's evolving bot management strategy.

Project Enigma is a SaaS service primarily designed for checking out sneakers. It supports setting up various profiles with multiple accounts, billing addresses, and payment information. Using numerous profiles makes each request appear unique and prevents orders from getting canceled. Before the sales events start, the operator can launch multiple browsers that automatically log in using the preconfigured accounts and then check out the items. Proxies are recommended; this product does not support CAPTCHA solving. A license initially costs $299. Long-term users may renew their licenses for three to six months for $30 and $60, respectively.

Unlike the web scraper/business intelligence use case previously discussed, we're not dealing with corporations that build these bots but more like a small group of individuals (like startups) that make a living building scalper bots. The preceding offerings are the most mainstream and established. Still, there are plenty of other *tailor-made bots* from independent freelance developers ready to develop custom bot solutions. From the defenders' point of view, this shows the extent of the bot management problem. Many professional developers are looking to produce software that will defeat detection to provide the best service to their users.

Anatomy of a Hype Event

A hype event is characterized by a massive change in traffic volume within a short period. The traffic ramps up quickly and reaches at least four times the normal volume for 30 minutes or less. The most extreme events may peak at more than 1,000 times the normal traffic volume and ramp up within a few seconds. These events catch the interest of large numbers of people.

Because the event lasts such a short time, it is challenging to manage from the defender's point of view and requires some preparation. The defense in place needs to detect the typical attack vectors by default and apply an adequate response strategy. During the event, there is no time for a security analyst to review the specificity of the attack, define a custom signature, adjust the detection setting, and deploy the changes to production. These steps take some time, even for a seasoned security analyst, and the event would likely be over by the time the changes are in place.

Let's look at a sample event to illustrate its intensity, timeline, and how it affects the traffic pattern on various endpoints. This example reflects the typical bot and human traffic patterns observed before and during a hype event.

Users who want to acquire the limited-edition item during a launch event must go through a specific workflow. The journey usually starts with the item being announced on social media and a dedicated web page on the site that describes the item that customers can buy. Some scalpers may scrape the site in an attempt to discover the main web page that corresponds to the launch. Once the item becomes available, the user can add it to their cart and complete the checkout process, which may involve logging in, entering the payment information and shipping address, and eventually completing the purchase.

For these hype events, the user must have a valid login. An increase in activity on the login endpoint is typically observed within the hour preceding the event. This corresponds to legitimate users getting ready for the event and some bot operators configuring their systems.

Shortly after the limited-edition items are made available for sale, we'll generally see a spike in login activity—mostly from humans and some bots (Figure 2.33).

Some users may have trouble remembering their credentials during login, which could translate to increased password reset before and during the event.

Once logged in, the user will enter their payment details. The activity coming from bots is particularly important. It indicates that legitimate users are also taking advantage of bot products to get a better chance at checking out the items and waiting until the last minute to configure their bot. Scalpers would typically have this step already configured in their system.

The bot traffic represented sometimes starts earlier and lasts longer than the event itself. Figure 2.34 shows a distinct increase in activity preceding the event. The tallest time series corresponds to the bot activity detected.

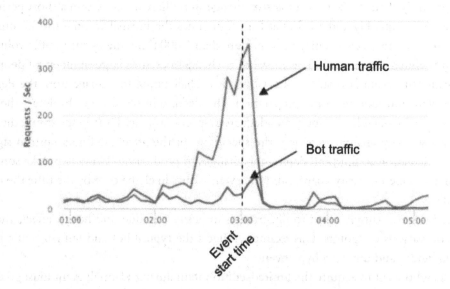

Figure 2.33   Impact of the hype event on the login endpoint

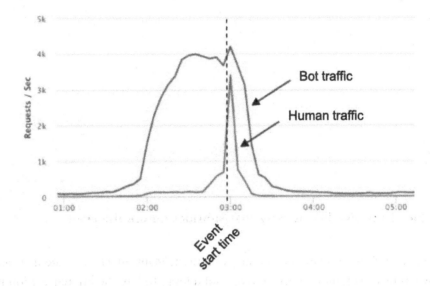

Figure 2.34   Increases in bot configuration activity preceding the events, as seen on the payment details endpoint

Finally, as soon as the event starts, we see a significant increase in activity on the checkout endpoint (Figure 2.35). The activity from bots (the tallest spike) at the checkout is generally substantial. All users may have to go through a waiting-room process, and only users who have completed the workflow will access the final checkout step while there is still some inventory available. The "wind down" period may vary depending on many factors, including how quickly the inventory sells out.

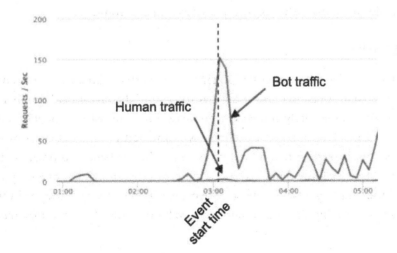

Figure 2.35   A significant increase in activity on the checkout endpoint

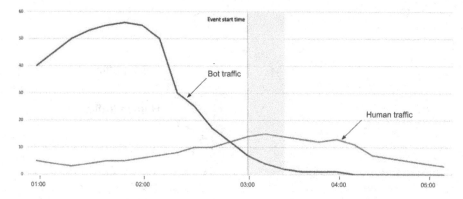

Figure 2.36   Excessive bot activity that subsides before the event

The bot activity often goes beyond the event itself. Many attackers create new accounts in advance when retailers require users to have a valid login to buy the limited-edition item. This commonly translates to recurring excessive bot activity on the account creation endpoint. Figure 2.36 shows excessive bot activity that subsides before the event. As seen in the account opening abuse attack discussion, attackers may create these accounts days or weeks before the events, let them age, and enroll them into exclusive groups as needed to get a better chance to check out an item successfully during the event.

Protecting each workflow step is essential to have as many opportunities as possible to screen the traffic to differentiate bots from humans. Bots detected at each stage should be mitigated most efficiently. For example, bot traffic can be denied on the page where the announcement is made—if they can't see the item, they can't buy it. Preventing bots from creating new accounts will also deny them the right to participate in the event.

Carding Attacks

Unlike other attacks that we've discussed so far that are part of a broader attack scheme, carding attacks are more "self-contained." All it takes is to "guess" the credit card number correctly to take advantage of it immediately and make a purchase. Any card with a monetary value, whether credit or gift card, involved in an attack scheme is considered a carding attack. Any e-commerce site has a checkout workflow that allows users to pay by card and can be abused as part of a carding attack. Most established brands have a gift card program, which opens up more opportunities for abuse. Carding attacks consist of two steps. The first step is the card validation step, which consists of verifying that a card number is valid or active. This step may require making a micro-purchase in the case of credit cards. The next step is card draining, where the attacker uses the card's funds to make a purchase.

Gift Cards

Gift cards are an easy way to show someone they are appreciated. Companies may use them to reward their employees for a job well done, and it also makes an easy gift for special occasions. Figure 2.37 shows the usage of gift cards during the holiday season, and you can clearly see an increase in payment by gift cards during sales events like Black Friday or Cyber Monday, but also during the week leading up to Christmas.

Most sites that allow payment by gift card have a separate application to allow consumers to check their gift card balance. One must provide the card number and associated PIN code to redeem a gift card. Once submitted, an API call to the server will validate the information entered. Those APIs are regular targets of attackers attempting to guess or validate the number/PIN combination. Sometimes, it's not so much a guess as it is more of a logical flaw in the card provider's number and safety PIN scheme that some clever attackers can reverse engineer. Another way for fraudsters to get these numbers is by collecting gift cards from the store, recording their numbers, replacing them at the store, and waiting for someone to buy and activate the card. The last step of monitoring the card activation can easily be automated with a botnet through the merchant's website. When a match on an active card is found, the attacker can set it aside and use it to purchase some items on the targeted website. The actual gift card owner will then be surprised that their credit has been drained when they try to use it. Alternatively, the attacker may sell the gift card on the dark web or some other public forum for a fraction of the total dollar value.

An analysis using data from the Federal Trade Commission in the United States found that gift card fraud cost consumers $148 million in 2023, a number on the rise compared to the previous year.

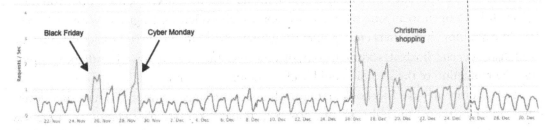

Figure 2.37 Gift cards used as payment method during the holiday shopping season

Credit Card Stuffing

Credentials or personal information are not the only type of data included in major data leaks mentioned previously. Attacks targeting e-commerce sites sometimes also include credit card information (credit card number, expiration date, CVV, and zip code associated with the account). Stolen credit card numbers can be found on marketplaces on the dark web. Fraudsters who purchase them need to validate them first. A list may contain thousands, but their owners may have already canceled their cards. Validating the credit card can easily be done by making a small purchase on an e-commerce website. Doing this manually would be time-consuming, and time is of the essence since the attacker must exploit the credit card before its owner cancels it.

Like attacks on gift cards, the most effective way to make the attack is by using a botnet that will go through the site, add a product to the cart, go through the checkout process, and use one of the stolen credit cards as payment information. If the purchase is successful, the fraudster can use the card to make additional and larger purchases or sell the verified card to other fraudsters.

Credit card stuffing generally results in an abnormally high number of declined transactions or a higher-than-usual shopping cart abandonment rate for a website owner. Credit card owners who are victims of the scheme must cancel their credit cards and call their bankers to ensure they are not liable for the purchase.

According to the 2023 Nilson Report, the global financial losses associated with credit card fraud are colossal, as they reached $28.64 billion in 2022.

Spam and Abusive Language

Many websites or web applications offer their users the possibility to interact with each other to share opinions and ask or answer questions. For example, media sites may allow users to share opinions on shows. Most tech companies have community websites where customers can get support or share best practices and product usage guidelines. E-commerce websites allow users to leave reviews on products they bought. Social media sites like LinkedIn, Facebook, YouTube, and TikTok are open to anyone who may use abusive and offensive language. With such freedom of expression, some users end up discussing unrelated or inappropriate topics that include spam, hate speech, clickbait, sexism, racism, or obscenity that are offensive to others, compromise the reputation of the site, and could lead to lawsuits and fines.

Today, companies like Facebook and LinkedIn dedicate large teams of data scientists, developers, and moderators to deal with this growing problem because allowing users to express themselves is core to their business. But for e-commerce, tech, or media companies for which the social aspect is not part of their core business, monitoring and curating user-created content is often reactive and relies on other users flagging inappropriate content before it is noticed and eventually removed.

Bot management products can help detect abusive language or spam since, in some cases, bots are used to spread toxic content on various platforms. To be most effective, the detection method also needs to look at the content submitted and look for signs of abusive language. One may look for specific keywords in a message and flag inappropriate ones. The challenge of this simple method is that it needs to consider the context of the message, which could lead to false positives. Also, attackers have learned to defeat the keyword detection approach by using slang or alternate words or adding special characters. For example, typical spam messages include the word *discount*. To avoid detection, the spammer may instead spell the word the following way: "di$count" or "d.i.s.c.o.u.n.t." A human reading the message will understand the message but a simple keyword approach would, in this case, likely fail to detect the spam. On the other hand, the word *discount* can be used in a completely legitimate message, which could lead to false positive.

A machine learning approach using the Term Frequency and Inverse Document Frequency (TF-IDF) approach may be more efficient by learning from labeled messages containing abusive language and ones with regular language. Term frequency consists of counting the times a term appears in a document. Inverse Document Frequency defines which frequent terms have the most weight and are the most relevant for a given topic, such as hate speech or spam. Dealing with multiple languages and slang adds another layer of complexity to the process.

Summary

This chapter reviewed the most common forms of abuse on the Internet that involve botnets. Not all that botnet activity, of course, is bad, especially in the case of "good bots" like web search engines or social media bots, which technically fall into the web scraping category but are critical to any business since they help make the site's content easier to find and attract new customers. But beyond the good bot traffic, there remains a significant amount of bot activity that needs to be addressed and managed to prevent the site owner and its users from falling victim to fraud schemes. The complexity of some attack schemes involves several steps, like the scalping attack that starts with account opening abuse, followed by scraping to finally complete with the purchase of the product and its resale on third-party marketplaces. Now that you understand the purpose of these botnets, the next chapter looks at the botnet infrastructure and how it typically evolves based on the defense in place to protect the targeted website.

3

The Evolution of Botnet Attacks

What are botnets, and how does their architecture evolve based on the defense strategy protecting a website when faced with a persistent bot operator driven by an economic incentive?

Incentive vs. Botnet Sophistication

The evolution of defense strategies has pushed botnet operators to become much more advanced. Because of the continuous advancement of web security products, some less sophisticated botnet developers have given up along the way. New entrants, however, will always find their way into the bot game to pick up where others left off and advance their tools and methods.

Back in the days when bot activity was perceived as DDoS, a simple web application firewall with rate limiting, IP blocking, and a custom rule builder was all that was needed to protect a website against attacks. These simpler methods still help today to detect bot activity, but not for long. Bot operators and fraudsters, in general, are motivated by the revenue gained from the data collected. After all, data is the new gold when one knows how to exploit it. The higher the revenue potential, the more persistent and sophisticated the attack strategy. For example, scalpers can make huge returns on reselling limited-edition shoes. Data extraction companies make big revenue by scraping and selling data from the Internet to their customers. ATO can also be lucrative. The level of sophistication of the botnet also largely depends on the sophistication of the defense in place. Bot operators are mindful of cost. A sophisticated botnet is more expensive to develop, maintain, operate, and ultimately impact their bottom line. So, bot operators typically deploy a botnet with just the right level of sophistication to defeat the defense. Figure 3.1 shows the evolution of the attack complexity compared with the revenue potential.

What typically triggers the evolution of botnets is powerful detection coupled with efficient mitigation strategies. As soon as you start mitigating the activity detected, you'll see a rapid shift in the botnet behavior and the overall attack strategy. The way an attack evolves follows always the same pattern, as described in the upcoming section "The Six Stages of a Botnet Evolution."

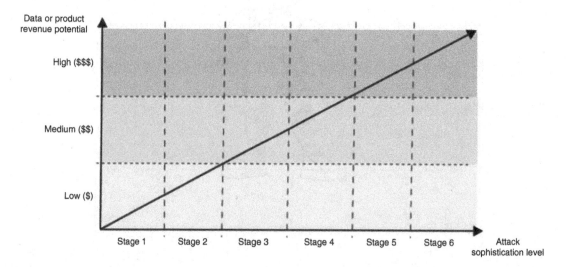

Figure 3.1   Attack sophistication vs. revenue potential

HTTP Headers 101

HTTP stands for HyperText Transfer Protocol. Several RFCs have been drafted over the years, corresponding to the various versions of the protocol. The latest HTTP version is version 3, also commonly referred to as HTTP/3 or H3 for short, and was officially standardized in 2022. H3 introduced several improvements to accelerate content delivery compared to the previous version by replacing the TCP protocol with UDP. H3 also improves security by enforcing the use of TLS v1.3. At the time of this writing, the adoption of H3 is still slow, and the most common protocol version on the Internet is still HTTP/2, or H2 for short.

Introduced in 2015, H2 is much faster and more efficient than HTTP/1.1, the original version introduced in 1997. One way H2 is faster is in how it prioritizes content during the page loading process. H2 also introduced multiplexing to load content using multiple streams to load the different elements in parallel. H2 also supports header compression to reduce the payload size. Although not required by the RFC, most browsers apply H2 only on secure connections (with TLS 1.2).

HTTP v1.1 has not totally disappeared yet, but today, it is mostly linked to nonsecure traffic, which is becoming rare, bot activity, or legitimate traffic coming through legacy corporate or public proxy services that have not yet been upgraded to support more recent protocol versions. When an HTTP message is sent, it includes a set of headers that are heavily used in bot detection to assess the traffic and detect bots.

Common HTTP Headers

A method to assess the sophistication of a botnet is to look at the HTTP headers sent with the request. Some of the standard headers are referenced throughout the sections that follow. Let's establish a baseline and define the most common HTTP headers one would expect a legitimate web browser to send with every request. The set and order of headers sent may vary from one browser vendor to another. Such variation helps establish a legitimate HTTP header signature.

The following table lists the standard headers across all browser vendors:

Header Name	Header Value Example	Purpose
User-Agent	Mozilla/5.0 (Macintosh; Intel Mac OS X 10.15; rv:109.0) Gecko/20100101 Firefox/113.0	Provides details about the system and application requesting the content (type of hardware, operating system, browser vendor).

(continued)

(continues)

Header Name	Header Value Example	Purpose
Accept	text/html,application/ xhtml+xml,application/ xml;q=0.9,image/avif,image/ webp,*/*;q=0.8	Indicates which content types, expressed as MIME types, the client is able to understand.
Accept-Language	en–US,en;q=0.5	Indicates the natural language and locale that the client prefers.
Accept-Encoding	gzip, deflate, br	Indicates the content encoding (usually a compression algorithm) that the client can understand.
Connection	keep-alive	Controls whether the network connection stays open after the current transaction finishes. Mostly linked to HTTP/1.1.
Cookie	sessionID=abc123	Contains stored session information associated with the website previously set with the client with the set-cookie header.

The following table lists the additional headers expected with the POST method:

Header Name	Header Value Example	Purpose
Content-Type	Application/json	Indicates the format the content included in the body of the request, typically URL-encoded, JSON, or plain text.
Content-Length	299	Indicates the size of the content included in the body of the request.

Client hint headers, as shown in the following table, were introduced as a more secure and privacy-oriented way to share information about the client with the server. The client hints header aims to replace the User-Agent header eventually. Most Chromium-based browsers (Chrome, Opera, Edge) support the new header set.

Header Name	Header Value Example	Purpose
`Sec-CH-UA`	Sec-CH-UA: " Not A;Brand";v="99", "Chromium";v="96", "Google Chrome";v="96"	Indicates the browser brand and major version.
`Sec-CH-Mobile`	?0	A binary value (0 or 1) that indicates if the browser is running on a mobile device.
`Sec-CH-Platform`	macOS	Indicates the operating system on which the browser is running.

As described in the following table, fetch metadata request headers were designed to provide additional information about the context from which the request originated and help prevent cross-site attacks. This allows the server to decide whether a request should be allowed based on where the request came from and how the resource will be used. Recent versions of all major browser brands support the fetch metadata request headers (MDN Web Docs, 2024a).

Header Name	Header Value Example	Purpose
`Sec-Fetch-Site`	Same-origin	Indicates the relation between a request initiator's origin and the origin of the requested source.
`Sec-Fetch-Mode`	navigate	Helps the server differentiate between requests that come from a user navigating between pages and requests to load images or other static resources.
`Sec-Fetch-User`	?1	Indicates if a user originated a navigation request from a document, iframe, and so forth.
`Sec-Fetch-Dest`	Document, embed, audio, etc.	Indicates how a resource will be used.

The following section includes examples of HTTP header signatures from various browsers. Note how the set of headers and their order change from one browser to another. Once you understand what legitimate HTTP header signatures look like, it becomes easier to spot bot traffic that may present a different set of headers in various orders.

Legitimate Browser Signatures

This section provides examples of HTTP headers, their values, and their exact order sent by various legitimate browsers with HTTP/2. One can notice some commonality in the set of headers sent, but the order varies slightly from one browser brand to the next. The `Host` header seems to always be in the first position for all the four brands presented, but the position of other headers, like the `Accept`, `Accept-Language`, or `User-Agent`, varies. Also, note the lack of `Sec-CH-UA` headers for Safari and Firefox compared with Chrome and Microsoft Edge.

Chrome running on Windows:

```
GET /url/path HTTPS/2.0
Host: www.mysite.com
Sec-CH-UA: "Google Chrome";v="113", "Chromium";v="113", "Not-A.Brand";v="24"
sec-ch-ua-mobile: ?0
sec-ch-ua-platform: "Windows"
upgrade-insecure-requests: 1
User-Agent: Mozilla/5.0 (Windows NT 10.0; Win64; x64) AppleWebKit/537.36
(KHTML, like Gecko) Chrome/113.0.0.0 Safari/537.36
Accept: text/html,application/xhtml+xml,application/xml;q=0.9,image/avif,
image/webp,image/apng,*/*;q=0.8,application/signed-exchange;v=b3;q=0.7
sec-fetch-site: same-origin
sec-fetch-mode: navigate
sec-fetch-dest: document
Accept-Encoding: gzip, deflate, br
Accept-Language: en-US,en;q=0.9
```

Edge running on Windows:

```
GET /url/path HTTPS/2.0
Host: www.mysite.com
Sec-CH-UA: "Microsoft Edge";v="113", "Chromium";v="113", "Not-A.Brand";
v="24"
Accept-Language: en-US,en;q=0.9
upgrade-insecure-requests: 1
sec-ch-ua-mobile: ?0
User-Agent: Mozilla/5.0 (Windows NT 10.0; Win64; x64) AppleWebKit/537.36
(KHTML, like Gecko) Chrome/113.0.0.0 Safari/537.36 Edg/113.0.1774.50
Accept: text/html,application/xhtml+xml,application/xml;q=0.9,image/avif,
image/webp,image/apng,*/*;q=0.8,application/signed-exchange;v=b3;q=0.9
Cache-Control: max-age=0
sec-ch-ua-platform: "Windows"
sec-fetch-site: none
```

```
sec-fetch-mode: cors
sec-fetch-dest: empty
Accept-Encoding: gzip, deflate, br
```

Firefox running on Windows:

```
GET /url/path HTTPS/2.0
Host: www.mysite.com
User-Agent: Mozilla/5.0 (Windows NT 10.0; Win64; x64; rv:109.0) Gecko/
20100101 Firefox/113.0
Accept: text/html,application/xhtml+xml,application/xml;q=0.9,image/avif,
image/webp,*/*;q=0.8
Accept-Language: en-US,en;q=0.5
Accept-Encoding: gzip, deflate, br
upgrade-insecure-requests: 1
sec-fetch-dest: document
sec-fetch-mode: navigate
sec-fetch-site: same-origin
sec-fetch-user: ?1
```

Safari running on macOS:

```
GET /url/path HTTPS/2.0
Host: www.mysite.com
Accept: text/html,application/xhtml+xml,application/xml;q=0.9,*/*;q=0.8
sec-fetch-site: same-origin
sec-fetch-dest: document
Accept-Language: en-US,en;q=0.9
sec-fetch-mode: navigate
User-Agent: Mozilla/5.0 (Macintosh; Intel Mac OS X 10_15_7) AppleWebKit/
605.1.15 (KHTML, like Gecko) Version/16.4 Safari/605.1.15
Accept-Encoding: gzip, deflate, br
```

Header Signatures from Bot Requests

The most advanced botnet sends the expected header set in the correct order. However, there are still botnets that do not make much effort to impersonate legitimate browsers.

The least advanced botnets can simply send the set of headers strictly required to make a successful request. In this example, the botnet only sends the Host and Accept header:

```
GET /url/path HTTPS/2.0
Host: www.mysite.com
Accept: */*
```

The following is a slightly more elaborate version—at least there is a `User-Agent` this time:

```
GET /url/path HTTPS/2.0
Host: www.mysite.com
User-Agent: Mozilla/5.0 (X11; Linux x86_64) AppleWebKit/537.36 (KHTML, like
Gecko) Chrome/106.0.0.0 Safari/537.36
Accept: */*
```

Here's an example where the client pretends to be a recent Chrome version, but the header signature is unlike the legitimate Chrome version. The fetch metadata request headers and client hint headers are missing. Some uncommon headers are also present, like the `Cache-Control` and `Pragma` headers with the `no-cache` directives, which are headers more commonly found in the response. Another giveaway from the following request is that the request is made over HTTP/1.1, which, at this point, is obsolete.

```
GET /url/path HTTPS/1.1
Host: www.mysite.com
User-Agent: Mozilla/5.0 (Windows NT 10.0; Win64; x64) AppleWebKit/537.36
(KHTML, like Gecko) Chrome/113.0.0.0 Safari/537.36
Accept-Encoding: gzip, deflate
Accept: application/json, text/plain, */*
Connection: keep-alive
Accept-Language: en-US,en;q=0.9,zh-CN;q=0.8,zh;q=0.7
Cache-Control: no-cache
Pragma: no-cache
Referer: https://www.mysite.com
```

Here's another example of a botnet missing some basic headers, such as the `Accept-Language`, `Connection`, `Sec-Fetch`, and client hint headers. The value of the `Accept-Encoding` header is also unusual, as we would expect the *gzip* and *deflate* values instead of identity.

```
GET /url/path HTTPS/1.1
Host: www.mysite.com
Accept-Encoding: identity
User-Agent: Mozilla/5.0 (Windows NT 10.0; Win64; x64) AppleWebKit/537.36
(KHTML, like Gecko) Chrome/90.0.4430.93 Safari/537.36
Accept: text/html,application/xhtml+xml,application/xml;q=0.9,image/webp,
*/*;q=0.8
```

Lastly, here's an example where the set of headers provided is mostly correct, but the order is inconsistent with the real Chrome browser:

```
GET /url/path HTTPS/1.1
Host: www.mysite.com
User-Agent: Mozilla/5.0 (Windows NT 10.0; Win64; x64) AppleWebKit/537.36
(KHTML, like Gecko) Chrome/100.0.4896.75 Safari/537.36
Accept-Encoding: gzip, deflate, br
Accept: application/json, text/plain, */*
Connection: keep-alive
Accept-Language: zh-CN,zh;q=0.9,en;q=0.8,en-GB;q=0.7,en-US;q=0.6
Cache-Control: no-cache
Pragma: no-cache
Sec-CH-UA: " Not A;Brand";v="99", "Chromium";v="100", "Google Chrome";
v="100"
sec-ch-ua-mobile: ?0
sec-ch-ua-platform: "Windows"
sec-fetch-dest: empty
sec-fetch-mode: cors
sec-fetch-site: same-origin
```

The Six Stages of a Botnet Evolution

Bot detection has advanced to curb the evolution of automated attacks. Fraudsters continuously study defense mechanisms that prevent large-scale fraud attempts. The strategy and infrastructure required to attack a website successfully are proportional to the defense in place. Website owners have a vast choice of technology with varying levels of sophistication when it comes to protecting their sites against attacks. Let's review the typical stages of attack evolution as the website owner enhances their web security strategy.

Stage 1: Deploy the Botnet on a Handful of Nodes Running a Simple Script

Attack strategy: Let's assume the attacker targets a site without protection against bots. In that case, they can keep their botnet very simple—a simple script designed to do a particular task and tailored to follow a given workflow, for example, creating accounts using a list of predefined credentials. The script is deployed on several nodes (say a dozen or so) to spread the traffic and stay under the radar of any DoS or WAF protection, which generally includes some rate-limiting features. The attacker may not take any particular care to make the request look like it's coming from a legitimate web browser by including all the expected HTTP headers in the requests, and it may look like one of the simple signatures shown in the previous section. Figure 3.2 shows the overall inexpensive and simple infrastructure.

Defense strategy: Because the number of nodes in the botnet is limited and may also be coming from the same subnet or data center, web security analysts will notice the obnoxious traffic rapidly. Also, because the script is simple, the HTTP header signature will likely look significantly different from regular traffic sent by legitimate web browsers.

If the web security administrator has a WAF at their disposal, they can quickly update the security policy and create rules to block the IP addresses causing problems and block the traffic based on its header signature. Creating a rule that looks for requests with the `User-Agent python_3.6` would be easy in this case. The security administrator at this stage may also take this opportunity to tighten the rate-limiting rules to completely block excessive amounts of traffic from individual IP addresses. For example, if the attack targeted the login endpoint, the security administrator could set up rules limiting the number of requests per IP on the URL to one request per minute or even less if the product allows a lower granularity.

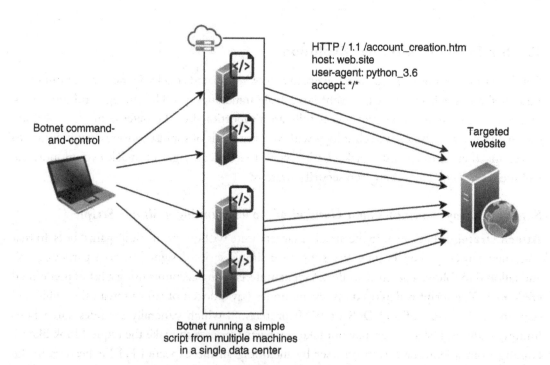

Figure 3.2 A simple botnet with a handful of nodes

Stage 2: Scale the Botnet and Impersonate the Browsers' Header Signatures

Attack strategy: To defeat the basic protection in place (custom signature and rate-limiting), the bot operator must scale up their botnet to hundreds of nodes. These nodes should be hosted in multiple cloud providers, and assuming the audience of the targeted website is global, the cloud providers should be located in various countries to make IP blocking more challenging and the bot traffic less noticeable.

At the same time, the attacker will update the set of headers sent with the requests to remove the obvious telling signs in the `User-Agent` header and instead craft an HTTP signature close to what a legitimate browser like Google Chrome or Firefox would send. Some key data points, like the `User-Agent`, will also be heavily randomized. Most attack tools include a comprehensive dictionary of User-Agents the attacker will cycle through with each request. Simpler attack tools may leverage a list of mostly obsolete User-Agents. More sophisticated ones will leverage a list of more up-to-date User-Agents generally within 10 releases of the current one, making the attack traffic less obvious to detect. Attackers can usually tell how they are being detected based on the request being blocked or challenged. They will adjust their signature through trial and error until some traffic is successful. As shown in Figure 3.3, the infrastructure is now slightly more sophisticated,

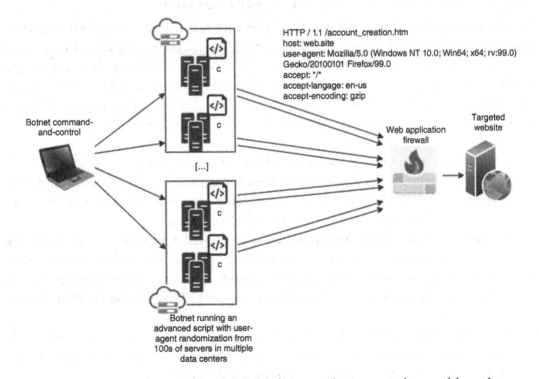

Figure 3.3 A more advanced botnet with browser impersonation and broader deployment

consequently increasing the operation cost due to the need to run the script from several cloud providers.

Defense strategy: Finding themselves unable to eliminate the bot traffic with a web application firewall and tired of playing the Whac-A-Mole game by blocking IPs or HTTP signatures that seem to change as soon as the new security policy is deployed, the web security administrator will opt for a more robust, purpose-built protection and add a bot management solution to defend the website.

Bot management solutions collect telemetry such as key presses or mouse movements and different device and browser characteristics (also known as a *fingerprint*) on the client side through JavaScript. Device and browser characteristics include the type of CPU, number of cores, screen size, platform, memory, graphic card, supported video and audio codecs, software version, and plug-ins. On the server side, additional data is collected and reflects the TLS, TCP, and HTTP protocol parameters the client negotiated when the connection was established. The detection engine processes the telemetry and fingerprint through different algorithms to differentiate bot from human traffic. Detailed discussions of the various detection methods included in most bot detection engines will follow in Chapter 4, "Detection Strategy."

Stage 3: Reverse Engineer JavaScript and Replay Fingerprints

Attack strategy: When bot operators realize the attack is failing, they re-evaluate the workflow. They will look for signs of web security protection, study them, and quickly learn that the work-flow has changed and that a new JavaScript that collects and sends data is running. They will pay particular attention to the JavaScript. When the code is obfuscated, they will spend time reverse engineering the obfuscation. Time for them to up their game. The attacker will identify the type of information the product collects and sends. Attackers, in this case, follow two strategies.

- **Telemetry and fingerprint replay:** They can record and replay good session data using the application as a regular user. However, replaying a limited number of finger-prints may be a dead giveaway. When investigating abnormal traffic on the site, most web security analysts usually look for the top offending signatures.
- **Telemetry and fingerprint randomization:** To avoid standing out too much, attackers typically randomize the rest of the data points in the fingerprint and telemetry to appear more unique and less noticeable. Essentially, they follow the same strategy as in stage 2 but go beyond simply randomizing the value from a specific HTTP header like the User-Agent.

If, as part of the workflow, the web security product generates tokens or cookies, the attacker will assume that they may provide some privileged access, attempt to harvest them from legit sessions, and replay them from a botnet at a later stage.

Defense strategy: The randomization patterns the attacker generates will typically create invalid combinations. When looking at the individual data points, the value is valid. However, when evaluated together, they are not. As defenders, that is when we typically see anomalous fingerprints such as incompatibility between the operating system advertised in the User-Agent, for example, macOS from Apple, and the platform it's running on, for example, Win32. The Windows and Macintel (Apple) combination is also quite common in attack traffic, something you'd never find in legitimate traffic. In other cases, we'll see iPhone as a platform with an impossible screen resolution (1080p).

Advanced bot detection products can typically identify these invalid combinations found in the fingerprint. It's worth also considering that the botnet can still not execute JavaScript at this level of attack sophistication. One way to weed out botnets that cannot run JavaScript is to introduce detection methods like proof of work (PoW) into the security policy. Chapter 4 discusses these different detection concepts in greater detail.

Stage 4: Force the Web Security Product to Fail Open

Attack strategy: Failing to defeat the detection through replay, the most persistent attackers will try sending malformed data to see if it triggers some exceptions. After all, bot operators are all developers, and they know that software exceptions can cause the product to "fail-safe" or "fail open." In effect, this means that tripping an exception or a bug in the product forces a bypass of the defenses. They also know that detection engines don't have infinite capacity, and the fail-safe mechanism may trigger if overwhelmed with traffic (back to the good old DDoS strategy). Bot developers are the best quality assurance engineers out there!

The best way to generate more traffic while not being blocked by the defenses in place is to load balance the traffic through even more proxies. As shown in Figure 3.4, the attacker at this stage may opt to leverage several proxy providers spanning dozens of countries to make the defender's task more complex. DoSing the web security infrastructure is risky, as the attacker could overwhelm their target. This would be counterproductive since they could not achieve their data collection or resource exploitation goals. In this case, they bet the targeted website has more capacity than the web security infrastructure, typically run by third-party Software-as-a-service (SaaS) providers.

Defense strategy: SaaS bot management or fraud detection solutions are best positioned to handle large volumes of attack traffic as they run on a cloud infrastructure like Amazon Web Services (AWS) or a CDN service. Although no SaaS infrastructure ever has infinite capacity, SaaS solutions are typically well-versed in adapting to large loads by scaling horizontally. Handling the load may be more challenging for hosted solutions if the system is not adequately provisioned. To determine the suitable capacity to provision, look at historical volumes on the endpoints you want to protect, including during an attack. The past does not always indicate what will happen in the future, but it certainly sets a baseline. Attackers' capacity depends on the size of their infrastructure and the cost they are willing to pay.

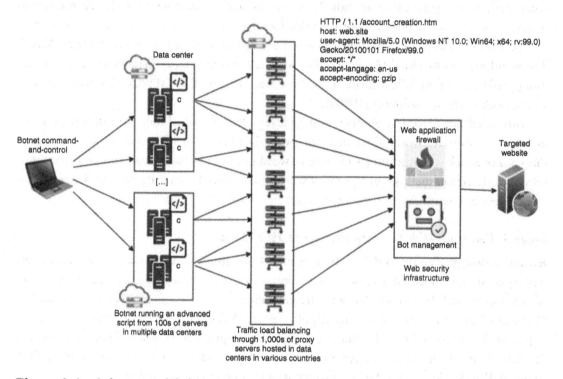

Figure 3.4 A botnet with increased scale leveraging cloud-based proxy services

Stage 5: Upgrade the Botnet to a Headless Browser

Attack strategy: At this point, the website is well protected against most forms of bot attacks using sophisticated scripts, and the best way forward for the most motivated attackers will be to upgrade their botnet with headless browser technology. Products like Selenium, headless Chrome, Playwright, and Puppeteer were built as a way for developers to automate the testing of their websites. However, these same tools are also commonly used to build more intelligent botnets that can run JavaScript natively. They can also be programmed to simulate human-like behaviors like mouse movement and key presses. For some frameworks like headless Chrome, the browser and device characteristics collected using JavaScript look very close to the regular version of Chrome, making detection methods that look for inconsistencies in the fingerprint ineffective. Headless browsers provide a regular-looking fingerprint and can also be programmed to simulate human behavior from keystrokes, mouse movements, and clicks. They can also resolve proof-of-work challenges, making this technology ineffective.

To make things even more challenging from the detection standpoint, attackers may also opt to upgrade their proxy infrastructure further. Instead of using the most basic proxy services running out of data centers, the attacker can use more advanced and expensive proxy services that leverage residential and mobile ISP IP addresses.

Figure 3.5 represents the infrastructure of the most advanced botnets. It shows that the required infrastructure is a lot more complex. It includes virtual machines hosted from data centers that load balance the traffic through advanced proxy services. This requires a lot more skill to develop and maintain. Additionally, such infrastructure is more expensive to run. If the average cost of cloud-hosted proxy services is about $50/month, a proxy service that provides access to millions of residential and mobile ISP IP addresses costs around $700/month. The cost also increases based on the traffic volume. Only attackers with a solid model to monetize the data harvested can justify the additional cost of pursuing their attack.

Defense strategy: Fortunately, headless browsers typically leave a few breadcrumbs within the Document Object Model (DOM), but skilled attackers may know how to remove them, making this traffic more difficult to detect. More advanced JavaScript-based methods are

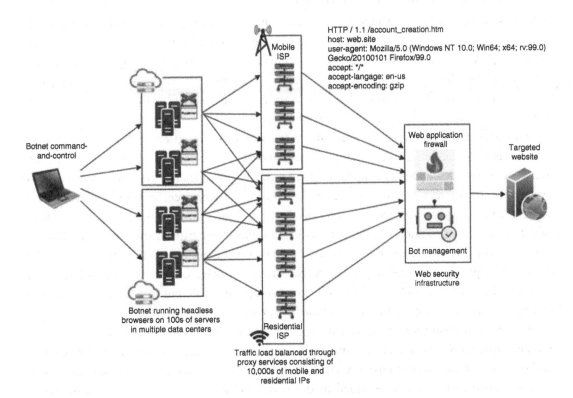

Figure 3.5   A headless browser botnet leveraging advanced proxy services

required to detect headless browsers in stealth mode. The detection method must focus on the particularities of headless browsers that typically run in a virtual machine environment. Several virtual machines may be running on a server, competing for resources. As a result, headless browsers may take more time to execute repetitive commands or run complex operations than regular devices. This concept is called the *red pill* in reference to the blockbuster movie from the late 1990s, *The Matrix*, which checks if the client can run JavaScript, tests its resources, and reveals its true nature (a bot).

Behavioral biometric detection that evaluates how the user interacts with the machine through mouse movement and key presses would also help here. The mouse movements, for example, may appear too smooth, straight, or repetitive from one session to another. Such characteristics in behavioral data are extremely unlikely with legitimate traffic as one cannot reproduce the same mouse movement or press keys at the same cadence within a somewhat short interval of time. I'll discuss the benefits of behavioral biometric detection in more detail in Chapter 4.

Stage 6: Resort to Human/Manual Attack

Attack strategy: Most will give up when the botnet attack becomes ineffective and the attacker is unsure of the best way to defeat the detection. Another factor that will cause attackers to give up is when the financial gains become uncertain. However, switching to manual fraud may make sense for some attack schemes and remain profitable. For example, creating new accounts on banking sites to take advantage of promotional cash offers for new members may make sense to carry out manually if the automation fails.

Defense strategy: Much more advanced techniques are required to detect human fraud. Human fraud is mainly a problem with account takeover, account opening abuse, and payment transactions. Bot detection techniques are ineffective in this scenario since the attack is using regular clients, the requests are coming at the regular "human pace," and unless the traffic is coming from a very unexpected location outside the website's usual market, the activity will be hard to notice. Some fraud detection products track the fingerprint of the device used by the user to detect inconsistencies. For example, a user may always check their bank account using their mobile phone. The mobile phone's fingerprint is recorded on the bank's fraud detection system and validated at each visit. Requests from completely different fingerprints require further validation, for example, through multifactor authentication.

Detecting human fraud requires paying particular attention to the data the user provides and detecting inconsistencies. In its simplest form, if the first and last names are not referenced in the email address, that can raise a red flag. Also, cross-checking the phone number and country code against the country provided in the postal address may show some inconsistencies.

Looking up the phone number against a phone number intelligence service may also reveal that this is a burner phone. There are legitimate scenarios where those inconsistencies would exist for a genuine user, but a collection of multiple anomalies found within the same application requires further evaluation. An unusual number of requests made with at least the same identifier (say, the email address or the phone number) should also be considered suspicious.

Botnets with CAPTCHA-Solving Capabilities

Some bot management systems may challenge users with a CAPTCHA as part of the detection process. CAPTCHA stands for Completely Automated Public Turing Test to Tell Computers and Humans Apart. In the early days of bot management solutions, asking a user to solve a CAPTCHA challenge was one of the first methods used to differentiate bots from humans, and it is still very prevalent today on the Internet. The most advanced bot management system usually combines transparent and interactive detection methods. Attacking a website with both technologies requires the most advanced infrastructure, software, and integration with a third-party CAPTCHA-solving service.

The botnet software will primarily focus on defeating the transparent detection layer. However, when the most advanced bot detection is in place, the attacker may have no other choice but to deal with solving the CAPTCHA challenge. The software, in this case, must be able to detect the condition and offload the solution to a third-party solver service. Figure 3.6 shows how attackers may integrate their advanced botnet with a third-party CAPTCHA-solving service, as seen in stage 5 of the attack. Depending on the complexity of the CAPTCHA, some services rely on computer vision to solve the challenge. Cheap human labor is used to handle the most complex designs.

Human-Assisted CAPTCHA Solver

Some CAPTCHA solver services rely entirely on human solvers. These services typically attract "freelance workers" in developing countries with access to a computer or a mobile device, looking to complement their income with a side hustle. Bot operators more commonly leverage CAPTCHA-solving services in the fake account creation use case. In this case, using CAPTCHA-solving services is viable since the attacker doesn't necessarily have specific time constraints to harvest new accounts, and the volume requirements are lower. CAPTCHA-solving services are used less for the account checking/credential stuffing use case, as the attacker, in this case, is looking to validate hundreds of thousands of credentials, and using a CAPTCHA-solving service wouldn't be efficient because of the 20-second or so delay completing the challenge and the associated cost. For example, considering a 20-second average challenge-solving rate, it would take more than 23 days to validate 100,000 credentials at a cost varying between

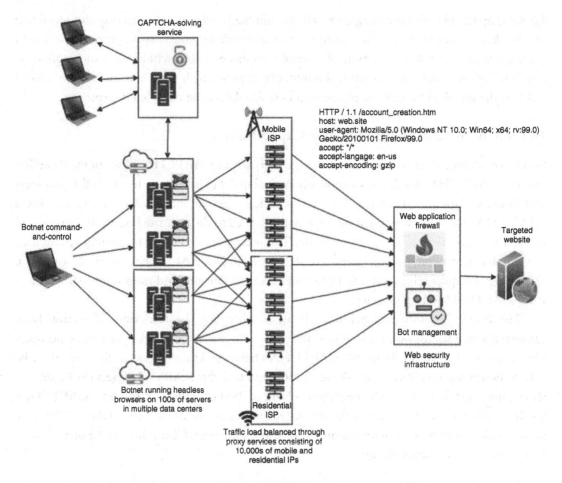

Figure 3.6   Advanced botnet with CAPTCHA-solving capabilities

$100 and $300, depending on the complexity of the CAPTCHA that protects the targeted website.

More than a dozen CAPTCHA-solving services are available (ProWebScraper, 2023), all of
which support reCAPTCHA (the solution most deployed on the Internet) and simpler homegrown word CAPTCHAs. Some support providers with a growing market share, like hCaptcha,
Geetest, and Arkose Labs. A few examples of these CAPTCHA-solving services include the
following:

- 2Captcha/RuCaptcha, hosted in Russia
- AntiCaptcha/Kolotibablo, hosted in the Netherlands

- Imagetyperz, hosted in the United States
- `Bestcaptchasolver.com`

CAPTCHA farm workers have to work hard to earn their money. On average, they get paid about $1 per 1,000 CAPTCHAs solved. The earnings vary depending on the difficulty of the CAPTCHA. For example, Arkose Lab's CAPTCHA can earn up to $1.3 per 1,000 solved because of its complexity. However, the earnings for solving simpler words may be as low as $0.5 per 1,000 solved. It would take a well-performing CAPTCHA farm worker working without interruption or distraction who can solve a challenge within 10 seconds, about 2 hours and 50 minutes to solve 1,000 challenges! Most workers, however, may have to wait several seconds between challenges. Wait time will vary depending on the number of workers connected, the workload, and the worker's performance and reputation. A worker's reputation can drop, or their account can be suspended if they don't solve the CAPTCHA fast enough or make too many mistakes. Assuming a 3-second wait time between each puzzle, it would take an average worker more than 3.5 hours to solve 1,000 challenges.

Because of the low wages, CAPTCHA farm workers are usually in developing countries such as Vietnam, India, Bangladesh, Pakistan, Indonesia, Russia, Ukraine, Venezuela, and the Philippines. Figure 3.7 shows the workforce distribution by countries that AntiCaptcha advertises.

Creating an account on these platforms is easy and takes only a few minutes. Some sites like 2Captcha/RuCaptcha require new workers to go through training by solving 50 different CAPTCHAs. Some platforms allow workers to choose the types of puzzles they want to solve.

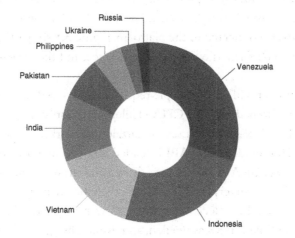

Figure 3.7 The workforce distribution by country according to AntiCaptcha

Computer Vision

Depending on the complexity of the visual challenge, one may be able to take advantage of computer vision to automate the solving of the CAPTCHA. If the CAPTCHA solution requires a user to select a picture depicting everyday objects or landmarks such as cars, buses, airplanes, traffic lights, or bridges (reCAPTCHA v2, hCaptcha), ML models like ResNet come pre-trained to recognize an extensive library of objects or locations. In this case, the bot operator may not need data labeling or model training to get a reasonable success rate. Simple word CAPTCHA from reCAPTCHA v1 or similar products can easily be solved with high accuracy through optical character recognition (OCR) models. Over the years, several research papers have been written describing how to automate the solving of CAPTCHAs with OCR and computer vision. Google, which runs the most popular CAPTCHA solution (reCAPTCHA), reacted by updating its product with more advanced techniques, but even more advanced research found ways to defeat reCAPTCHA time and time again (`Usenix.org` conference, 2020).

When the design of the challenge is more complex, custom, or includes multiple variables, pre-trained computer vision models may not perform as well out of the box. In this case, some level of image labeling to train the AI model will be required to obtain good performances. Unfortunately, this represents only a small obstacle, as attackers may leverage CAPTCHA solver workers to label the images and help train the model.

The CAPTCHA Solver Workflow

Two of the most common CAPTCHA-solving services that bot operators integrate with include 2Captcha or AntiCaptcha. They both have a SaaS offering where bot operators can offload the CAPTCHA resolution by prepaying solved CAPTCHAs and sending the page with the CAPTCHA to be resolved through an API. The CAPTCHA-solving service distributes the tasks to one of the workers connected to the platform. Figure 3.8 shows the interaction between the botnet, the CAPTCHA farm, the CAPTCHA service, and the targeted website.

1. The attacker's botnet will send multiple requests to the CAPTCHA solver API referencing the page that hosts the CAPTCHA challenge to resolve.
2. The CAPTCHA solver service passes the puzzle to a worker connected to the platform.
3. The CAPTCHA provider client API is loaded and executed on the worker's machine. The CAPTCHA client API may collect device and browser characteristics from the worker's machine for fingerprinting and adapting the challenge strategy. The challenge is loaded, and the worker selects the correct answer corresponding to the question, goes through multiple rounds as needed, and eventually gets a token back from the CAPTCHA provider that is passed back to the CAPTCHA solver service.
4. The attacker's botnet retrieves the tokens for the solved CAPTCHAs from the service.

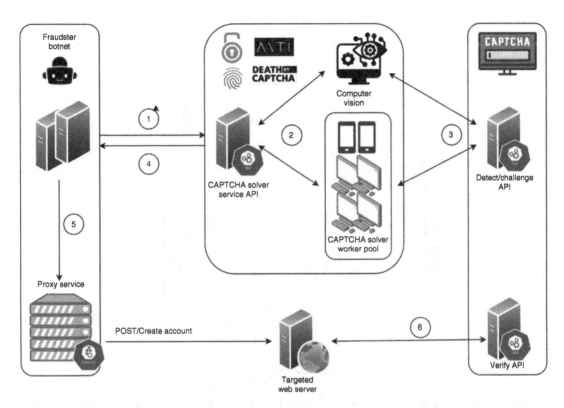

Figure 3.8   The CAPTCHA solver workflow

5. The valid tokens are distributed to the botnet to send requests to the protected endpoint (for example, a POST request that includes all relevant information to create a new account), including the token. The attacker may use a proxy or VPN service to make the requests less obvious to our detection engine.

6. The customer's web server extracts the CAPTCHA provider's token from the incoming POST request and makes an API call to their API to verify the token. If the service returns `solved=true` (or equivalent), the targeted web server will create a new account, which the attacker may use later for some fraud schemes.

AI Botnets

In 2023, a new buzzword has appeared in the industry, *AI botnets*, which assumes a botnet is running with artificial intelligence. Like bot management solutions, which have complex workflows to detect bots, advanced botnets have advanced workflows to detect bot management solutions to ensure the success of their activity. This "anti-ban" workflow may look like the one in Figure 3.9, with a decision tree detecting various aspects of possible protection in place.

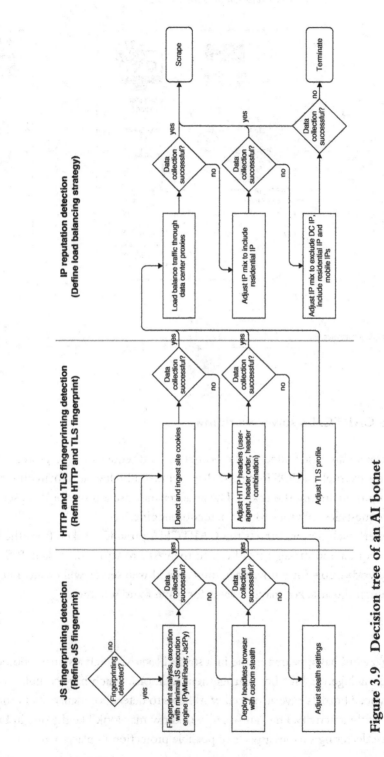

JS fingerprinting detection (Refine JS fingerprint)

HTTP and TLS fingerprinting detection (Refine HTTP and TLS fingerprint)

IP reputation detection (Define load balancing strategy)

Fingerprinting detected?

no

yes

Fingerprint analysis, execution with minimal JS execution engine (PyMiniRacer, Js2Py)

Data collection successful?

yes

no

Deploy headless browser with custom stealth

Data collection successful?

yes

no

Adjust stealth settings

Detect and ingest site cookies

Data collection successful?

yes

no

Adjust HTTP headers (user-agent, header order, header combination)

Data collection successful?

yes

no

Adjust TLS profile

Load balance traffic through data center proxies

Data collection successful?

yes

no

Adjust IP mix to include residential IP

Data collection successful?

yes

no

Adjust IP mix to exclude DC IP, include residential IP and mobile IPs

Data collection successful?

yes

no

Scrape

Terminate

Figure 3.9 Decision tree of an AI botnet

90

1. Suppose the bot management solution collects a fingerprint through JavaScript and does more advanced validation on the client side, such as a proof-of-work challenge. In that case, the scraper may need to execute the JavaScript. To counteract these methods, the scraper may attempt to do the following:
   (a) Run the JavaScript through a minimal JS execution engine like Js2Py or equivalent frameworks, which may be enough to generate an adequate fingerprint and execute the custom logic.
   (b) If this doesn't work, running the botnet on a headless browser may be necessary.
   (c) Tuning the headless settings to stealth mode may be required to avoid detection by advanced bot management solutions.

2. Most bot management solutions evaluate the HTTP headers. Some even assess the TLS handshake when the secure connection is established. To defeat the bot detection, the scraper will need to do the following:
   (a) Evaluate the set of cookies and assess which one to ingest and replay to successfully collect data from the site.
   (b) Adjust the HTTP header set sent, its order, and its values to match the system it pretends to be (Chrome on Windows, Firefox on macOS, Edge on Windows, Safari on iPhone, etc.).
   (c) Adjust their TLS handshake settings to match the OS and browser they claim to be.

3. To defeat IP reputation systems, they must load balance their traffic through a large set of IP addresses.
   (a) Start with data center IP addresses.
   (b) In case of failure, add some residential IP addresses into the mix.
   (c) Further adjust the "IP address" mix (data center, residential, and mobile network IP) as needed to achieve the lowest block level.

In the end, my interpretation of an AI botnet reflects its ability to dynamically adapt to the defense in place and configure itself to look like any of the botnet architectures discussed previously in this chapter. When little protection is in place on the targeted website, the botnet would only need to run the minimum architecture described in Figure 3.3. However, if strong protection is in place, the botnet will need the more advanced infrastructure described in Figure 3.5 or Figure 3.6. Some of the previous workflows may involve machine learning, especially when evaluating the JavaScript fingerprinting code, adjusting to the cookie strategy, HTTP header, and TLS parameters, and collecting statistics on the success rate.

The Botnet Market

There are a number of service offerings supporting the botnet market. Some of these offerings come from legitimate companies, as you saw in the web scraping use case. For the rest, the legitimacy is a lot more questionable, yet there are, most of the time, no clear laws that outright classify the activity as illegal. The market is split into several specialized segments based on use cases:

Sneaker Bots   Sneaker bot developers know that bot protection defending their primary targets (Nike, Adidas, and some of their retailers participating in sneaker drop events) evolves rapidly. To adapt to that and keep their customers happy, they offer their product as a yearly or monthly subscription and provide regular updates to counter the new detection methods. One configures the product to buy a specific pair of a specific size and automates the checkout process, including logging in, adding the item to the cart, adding the shipping address and payment details, and completing the transaction. The price of the software may fluctuate depending on its reputation and success rate in defeating bot detection.

Generic Attack Automation Tools   Plenty of independent developers build their own attack tools, and some publish them on public repositories like GitHub. Some of these developers have quite good intent and develop these tools from a "white hat" or ethical hacker perspective to raise awareness of the ease of performing certain attacks like credential stuffing. Except, of course, these tools, when available on a public repository, can be easily downloaded and used for ill intent. A quick search for the credential stuffing attack tool on the Internet yields several results pointing to various Git repositories.

Other tools like OpenBullet or Sentry MBA may be provided for free, but the configuration file for a specific target website may require a fee. Similar to headless browser products like Playwright and Puppeteer, OpenBullet was originally intended as an automation tool for QA but can easily be used for web scraping or various not-so-legitimate activities like account opening abuse or credential stuffing. Sentry MBA, on the other hand, has clearly been purpose-built for credential stuffing attacks.

Scraper as a Service   As discussed in the web scraping use case discussion, dozens of legitimate companies offer web data extraction and analytics services and operate botnets to scrape websites regularly to collect data. The data gathered is used to produce market, competitive, and user sentiment intelligence, among other things. Most of them also offer custom data collection and analysis services. These organizations have well-known household brands as reference customers, which shows that, contrary to popular belief, scraping services are not handled by criminals running an underground market. They exist because there is a demand for their services, and the intelligence they provide helps their customers adjust their product strategy and positioning to gain a competitive edge. The leading players in the scraping space at the time of this writing are DataMam, CrawlNow, Smartproxy, Outsourced BigData, Bright Data,

ScrapeHero, Grepsr, Zyte, and BotScraper, to name a few. These organizations hire talented developers, data scientists, and product managers to operate advanced botnets designed to defeat bot detection and transform the data collected into business intelligence. Scraper as a service belongs to the data extraction software market segment, which, according to the research firm Verified Market Research, had a market size of more than $1.2 billion in 2021 and is expected to triple by 2030.

Token or Cookie Harvesters Most bot management solutions leverage tokens or cookies to track the status of a given user who has already been evaluated. A "good" user may be given limited privileges to ensure a good user experience on subsequent visits. Some have made it a business of harvesting these tokens and cookies and reselling them to wannabe fraudsters looking to take advantage of them as part of their attack to bypass the protection in place.

Little regulation exists to control bot activity. Although some botnets are regularly taken down, those are still anecdotal events. When it comes to the data extraction industry, tighter regulation on data privacy and acceptable usage policies could disrupt that market in the future. However, currently, bot management solutions are best positioned to protect sites from abuses and enforce acceptable site usage.

Summary

Botnets come in all shapes and sizes with various levels of complexity in their technology stack. Some botnets are advanced scripts designed to run through a workflow with various fingerprint randomization patterns. In contrast, others have the same ability as a web browser to load and parse the content returned by the web server, execute JavaScript, and interact with the UI. Most botnets load balance their traffic through proxy infrastructures ranging from a set of machines hosted in cloud providers to a vast network of relays hosted on mobile devices, desktops, laptops, or even smart TVs. The most advanced botnets yet, operated by major data extraction companies, can adapt their configuration based on the defense in place on the targeted website. This results in much of the bot traffic originating from devices connected to residential and mobile Internet service providers. With this knowledge, let's look at various methods to detect botnets.

4

Detection Strategy

Building an efficient and accurate bot detection strategy is a real challenge and can be as difficult as herding cats! As discussed in Chapter 1, "A Short History of the Internet," the Internet has been built around well-thought-out principles and protocols, but the ecosystem evolves constantly, with new devices and software being released regularly. The raw material required to build efficient detection methods is data—specifically, data collected on the client side through JavaScript, which represents the client configuration and user settings, and data on the server side, that represents the network and communication protocols characteristics used. The data is used to differentiate between the ever-changing Internet ecosystem that represents valid user traffic and the dynamic attack traffic. This chapter discusses the different types of data points collected, the complexity of the Internet ecosystem, the various detection approaches, and how they have evolved over time.

Data Collection Strategy

Each interaction between a client and a server generates data used to research and differentiate what constitutes good or bad traffic. Different types of data are required to look at the request from various points of view and build resilient detection methods. Most bot management products collect data on the client side through JavaScript running on the page hosting the protected resource. For example, suppose the endpoint to protect is a login POST request. In this case, JavaScript will be injected into the page with the login form. The website administrator may add JavaScript to the relevant web pages, or the bot management product may dynamically inject it. Data can also be collected from native mobile applications. If you are working with a bot management vendor, this usually requires updating the application with the vendor's software development kit (SDK) to enable the data collection. The following table provides a high-level overview of the different types of data collected while the user interacts with the site:

Data Type	Description
Network	Describes the connection of the user. The primary data point is the IP address. Additional information can be derived from the IP address through an IP intelligence service. It includes the Autonomous System (AS) number that identifies a network in the Border Gateway Protocol (BGP), which enables data exchanges on the Internet. The company name owning the IP address and the type of connection (cloud provider, residential, or mobile) can also be derived depending on the richness of the IP intelligence solution.
Geolocation	Describes where the user is in the world. It includes the country and may also include the state and city. The location can be derived from the IP address or from the longitude and latitude information collected from the client.
Protocol information	Describes the protocol-level settings used by the client when connecting to the server at the TCP and TLS levels. It also includes the HTTP protocol settings (headers) used by the client when requesting content from the web server, as described in the "HTTP Headers 101" section in Chapter 3, "The Evolution of Botnet Attacks."
Device characteristics	Describes the hardware characteristics of the client. It includes the CPU type, hardware concurrency (number of CPU cores), graphic card model, memory available, installed peripherals, display screen size, audio, and video fingerprint.

Data Type	Description
Browser and OS characteristics	Describes the software running on the client. It includes the browser name and version, OS name and version, and browser plug-ins and extensions installed.
Behavioral data	Describes how the user interacts with the web interface and the device. It includes mouse movements, mouse clicks, keystroke events, and touch-screen interaction. For mobile devices, this may also include gyroscope and accelerometer data.
User preferences	Describes the user-specific software settings. It includes the preferred language, supported languages, time zone, screen orientation, display mode, and cookie support.
Site context information	Describes the user activity on the site. It includes permanent or session site cookies, URL visited, and time of visit.

Note that the list of data points represents what bot and fraud detection solutions collect, but it is not exhaustive. The list may vary from one solution to another and change over time to adapt to the Internet ecosystem and attack pattern evolution.

Most bot management products collect hundreds of data points while the user interacts with the website. The data collected is often referred to as a *fingerprint* or *telemetry*. Bot management and fraud detection products use the data only to protect the website and its users; the data is never used for any other purpose. The data is collected using secure transport protocols and encrypted before being stored. The data is typically deleted after some time following international and local privacy laws. Issues related to user privacy will be covered in Chapter 7, "Internet User Privacy."

Detection methods may use each data point individually or in combination with others. They may be as simple as a static ruleset designed to detect well-known anomalies from attack traffic or as part of a more advanced machine learning model.

The complex combination of data points and detection methods is essential to make it more challenging for an attacker to defeat the protection in place. For example, an attacker may be able to successfully craft their request to send data collected on the client side to look identical to what a legitimate browser might send. However, it will be much more difficult for them to control how their client communicates with the server at the protocol level (HTTP, TLS, TCP, and IP).

Positive vs. Negative Security

When it comes to developing detection methods, there are two main strategies:

Positive Security   Positive security focuses on identifying what is legitimate. The theory behind this strategy is that if one can accurately identify what is good, it is by opposition possible to determine what is bad. The data representing good traffic is abundant, but this strategy can be challenging because the digital Internet ecosystem is continuously evolving. Major software vendors like Windows, Apple, Google, Samsung, and Mozilla release new versions of their products regularly. Hardware vendors also release new products to the market regularly. Protocols like HTTP and TLS also evolve. Despite this fluid ecosystem evolution, the various data types mentioned in the previous section stay relatively stable from one version to the next. However, significant changes are introduced once or twice a year that can cause a major shift in how good traffic is identified. Such a shift is happening today as we see more adoption of the HTTP/3 protocol, which forces the adoption of the TLS 1.3 secure connection protocol and significantly changes the setting clients send when establishing a secure connection. As discussed in Chapter 7, the adoption of features designed to give users a more private online experience also forces a shift in how good traffic can be identified. Keeping up with the evolution requires constant learning and re-establishing the ground truth by combining heuristics, statistical models, or machine learning.

Negative Security   Negative security focuses on identifying what is bad. The challenge with this strategy is that the attacks evolve very rapidly, so identifying and harvesting attack signatures is a constant struggle. Attackers work hard to make their traffic look as close as possible to legitimate traffic to stay undetected, making finding a clearly differentiating signature difficult.

The best strategy is to combine both approaches to reduce the need for each strategy to be very accurate. This helps keep the attack surface as narrow as possible, significantly reducing the attacker's ability to complete their attack (see Figure 4.1).

In a dual-strategies approach, both methods compensate for each other's flaws. For example, a negative security model may also partially catch legitimate traffic (false positive). In this case, a positive security model can correct and balance the negative security model.

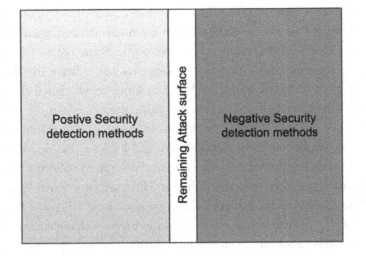

Positive Security detection methods

Remaining Attack surface

Negative Security detection methods

Figure 4.1 Coverage of the attack surface with negative and positive security model

The Evolution of the Internet Ecosystem

In the early 2000s, the Internet ecosystem was simpler and mostly populated with desktops and laptops. The traffic mostly came from a small number of web browsers. However, the release of the first iPhone in 2007 changed everything. Users could access the Internet from these powerful new devices wherever they went. The years that followed saw a dramatic evolution in mobile devices, with vendors like Sony and Samsung launching their own smartphones. As screens got bigger with the introduction of tablets like the iPad in 2010, navigating the Internet from mobile devices became even easier. Website owners adapted to the new platforms and developed new applications to reach their users on the go. The last 15 years saw a significant shift in Internet traffic from traditional desktops or laptops to mobile devices. Today, in some countries like India, users mainly browse the Internet from more affordable mobile devices.

Around the same time, smart TV started to emerge. Connecting more household devices to the Internet, like DVD/Blu-ray players, game consoles, watches, and even fridges, also became possible. These Internet of Things (IoT) devices became new interfaces to interact with web services and, simultaneously, became a new entry point that attackers could exploit. Web security vendors had to adapt to native mobile applications and develop SDKs to help secure the traffic.

Referring to the aforementioned positive security model, all these IoT devices make it much more difficult for web security vendors to learn what is legitimate online due to the sheer variety of hardware, software, and configuration. Some of these variations may also be specific to an industry. For example, gaming consoles and mobile devices dominate the gaming industry. At the same time, smart TVs are more common in the media streaming industry. E-commerce sites will mostly see mobile and desktop/laptop web traffic. Some types of devices may be specific to geography. For example, a hardware vendor may concentrate its sales on a restricted market instead of more global vendors like Apple or Google, which sell their devices worldwide. This variety allows attackers to blend in and make their attacks more successful.

IoT devices don't always have the same abilities as laptops or smartphones. They sometimes run a proprietary and lightweight operating system and browser that doesn't behave the same way as a regular browser and, for example, may be unable to run JavaScript. The interface available to interact with these devices is also different. This may be a touch screen for a fridge, a remote control from a TV, and a gamepad for a game console. All these factors impact web security vendors' ability to collect valuable devices and browser characteristics or rich behavioral telemetry normally available from mobile devices or laptops and impact detection effectiveness.

The evolution of web standards and trends in website and native app development can also disrupt the web security world. Web 1.0 had a very predictable traffic pattern, with at least one HTML page loading with each interaction from the user, followed by a multitude of images, JavaScript, and style sheets to render the content. Web 2.0 introduced a more dynamic model with the concept of APIs. This made the user experience on websites more fluid and engaging. Single-page applications made it feel like pages were loading instantly. The faster the page loads, the more likely the user will stay on the site longer and eventually make a purchase. The promise of Web 3.0 is about the decentralization of the content. I have yet to see a website embrace this model, but Web 2.0 took several years before being truly adopted by website owners, so I know this will come. This shift of interaction always requires adapting the detection technology to make sure it will perform with the same level of accuracy.

The Evolution of Detection Methods

Over the years, two schools of thought regarding detection methods have existed. Both have evolved in parallel and are progressively merging. First emerged interactive detection methods with CAPTCHA challenges and later transparent detection methods, which, unlike interactive detection methods, don't require any user interaction and instead focus on identifying the system making the request and detecting anomalies usually associated with malicious traffic.

Interactive Detection

Interactive detection methods, more commonly known as CAPTCHAs, are designed to present a simple puzzle that the user must interact with and resolve to prove they are human. Different types of puzzles have been invented over the years. Let's review the history.

Word Puzzles   Word puzzles were first invented in 1997 and progressively adopted by companies like PayPal in the early 2000s to protect against fraud. One of the most widespread deployments, reCAPTCHA, was released in 2007 and acquired by Google in 2009. reCAPTCHA helped protect websites against automation and helped digitize books from the public domain at the same time. Users were presented with a series of alpha characters they needed to type in a field to access the protected resources.

The system relied on optical character recognition (OCR) technology to validate the user's answer. However, as the OCR technology improved, fraudsters also used it to automate solving puzzles.

To compensate for this, CAPTCHA solutions were enhanced. As shown in Figure 4.2, various types of distortions, color schemes, and noisy backgrounds were added to the string of characters to make it harder for machines to recognize. The problem is that this also made it significantly harder and more frustrating for humans to recognize the characters. It was increasingly difficult to distinguish a U from a V or an O from a 0! Meanwhile, the evolving OCR technology was getting better at resolving these challenges.

Image Puzzles   Image puzzles were introduced to compensate for the evolution of OCR and make CAPTCHAs more human-friendly. reCAPTCHA introduced version 2 with image puzzles in 2012. Users were presented with a description and a set of images, as shown in Figure 4.3. Users had to select the images corresponding to the description to complete the puzzle. Intuition Machines, a company that offers image and text recognition services using artificial intelligence, also introduced the hCaptcha service in 2017 to help with its image labeling service while protecting websites against bots.

Introducing this new type of puzzle caught bot operators off guard, as their botnets outfitted with OCRs could not deal with image puzzles. Humans, meanwhile, welcomed the more user-friendly challenges. However, over the last 10 years, computer vision has dramatically

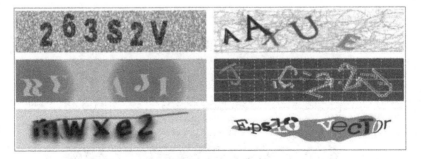

Figure 4.2   Example of word CAPTCHAs

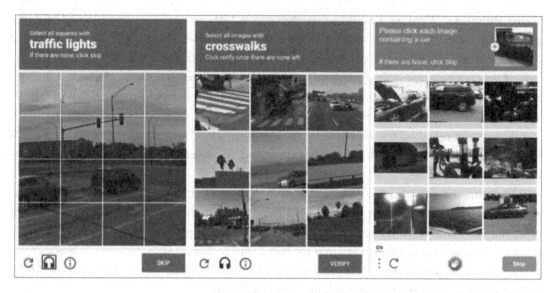

Figure 4.3   Examples of image CAPTCHAs

improved with pre-trained models like ResNet that recognize various objects, landmarks, or animals out of the box. This made image recognition more accessible to all, and it wasn't long before new botnets outfitted with computer vision emerged. Meanwhile, Internet users started to tire of proving their humanness by picking images with crosswalks, cars, buses, bridges, and my all-time favorite (sigh), traffic lights.

Mini-games   Around the same time image puzzles appeared, companies like Are You a Human introduced a different alternative to CAPTCHA puzzles with mini-games. This option was certainly more appealing and fun to at least the younger generation. Companies like Fun-Captcha and GeeTest also introduced their version of the mini-game CAPTCHAs. Figure 4.4 shows some examples of mini-game CAPTCHAs.

Figure 4.4   Examples of mini-game CAPTCHAs

Mini-game CAPTCHAs can be a fun interaction, but they can also create friction that most users find cumbersome if they have to go through the process several times during a session while interacting with a site.

Behavioral Challenges   The novelty of mini-games and image puzzles eventually wore off. These types of challenges may be popular on gaming websites but may not be as fitting for a banking or e-commerce website. Website owners were looking for solutions that require as little interaction as possible to limit friction. In 2014, Google reCAPTCHA introduced No CAPTCHA, which only required the user to check a box (see Figure 4.5). Cloudflare's Turnstile application and Akamai Technologies' advanced behavioral challenge follow the same principle. During this simple interaction, the software collects telemetry on the client side to assess the risk based on the device fingerprint and how the user interacts with the challenge. The fingerprint, mouse movement, touch events, or keystrokes are evaluated to ensure they look human-like. User interaction that presents anomalies while going through this initial check can be challenged with an image puzzle.

Figure 4.5   Behavioral CAPTCHA

Transparent Detection

Transparent detection methods take advantage of various signals collected from the client through JavaScript or an SDK or mobile application and information collected from how the client communicates with the server, mainly through the HTTP, TCP, IP, and TLS protocols. Transparent detection methods don't require any user interaction. This section discusses how transparent detection methods have evolved over the years to keep up with the evolution of botnets.

Web Application Firewalls   Back around 2010, attacks mainly came from small botnets, which consisted of a handful of nodes, and the scripts they were running were simplistic. The botnet request rate would typically be very high, so detecting and blocking it was relatively

IP   IP rate   Traffic filtering/
blocklist   limiting   custom rule

Figure 4.6   Detection methods included in a web application firewall

straightforward. As described in Figure 4.6, all you need in this scenario is a web application firewall (WAF) with IP blocking and rate-limiting capabilities and the ability to build custom rules.

Because the number of nodes within the botnet was small, web security professionals could get away with adding individual IP addresses to a blocklist. Better yet, implementing rate limiting with a low threshold on the critical resources would automatically detect and mitigate clients sending requests with high velocity. Lastly, because the scripts were so simplistic, their HTTP header signature looked far from what is expected from a regular request from legitimate browsers like Chrome or Firefox. Developing and adding a custom rule in the WAF policy was easy enough to block the bot activity.

Bot Management   In the 2012 time frame, as WAFs were commonly deployed to protect websites, bot operators evolved their botnets. They got bigger, and their scripts became more advanced. Instead of a few dozen nodes, a botnet would consist of a few hundred nodes. That way, the fraudster could spread the traffic, reduce the request velocity of each node, defeat any attempt at rate control, and make the IP blocking strategy ineffective. The header signature also blended more with requests from real browsers and became more complex. Bot operators designed their botnets to randomize specific device characteristics like the value of the User-Agent HTTP header. This shift in the attack strategy required defenders to continuously update their WAF custom rules to keep up with the evolution of attacks. At this point, purpose-built products designed to detect bots were required. As seen in Figure 4.7, bot management solutions needed the basic detection methods from a WAF, but also new methods specifically designed to detect bots, including the ability to calculate the reputation of the IP address, evaluate support for JavaScript, collect a fingerprint, and detect anomalies typical of bot traffic.

The company Distil Networks was a pioneer in the space and introduced its bot management product in 2011. Following strong interest from e-commerce, travel, and hospitality companies, other web security vendors like Akamai Technologies and Cloudflare followed.

Figure 4.7   Detection methods included in bot management products

Advanced Bot Management   By 2016, bot management solutions became the product of choice to protect websites against bots. This forced bot operators to enhance their scripts to defeat the new detection methods. To overcome IP reputation, they increased the size of their botnets to thousands of nodes, making IP reputation far less effective. Bot operators also found ways to mimic the execution of the bot manager JavaScript by harvesting good fingerprints from legitimate systems and replaying them from their botnet. The most advanced bot operators understood that fingerprints were used to identify users uniquely. To defeat such techniques, attackers randomized the fingerprint data points to make each request look like it was coming from a different user. As seen in Figure 4.8, more advanced bot management solutions were required, including methods previously cited and additional ones such as more advanced client-side data collection and fingerprint validation technology, as well as advanced techniques like proof of work to force the execution of JavaScript.

Figure 4.8   Detection methods included in an advanced bot management product

More security vendors entered the bot management market to help solve the ever-growing and complex bot problem. These included Shape Security, DataDome, HUMAN, and Kasada, to name a few.

Advanced Fraud and Abuse Detection   No challenge is too big for the most sophisticated, advanced, and motivated attackers. They found efficiency by taking advantage of the ever-increasing number of cheap anonymous proxy or virtual private network (VPN) services popping up around the world. By 2018, it was common to find botnets consisting of hundreds of thousands of nodes. To overcome the PoW and device intelligence detection methods, some of the most advanced bot operators outfitted their botnets with a minimal JavaScript execution engine like Js2Py that turns JavaScript code into Python code. Others upgraded their botnets with headless browser technology to natively execute JavaScript, thus reducing the efficacy of the PoW and device reputation technology methods. As seen in Figure 4.9, more advanced upgrades in the toolset were yet again required, including behavioral and headless browser detection.

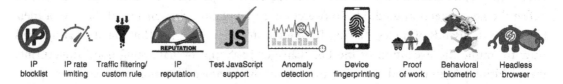

Figure 4.9   Detection methods included in fraud detection product

More complex JavaScript code and fingerprint payload obfuscation methods were required to force the client to execute JavaScript. To better detect headless browsers, advanced client fingerprinting methods were developed to detect the most complex botnets running headless browsers in stealth mode. Behavioral biometric detection processing mouse movements, keyboard keystrokes events, or mobile device motion sensors helped check whether a human is interacting with the machine.

As seen in Chapter 3, despite the continuous evolution, botnets that target a website at any given time vary in sophistication. Web security teams cannot bet on simple detection methods, assuming they're only targeted by simple bots. Bots can evolve their strategy rapidly when their activity is mitigated. The combination of detection techniques described previously is required today in a bot management offering to match the different levels of botnet sophistication and build a cost-effective and efficient product.

The State of the Art

The interactive and transparent detection strategies described previously have merits and flaws. Interactive detections disturb the natural flow of the site, and Internet users have grown tired of typing a random text, choosing the right image, or playing mini-games. Ultimately, they want to avoid having to prove they are human before they can interact with a website. Transparent detection offers a better user experience most of the time since the user doesn't have to do anything. Only their system and their overall behavior are being evaluated. However, despite all bot managers' and fraud vendors' best efforts to develop detection methods as accurate as possible, it's simply impossible to reach 100% accuracy. False positives

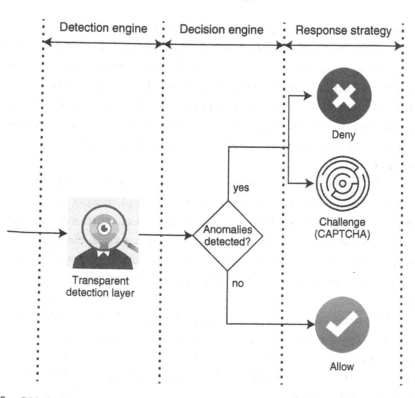

Figure 4.10 High-level bot management architecture

are a fact of life for defenders, and a small percentage of legitimate users may occasionally be incorrectly classified as bots, which could have some impact on the website's revenue. Figure 4.10 shows the ideal bot management solution. It must combine both types of detection through a decision engine:

- **Transparent detection layer:** This layer assesses the device and the user based on past and current behavior.
- **Decision engine:** This layer decides how to handle the request based on the anomalies found by the transparent detection layer. In effect, this layer defines the response strategy and, consequently, how this will affect the user experience. When no anomaly is detected, the user can access the requested resource. When some anomalies are found, the user may be challenged, and if the anomalies detected clearly indicate that the request is coming from a bot, the user will be denied access.
- **Response strategy:** This layer consists of a set of response strategies, including simply denying the request, delaying, or challenging the client with a secondary interactive detection method.

Owner	User-Agent
Google	Google read aloud bot Mozilla/5.0 (Linux; Android 7.0; SM-G930V Build/NRD90M) AppleWebKit/537.36 (KHTML, like Gecko) Chrome/59.0.3071.125 Mobile Safari/537.36 (compatible; Google-Read-Aloud; +https://support .google.com/webmasters/answer/1061943) Google Bot, supports the search engine Mozilla/5.0 (Linux; Android 6.0.1; Nexus 5X Build/MMB29P) AppleWebKit/537.36 (KHTML, like Gecko) Chrome/107.0.5304.115 Mobile Safari/537.36 (compatible; Googlebot/2.1; +http://www.google .com/bot.html) Google advertisement service Mozilla/5.0 (Linux; Android 5.0; SM-G920A) AppleWebKit (KHTML, like Gecko) Chrome Mobile Safari (compatible; AdsBot-Google-Mobile; +http://www.google.com/mobile/adsbot.html)
Microsoft	Bing bot, supports the Bing search engine Mozilla/5.0 (compatible; bingbot/2.0; +http://www.bing.com/ bingbot.htm) Mozilla/5.0 AppleWebKit/537.36 (KHTML, like Gecko; compatible; bingbot/2.0; +http://www.bing.com/bingbot.htm) Chrome/103.0.5060.134 Safari/537.36
Facebook	Bots used to preload a page shared on the social media site facebookexternalhit/1.1 (+http://www.facebook.com/externalhit_ uatext.php)
Pinterest	Bots used to preload a page shared on the social media site Mozilla/5.0 (compatible; Pinterestbot/1.0; +http://www.pinterest.com/ bot.html)
UptimeRobot	Checks the site availability from various geographical locations Mozilla/5.0+(compatible; UptimeRobot/2.0; http://www.uptimerobot .com/)

Another characteristic these bots have in common is that they typically follow the robot exclusion protocol directives (Wikipedia, 2024) found in most websites' robots.txt me. Good bots that want to crawl a website will first check the robots.txt field that can be found in the site's root directory, for example, `http://www.example.com/robots.txt`. The file may look as follows:

```
User-agent: Pinterestbot
Allow: /products/
User-agent: *
Disallow: /admin/
```

The preceding instructions tell the Pinterest bot that it is only allowed to crawl the products section of the site and that all bots must stay away from the admin section. The file may also include additional directives to limit the crawl rate for specific bots. Using `robots.txt` is still a good and relevant way to manage most good bots today.

Good Bot Categories

The problem with the simple keyword detection logic approach is that on any given website, you'll end up with hundreds of bot `User-Agent` header values to review. Some are common and easy to recognize (Googlebot or Bingbot, for example), but others are far less obvious. Looking up every single one of them is a tedious task; a good bot management system should be able to detect and categorize them automatically. Good bots will typically fit into the following categories:

Web Search Engines   Web search engines are systems designed to help users find information on the Internet. Google, Bing, Baidu, and Yandex are by far the most well-known worldwide, but more than 100 web search engines support local markets like 360.cn or Sogou in China, Coc Coc in Vietnam, or the privacy-focused search engine DuckDuckGo. Some search engines also support vocal assistants like Applebot for Siri. Bots continuously crawl the Internet to find new sites and index their pages to make their content available and easy to find for users.

Commerce Search Engines   Commerce search engines are like web search engines, except that they specialize in specific types of goods or services such as cars (CarGurus), fashion (Lyst), interior design (Houzz), price comparison (`shopping.com`), books (BookFinder), travel (Skyscanner), etc. These companies use bots to crawl retailers in their targeted product or service category to retrieve product descriptions, images, and prices they reference on their sites. Like a web search engine, the user will be redirected to the site offering the product or service when clicking any of the links.

Search Engine Optimization, Audience Analytics, and Marketing Services   SEO is the process of improving the visibility of a website's content in a search engine's "natural" or unpaid ("organic") search results. In general, ranking a site on a search engine can directly impact the number of visitors and potentially the company's revenue. SEO may target different kinds of searches, including image, video, academic, news, and industry-specific vertical or localized search engines.

As an Internet marketing strategy, SEO considers how search engines work, what people search for, the search terms or keywords typed into search engines, and which search engines are preferred by their targeted audience. Optimizing a website may involve editing its content to increase its relevance to specific keywords and remove barriers to the indexing activities of search engines. SEO companies may also provide audience analytics and marketing services to help site owners better understand customer behavior. To provide analytical information, SEO companies operate bots to crawl a wide variety of websites and provide their customers with key data regarding their positioning on the market compared to their competitors. The information collected may not directly benefit the company that receives the scraping activity unless they are in contract with the SEO company. Companies operating bots in that space include Semrush, Ahrefs, and Botify.

Online Advertising   Online advertising optimization helps businesses refine their product positioning and online advertising strategy to attract as many customers to their websites as possible. We've all experienced online ads pointing us to a site we visited days ago, following us around the Internet. Information about user behavior is collected as users visit various sites. When a user visits a site where the online advertising company owns an ad space, it will present ads related to the user's past interest. This strategy will likely lead the consumer to return to the site and buy products or services.

Online advertising companies use bots to scrape their clients' and competitors' websites. Companies operating bots in this space include Adbeat, Comscore, and Google.

Social Media   Social media is a two-way form of communication that allows users to share ideas and interact with the information being transmitted. It encompasses various online content, from social networking sites like Facebook or Instagram to interactive information-sharing forums like Wikipedia or Quora. Social media is at the center of the marketing strategy of most online businesses. It complements or replaces the traditional newsletter sent by email.

On most social media sites, users can share links. When this happens, the social media bot will scrape the page that has been shared so that a summary of the content can be displayed on the user feed. Only shared content will be scraped. Social media companies that operate bots include Facebook, LinkedIn, and Pinterest.

Job Search Engines   Job search engines primarily use the career section of websites to collect the list of jobs available. Listings are then republished on job portals, such as dice.com. Job portals may earn revenue from advertising or partnership agreements with the company that advertises the job.

Web Archives   Web content is ephemeral, and its content is continuously updated. Some organizations like `archive.org` have decided to archive the Web to "save websites or data in danger of being lost." Regular users can then visit these websites and look for previously available information or look back at website designs for research purposes. These services are similar to search engines, but the data reference is outdated. Organizations running archiving services crawl popular websites regularly to preserve a copy of their content. Companies in this category include `archive.org`, which operates the *Wayback Machine*.

Site Development and Monitoring Services   Many services and tools are available online to help site owners ensure their website is fully functional and performs well worldwide. The services offered may include the following:

- End-user experience monitoring
- Site availability monitoring from different geographies
- Site load time from different geographies
- Checking for broken links
- Domain name availability
- Checking for DNS resolution issues
- Checking for appropriate TLS support

Companies generally have a service agreement with the service provider if the service is chargeable and provision these activities themselves. The bots will regularly retrieve specific site pages to run some diagnostics. Hundreds of companies exist in this space, such as Akamai Technologies, Catchpoint, and Pingdom.

Media and Entertainment Search Engines and Aggregators   This category includes specialized search engines that focus on various media types: news, music, video, and images. News aggregator companies like `Mashable.com`, `Wired.com`, or `Newsnow.com` scrape news outlets' websites to collect articles, see what is trending, and reference the most relevant content on their sites. Scraped websites may include regional, national, or international news agencies. The referenced content may complement the site's content, and the content displayed to a user may depend on their geolocation and personal preferences based on previously accessed articles. People who click one of the referenced links will be redirected to the site that originally published the content. News agencies should welcome the scraping activity of media and news aggregators since it can increase their audience and thus increase their advertisement revenue when users visit their sites.

RSS Feed Readers   Rich Site Summary (RSS), often called *Really Simple Syndication*, uses standard web feed formats to publish frequently updated information: blog entries, news headlines, audio, and video. An RSS document (called a *feed*, *web feed*, or *channel*) includes complete or summarized text and metadata, like publishing date and author's name.

RSS feeds enable publishers to syndicate data automatically. A standard XML file format ensures compatibility with many different machines/programs. RSS feeds also benefit users who want timely updates from their favorite websites or aggregate data from many sites.

Some Internet services use bots to retrieve information from these RSS feeds and make them available to users.

Financial Aggregators   Companies like `Mint.com` or Plaid offer services that allow users to centralize bank and credit card account management into a single portal. Financial aggregators use botnets to log in to all the user's accounts regularly and retrieve the latest financial information. Users can also transfer money from one account to another from the aggregator's portal. Partnership agreements are typically required between the aggregator and the financial institution since the latter closely monitors any account transaction to prevent fraud.

Stock Market Tickers   Many companies or individuals trading securities use bots to get the latest quotes on various stocks to make their buy/sell/hold decisions. The information may be fed into an algorithm that automatically evaluates the market trends and news to decide how to handle specific securities.

Enterprise Data Aggregators   Some companies offer scraping services to their customers to gain a competitive edge in the market. These companies are, in effect, like SEO companies, but the data collected and the outcome are more focused on driving the company strategy to gain market share.

As described in Chapter 2, "The Most Common Attacks Using Botnets," companies that fit this category don't always clearly identify themselves in the `User-Agent` string and may employ techniques to defeat bot detection features. Depending on how the data is used, this can have a negative business impact on the company receiving the scraping activity.

Academic and Research Bots   Corporate or academic researchers may need to scrape data from various Internet companies to research a particular topic. For example, a researcher may want to scrape multiple news outlets and social media to study how fake news spread and become viral. Web security researchers may scan websites to look for common vulnerabilities and develop a state of the Internet web security report. The intent of the bot activity is not malicious, and their goal is to develop reports, products, or services that will help raise awareness of certain issues and propose solutions to fix them. Institutions that generate the traffic will advertise a URL in the header signature that one can visit to learn more about their intent, purpose, or how to reach out to get the activity to stop if the scraped company does not wish to participate in their efforts.

Handling Good Bots Traffic   Not everyone would agree on the definition of "good bots" described here. The context of the website and the market it operates in must be considered to decide whether one category is good or even relevant for the site or not. Over the years, I've seen few issues caused by "good bots."

Companies that want to limit good bot activity should consider the following principles:

- All bots from the web search engine or social media category should be considered "good," whether significant players like Googlebot or Facebook or smaller players like DuckDuckGo. One never knows which search engine potential customers may decide to use or which social media a particular page will be shared on. Only allowing the major players could result in a missed opportunity.
- Companies should work with their business team for SEO and online advertising to understand which company has been hired to help in their web strategy. Allowing your SEO and online advertiser bot is critical, while the rest may bring less value.
- E-commerce and media sites should embrace commerce and media search engines, respectively, since they are just as valuable as web search engines for them.
- Web Archiver, RSS feed readers, and academic and research bots, however, may not be critical to the business goals and can potentially be blocked.

Good Bot Impersonators   New "good bots" emerge regularly, and previously known ones may disappear as companies that run them may go out of business, merge with larger groups, change their focus, or diversify their data collection to achieve their product and financial goals. Maintaining an up-to-date dictionary of "good bots" is a constant effort. Attackers understand that bots operated by companies like Google, Microsoft, X (Twitter), and Facebook may be allowed by most companies, considering the value they can bring to the business regarding new audiences and potential revenue. Bot operators will capitalize on this and sometimes impersonate them to stay under the radar and conduct malicious activity. For example, an e-commerce website may expect and want to see web search engines like Googlebot scrape their product pages regularly. However, seeing the same Googlebot attempting to log in to too many accounts in a credential stuffing scheme or create multiple accounts should be considered abnormal.

To prevent bot impersonation of well-known good bots, it is essential to identify them using multiple factors, including the network of origin (AS number), IP address, HTTP header signature, TLS signature, or other uniquely identifying factors.

IP Intelligence

As discussed previously, bot operators and fraudsters commonly use proxy services to spread their attack traffic. They also typically deploy their botnet on cloud computing services. Simpler attacks may come from a handful of countries, but more advanced ones, especially when using proxy services, may have a global footprint. IP intelligence can detect and defend against these advanced attack strategies.

IP intelligence consists of information inferred from the IP address about the user's geolocation (country, state, county, city, longitude, and latitude) and the network the IP address belongs to (AS number, company name, type of connection). The reputation of the IP address is based on past behavior and, finally, whether it is associated with a proxy or VPN service. Several vendors like Neustar, IPQualityScore, MaxMind, and others provide data feeds. Note that not all providers offer the same level of quality and coverage. The information concerning a specific IP address may vary from one provider to the next. The various data points used in the context of a website can be very valuable in detecting malicious activity. Here are some guidelines on using some of the most helpful IP intelligence indicators:

Geolocation

Country	Some websites have a global audience, so website owners expect traffic to come from all corners of the world. But most websites only have a regional audience that corresponds to their market reach. For example, a retailer or a bank in Europe with outlets, say, in France, Germany, and the United Kingdom, may expect that most of the traffic coming to their websites will come from their typical market. Traffic coming from North America, Asia, or Africa, especially in high volume would in this case be highly unexpected. Rate-limiting traffic coming from unexpected countries can help reduce the attack surface. Outright blocking traffic from countries you do not do business with is usually not a good idea since you need to account for legitimate users needing to access the site while they are traveling. The rate-limiting logic may need to be adjusted over time based on the company's market growth strategy.

Network

Connection type	IP intelligence providers may provide insight on whether the IP address belongs to a corporate business, educational institution, residential Internet services provider (ISP), mobile network, or cloud provider. Most websites receive the bulk of their traffic from residential ISPs and mobile networks. They may also receive a small percentage of traffic from corporations or universities. However, traffic coming from cloud providers is usually unexpected especially if it comes at a large volume so this is usually a sign of bot activity.

Network

Company name	The company name directly identifies the entity that is assigned the IP address, which significantly helps provide context for the traffic. For example, traffic coming from the residential ISP Comcast or AT&T in the United States or Orange in Europe would be expected. However, seeing traffic from cloud computing services, servers hosting companies, or VPN service companies is something to watch for.
ASN	The Autonomous System (AS) number identifies a network or organization and is used to route traffic in the Border Gateway Protocol (BGP), the main routing protocol used on the Internet. Most IP intelligence providers offer this information, which is a good alternative to the connection type, or company name information if those are not available.
VPN, proxy	The usage of virtual private networks (VPNs) and proxy services have gained in popularity over recent years with legitimate users concerned with their privacy on the Internet. It is estimated that about 10% of legitimate Internet users use proxies and VPNs on a regular basis. Some web browsers like Opera, Brave, and Firefox offer features to facilitate browsing the Internet through proxy or VPN services. Several browser add-ons are also available for popular browsers like Chrome and Firefox. The use of proxies or VPNs are also a very common method for bot operators to load balance their traffic to help evade detection but also stay anonymous. An abnormal ratio (exceeding 10%) of proxy and VPN traffic may be a clear indication of malicious intent.

IP Reputation

Reputation score	The reputation is calculated based on various risk factors that may include the risk associated with traffic coming from specific countries in the context of a website, past behavior of the IP address or subnet, company, and connection type it is affiliated with, and whether it's part of a proxy or VPN network. Different vendors use different heuristics and methodology to produce a risk score out of the different indicators. The score typically ranges from 0 (low risk) to 100 (high risk).

None of the IP intelligence signals is deterministic enough to use for directly blocking since, as we've seen, there are legitimate reasons to use a proxy or VPN or to access the protected resources from an unusual country. However, when combined with indicators from other detection methods within the context of the protected resource, IP intelligence can help differentiate between legitimate and malicious traffic.

Cookie Handling

Cookies contain information about the user's session, preferences, or states. They are much talked about in the context of user privacy but are also generally an essential part of a bot and fraud detection strategy. Consequently, botnets have an interesting relationship with cookies. They will either go after them if they hold special privileges, drop them for fear that they will make their activity stand out in analytics platforms, or neglect them. So, evaluating the cookies included in the request can be revealing.

Cookies with Privileges   First, let's look at cases where bots go after cookies that may hold privileges. Bot and fraud detection solutions sometimes use cookies to track certain states. This can be done, for example, so the client-side data collection limits the solution's impact on user privacy. Bot operators discovering a cookie is associated with certain statuses and privileges will start harvesting it and replaying it within their botnets. Cookies that hold states must be protected to prevent their abuse through replays.

A cookie is always specific to a browser, device, and hostname. Cookies cannot and should not be shared with other devices or across websites. This rule of thumb can be enforced by including information about the device and the site context when it is set. The cookies should hold some basic information about the device, such as the operating system (Windows, iOS, macOS), browser brand (Chrome, Firefox, Edge, Brave), specific user preferences like preferred languages, and other essential information like creation date and time and the hostname it was created for. The cookie value must be encrypted, and the bot management solution must validate the cookie at each request and flag the request when inconsistencies are found.

Cookies for Evaluating User Behavior   Now, cookies are the best way to identify a user uniquely. Most bot and fraud management solutions use them to assess user behavior over time. When bot operators detect such behavior, they may be tempted to drop the cookies.

Evaluating user behavior can be as simple as counting the requests with the same cookie on specific workflows. Seeing the same cookie attempting to log in, create new accounts, or add credit or gift cards in the checkout workflow an abnormal number of times would be a strong signal of credential stuffing, account opening abuse, or carding attack behavior, respectively. What "abnormal" means may vary from site to site, but anything above five daily requests on each of these workflows should raise suspicion. The solution must be able to track the number of requests on these critical workflows and flag the request when the count exceeds a predefined threshold. The threshold may be adjusted dynamically to avoid manual tuning but must be kept as low as possible for the best effectiveness.

Other Site Cookies   Beyond the cookies set by the bot and fraud detection solution, most sites use cookies extensively to track various activities, such as whether a user is logged in, items in the shopping cart, user preferences, geolocation, etc. Online ads, SEO, or third-party analytics services integrated into the site will track additional information like a fingerprint to understand the user behavior over time.

Humans go to various areas of the site and collect dozens of cookies throughout their journey. At the same time, bots sometimes limit their activity to a particular workflow, for example, login, account creation, or product pages. Therefore, the cookies set for legitimate users versus bots may diverge significantly. Also, as mentioned previously, botnets may be selective with cookies and only retain the ones that seem essential to the success of their attack strategy. Evaluating the diversity of cookies from legitimate users versus requests coming from adversaries can help set them apart.

JavaScript Execution Handling

Sometimes, what matters is not what one sees but what one doesn't see. Most bot management solutions collect a fingerprint and telemetry from the client through JavaScript. The data may be sent synchronously (along with the protected request) or asynchronously (at various pages and intervals while the user is interacting with the protected website). The great majority of botnets out there are unable to execute JavaScript natively. Therefore, testing a client's ability to execute JavaScript is still a strong and relevant detection method. A client that doesn't send a fingerprint or telemetry would be considered unable to execute JavaScript. The bot detection engine must keep track of clients that do not send fingerprints or do so inconsistently.

Judging a client by its ability to run JavaScript can sound harsh to legitimate security and privacy-conscious users who selectively disable JavaScript on their browsers. Some bot and fraud detection solutions are more forgiving than others regarding client-site data collection. Some solutions take a "guilty until proven innocent" approach, meaning that a client is considered bad (a bot) by default, and the client must send a fingerprint and telemetry to prove its "innocence/ legitimacy" to the detection engine. These systems would strongly impact legitimate users who disable JavaScript. Other systems take the opposite approach, consider everyone innocent, and detect bad behavior over time. Most websites, especially single-page applications, require JavaScript to render and function properly. Therefore, the argument about the impact on legitimate users when strictly enforcing JavaScript support is not as strong as it used to be 5–10 years ago.

When a bot management solution is first introduced to a site but no mitigation is applied, botnet operators are generally unaware of the bot management solution, and their botnets do not send any fingerprint. Once mitigation is applied to the traffic, it usually doesn't take long for the adversary to realize their attack is failing and discover the required data collection. This short advantage can be exploited during the solution's initial rollout and repeatedly by introducing regular changes to the JavaScript data collection, which, over time, helps weed out the least sophisticated botnets that cannot execute JavaScript natively.

Device Intelligence

Some bot operators developed a fingerprint generator that randomizes some data points expected by the bot management solution to make their signature appear unique from one request to the next. To protect against these attack scenarios, defenders commonly follow the negative security model and try to find the signatures that identify the attack traffic. Defining attack signatures requires identifying the parts of the fingerprint that are not randomized. In this context, this corresponds to the stable part of the fingerprint and will uniquely identify the attack traffic. The attack signature must not overlap with legitimate traffic fingerprints to prevent false positives. Depending on the sophistication of the randomization pattern, this can be a complex task. For example, let's assume the full fingerprint consists of the following data points:

```
Browser name/version + OS name/version + screen size + CPU + memory size
```

Suppose the attacker heavily randomizes the browser name and version (a common scenario), but the rest of the data points are stable. In that case, the defender may be able to identify the attack using the following signature structure:

```
OS name/version + screen size + CPU + memory size
```

Now, here's an example of fingerprints sent by a botnet. As you can see, the part of the fingerprint in bold varies, while the other part stays the same.

```
Chrome 90 + Windows 10 + 800x600 + Macintel + 2GB
Edge 91 + Windows 10 + 800x600 + Macintel + 2GB
Chrome 92 + Windows 10 + 800x600 + Macintel + 2GB
Firefox 93 + Windows 10 + 800x600 + Macintel + 2GB
Chrome 90 + Windows 10 + 800x600 + Macintel + 2GB
Firefox 91 + Windows 10 + 800x600 + Macintel + 2GB
```

```
Edge 92 + Windows 10 + 800x600 + Macintel + 2GB
Chrome 93 + Windows 10 + 800x600 + Macintel + 2GB
```

Therefore, the signature "`Windows 10 + 800x600 + Macintel + 2GB`" can accurately identify the attack traffic. In this case, we can also guarantee no overlap with legitimate traffic. Here, the bot operator made an obvious mistake in building the fake fingerprint: a Windows OS (Microsoft) is incompatible with a Macintel chip (Apple). Such mistakes are surprisingly common, but attackers won't always be this generous with the defenders. Here's another example with the same randomization pattern, but this time with no obvious incompatibilities in the stable part of the fingerprint:

```
Chrome 90 + Windows 10 + 800x600 + Win32 + 2GB
Edge 91 + Windows 10 + 800x600 + Win32 + 2GB
Chrome 92 + Windows 10 + 800x600 + Win32 + 2GB
Firefox 93 + Windows 10 + 800x600 + Win32 + 2GB
Chrome 90 + Windows 10 + 800x600 + Win32 + 2GB
Firefox 91 + Windows 10 + 800x600 + Win32 + 2GB
Edge 92 + Windows 10 + 800x600 + Win32 + 2GB
Chrome 93 + Windows 10 + 800x600 + Win32 + 2GB
```

In this example, the signature "`Windows 10 + 800x600 + Win32 + 2GB`" can still be used to identify the attack. However, because this is a prevalent signature with legitimate traffic, it must be combined with additional differentiating conditions to eliminate false positives. Thankfully, the attacker uses older versions of Chrome, Edge, and Firefox in the randomization pattern. At the time of this writing, the latest version for these browser brands is 124, which means the versions in the attack traffic are more than two years old, which is unusual considering these browsers are designed to auto-update. Adoption of new versions is usually fast. To accurately detect the preceding attack pattern, the defender may use the following signature:

```
Fingerprint contains "Windows 10 + 800x600 + Win32 + 2GB"
AND browser name is Chrome OR Edge OR Firefox
AND browser version is < = 93
```

Such rules are effective in blocking an attack but will be quickly rendered ineffective when the attacker updates their script to correct their fingerprint. Finding an attack signature can be automated through machine learning models. However, that also has limitations and could lead to thousands of combinations that could be more challenging to maintain.

Device intelligence is a positive security approach complementary to the preceding method. A device intelligence method aims to learn and identify what legitimate traffic fingerprints look like. Thousands of different devices on the market run various software combinations, potentially leading to tens of thousands of unique fingerprints. Like the negative security model, the structure of the "good device" signature must consist of data points that are the least likely to change over time to improve stability. The changes largely depend on software and hardware release by vendors worldwide and user adoption. If one can recognize good signatures, it makes it easy to identify bad signatures. Identifying good user signatures helps better detect bot traffic with randomization patterns. Harvesting good device signatures manually would be impossible. That's where a statistical or machine learning model can help automate the process. Different companies may use different algorithms, and their efficiency will depend on the quality and diversity of the available data.

Going back to the signature structure from the traditional negative security model, let's assess what can change as new software or hardware gets released:

```
Browser name/version + OS name/version + screen size + CPU + memory size
```

New software that affects the browser and OS version is released every four to six weeks. New hardware that can affect the screen size, CPU, and memory size is released every 6 to 12 months. The version numbers are ephemeral. Hardware characteristics are stable for several months. If someone wants to build a device intelligence database with signatures that will be stable for months, using the following combination would only require retraining the model occasionally:

```
Browser name + OS name + screen size + CPU + memory size
```

After training this model with legitimate traffic, it will be able to recognize inconsistencies like Windows running on a Macintel CPU, macOS running on a Win32 CPU, or iOS running on a device with a screen resolution of 2560x1080, which is highly unexpected for an iPhone or even with the largest iPad. However, it will not be able to recognize the more subtle and common inconsistencies relative to the OS or browser version. That's where including the browser and OS version makes sense to help increase the detection effectiveness:

```
Browser name/version + OS name/version + screen size + CPU + memory size
```

Including the versions in the structure of the device intelligence signature requires more regular training of the model (at least once a day) to keep up with the introduction of new browser versions and their rapid adoption. This more advanced signature will recognize strong outliers like requests from systems that advertise obsolete browser versions like Firefox v10 or obsolete OS versions like Windows 98, which, surprisingly, I still see regularly. However, it will also help recognize more subtle anomalies, such as requests from systems that advertise a browser version over five versions behind, which have become rare.

The signature used to illustrate this section is one of the many possible combinations that can be used to build an effective device intelligence detection method. Consider using several formulas or types of data to structure the device intelligence signature.

Proof of Work

Since most botnets are sophisticated scripts but generally cannot run more complex JavaScript code, one of the common methods to detect bots is to check if they support JavaScript. Even if a bot or fraud detection product collects a fingerprint on the client side through JavaScript or an SDK installed in a mobile application, receiving the fingerprint does not guarantee the client has executed the code. As we've already seen, attackers commonly harvest and replay fingerprints. One way to raise the bar on JavaScript support detection is with the PoW detection method. The primary purpose of the PoW detection method is to verify that the client can solve complex operations through JavaScript using a specific code.

The main characteristic of PoW is its asymmetry: the work must be moderately hard (yet feasible) on the client side but easy to check on the server side. The PoW challenge is typically a complex mathematical or cryptographic puzzle the client must resolve through brute force. The challenge to be solved must be unique with each request, and its answer cannot be predictable, repeatable, or easy to precompute.

When building a PoW detection, one must decide on the formula or equation the client must solve. An example of a puzzle consists of computing a hash where the resulting value must have a certain number of leading zeros in the response based on a unique seed value for each session. The compute time may also be modulated with a difficulty parameter. The following is an example of a Proof of Work equation:

$$\texttt{sha256}(\texttt{Seed} + \texttt{difficulty} + \texttt{answer}) = \texttt{0000}[\texttt{0-9a-f}]+$$

The server will provide the following three parameters to the user:

- A *seed*, which is a value the server generates dynamically with each request
- A *difficulty* is a value that can vary depending on the type of threat detected and the context of the request. The difficulty will directly influence how long the client will take to solve the challenge.

represented with a plain X. A click up (when the user releases the button) is represented as a clear X. As shown in Figure 4.13, human behavior is complex and erratic whereas bot behavior is sometimes a lot simpler and minimalist.

Companies specializing in analyzing user experience and marketing collect mouse events and focus mainly on where users move their mouse or click. In the web security field, how the user interacts with the page is less important than how the user interacts with the device using the mouse. According to Stork, "Looking at the X-coordinate of the mouse cursor on a page versus time can help differentiate the human from the bot. With human-mouse motions (Figure 4.14, left), coordinate paths are often inconsistent, have clusters of points, and have "smooth" curves when changing position. Many discontinuities can be seen when comparing the plot (Figure 4.14, right) to a simple automated program controlling the mouse on the same web interface. Often, the time between each event is evenly spaced out. In this case, the bot only sends click events, not mouse move events".

More differences become apparent when evaluating the same mouse trajectory's velocity. Stork observed, "With human-mouse velocity (Figure 4.15, left), many inconsistencies are obvious, and many sharp increases in the speed of the mouse motions can be seen over time.

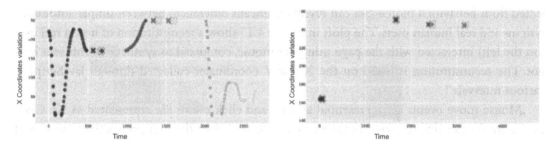

Figure 4.14   Human vs. bot mouse pointer movement over time

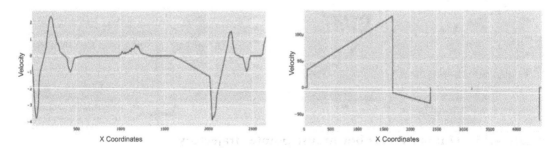

Figure 4.15   Human vs. bot mouse pointer velocity

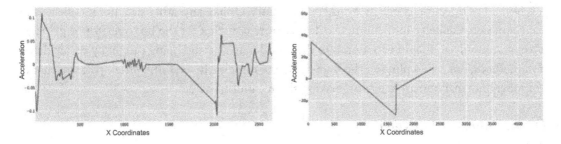

Figure 4.16 Human vs. bot mouse pointer acceleration

With basic automated systems (Figure 4.15, right), the cursor's velocity is often linear between movements and much less variable than human motion."

When looking at the acceleration profile of the mouse, motion bots show a more linear behavior (Figure 4.16, right) than significant variability across time observed with human-generated mouse movements (Figure 4.16, left).

According to Stork, "This same type of analysis can be applied to any interface control, from the speed of keypress events to the patterns of touchscreen interactions. All these dimensions can be combined to create a rich feature set for bot detection."

Other Caveats and Benefits One can detect familiarity with the data with keystrokes. Legitimate users logging into their online accounts are expected to be familiar with their username and password and type them faster than a fraudster trying to impersonate and take over the account. A machine learning model may also be trained to recognize the exact cadence users apply when typing their credentials, which can further help detect fraudsters.

Behavioral biometrics must consider the overall context of the request: Security-conscious users may take advantage of a password manager, which will automatically fill out the credentials on behalf of the user. The lack of keystrokes in this case and the presence of the password manager add-on on the browser can become a trust factor in explaining the limited behavioral data.

Regarding mobile devices, data from the gyroscope and accelerometer sensors can be used to evaluate how the user handles the devices. Fraudsters regularly spoof their traffic to make it appear like it is coming from a mobile device like an iPhone. These devices are so common that it can be complex to differentiate between similar devices, making behavioral anomaly detection more challenging. However, we expect the device to send data from the gyroscope and accelerometer in this case. The lack of telemetry sent by the device could strongly indicate that the fingerprint sent is spoofed.

Some bot operators generate synthetic telemetry. Unlike any other data point collected on the client side, the behavioral biometric data is more complex for the bot operator to get right. They commonly add slight variation into the coordinate to avoid being caught by replay detection methods, but when plotting the trajectory, one can clearly see some jittery patterns that do not reflect normal human behavior, making them easier to detect.

Headless Browser Detection

Websites can offer a wide variety of services and are critical to the operation of a company. Many businesses do not have a physical presence with brick-and-mortar shops in various locations and only have a presence on the Internet. They entirely depend on their website to generate revenue. The business logic may be complex, and completing a comprehensive test of the website before any new release will help prevent any downtime and impact on revenue. Several frameworks exist to help quality assurance teams automate site testing. These tools are known as *headless browsers*. A headless browser is a web browser without a graphical user interface controlled through a script.

Headless browsers provide automated web page control in an environment similar to popular web browsers like Chromium products, Firefox, or Apple WebKit. They are useful for testing web pages as they can render and understand HTML the same way a browser would, including styling elements such as page layout, color, font selection, and execution of JavaScript and Ajax, which are usually unavailable when using other testing methods.

Several frameworks have been developed over the years, the most relevant at the moment include the following:

- Selenium is an open-source project for various tools and libraries to support browser automation.
- Playwright, developed by Microsoft, supports all modern rendering engines, including Chromium, WebKit, and Firefox.
- Puppeteer and Headless Chrome, developed by Google, are designed to automate Chrome.
- Firefox, developed by Mozilla, also has a headless mode.

These automation frameworks were primarily developed to help automate website testing, but they can just as well be used to scrape websites or perform other attacks. These tools can be configured to automatically fill out forms, for example, in account registration abuse or credential stuffing attacks. They can also be used to parse web pages to extract product inventory or pricing in web scraping scenarios.

Detecting headless browsers can be very tricky. Indeed, because they run a real web browser, their fingerprint (device and browser characteristics and protocol parameters) looks identical to those of real browsers, making detection methods previously discussed inefficient. A headless botnet will handle cookies and JavaScript well, have a legitimate signature, and can execute a PoW challenge. But then again, it depends on how sophisticated the bot operator is. Detecting headless browsers can sometimes be as simple as looking for specific keywords in the `User-Agent` HTTP header or the `navigator.userAgent` object. For example, a vanilla integration of Headless Chrome would show the string `HeadlessChrome` in the User-Agent. But suppose a bot operator has gone through the trouble of deploying a botnet with a headless browser. It is very likely that they also did their due diligence and hid the characteristics that could easily give them away.

To detect headless browsers, one can test for the presence of various properties and variables using JavaScript to reveal them. The following table shows a few examples of variables and properties that can be queried:

Description	Characteristics
This property is available only in Headless Chrome and not available in the regular Chrome product.	`Navigator.webdriver`
`Window.document` objects	`__webdriver_evaluate`
	`__selenium_evaluate`
	`__webdriver_script_function`
	`__webdriver_script_func`
	`__webdriver_script_fn`
	`__fxdriver_evaluate`
	`__driver_unwrapped`
	`__webdriver_unwrapped`
	`__driver_evaluate`
	`__selenium_unwrapped`
	`__fxdriver_unwrapped`
Window properties	`_phantom`
	`__nightmare`
	`_selenium`
	`callPhantom`
	`callSelenium`
	`_Selenium_IDE_Recorder`

Bot operators may adopt advanced techniques to hide these properties and variables, which requires more "stealth mode" detection methods. More advanced detection methods are protected intellectual properties and cannot be shared in this book.

User-Behavior Anomaly Detection

User-behavior anomaly detection looks at how a client interacts with a website over time. Users may be identified based on their IP address, a cookie, or a device ID. User behavior anomaly detection looks for users who deviate from the normal usage pattern.

As shown in Figure 4.17, characteristics such as geolocation, navigation patterns, time spent on the site, and the number of pages visited are considered in the evaluation. This method can be powerful in detecting bot activity and human fraud activity.

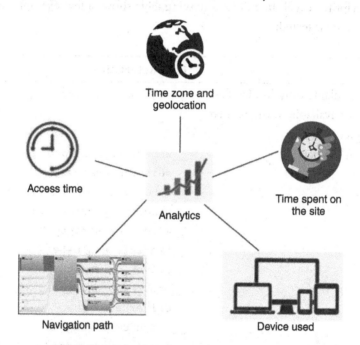

Figure 4.17   User-behavior anomaly detection

User Identifiers   One of the main requirements of user-behavior anomaly detection is identifying the user. Identifying users on the Internet is a controversial topic that we'll discuss in detail in Chapter 7. The following three primary identifiers are commonly used:

Cookies   A cookie is a piece of information that is dropped on the client's browser when they first visit a site. Various cookies may be designed to optimize the user experience on a site and include different types of information, from their shopping cart history to their geolocation. From a security point of view, cookies are also used as a token to attest that a user is logged in or retains certain states and characteristics of a user's device that can be reused during future visits to the website to evaluate any fraud risks.

Session cookies may expire when the user closes their browser or may have a specific expiry time after a few minutes or far in the future. They cannot be shared across domains or across platforms. Because of their characteristics, cookies are valuable in uniquely identifying a user. However, users may clear their cookies at any time. Attackers may drop or replay the cookies to fool the protection that depends on them.

Device IDs As mentioned previously, security products commonly inject JavaScript client-side and collect a fingerprint that reflects the device's characteristics, the browser used, and the user's preferences. Additional data points are collected server-side relative to the settings the client negotiated with the server when establishing the connection at the TCP, TLS, and HTTP layers. A subset of the previous data points can be used to compute a device ID.

If the structure of the device ID consists of data points that don't change too often, it may have a durability of several weeks. It will be able to detect a class of users that share the same type of device characteristics, browser, and user preferences but, on its own, cannot uniquely identify a user. In fact, with certain classes of very popular mobile devices like iPhones, it is difficult to differentiate between users. However, it is the second-best choice to identify a user when the cookie is missing.

IP Addresses Since the early days of the Internet, the IP address assigned to a client machine by the ISP has been used to identify users uniquely. However, user behavior has changed over time, especially with mobile devices. Users may use several IP addresses throughout the day at home, school or office or on public transport.

Various network architectures may also significantly influence the usability of the IP address. Corporations and ISPs commonly use proxy services or Internet gateways to optimize, accelerate, and secure the delivery of Internet traffic to their users, leading to hundreds of users behind a single IP address. Also, the use of privacy-preserving proxy services like Apple Private Relay has become more mainstream.

These changes make the IP address a less reliable identifier for user behavior analysis, but it is still commonly used.

Identity Graph As previously discussed, each identifier has its strengths and weaknesses, and none is perfect. To make good use of them, one needs an intelligent layer, sometimes referred to in the industry as an *identity graph*, to correlate the different identifiers and other pieces of information to identify a user.

An identity graph consists of a collection of profiles that may be interconnected with each other. A profile with various identifiers linked to each other represents a user. In its simplest form, a profile may look like the one shown in Figure 4.18, where a user cookie is linked to a single device ID linked to three different IP addresses. We'll typically find this for a user who connects to a website using the same device from three different networks or locations and never clears their cookies.

The picture may look a lot more complex for users who occasionally clear their cookies or connect using proxy services, with interconnections between different profiles. In the example shown in Figure 4.19, profile 1 has two cookies linked, either because the user has cleared their cookies at some point or because two distinct users have the same device ID (their software and hardware characteristics and user preferences are the same). We also see a link between two profiles that share some of the same IP addresses. This would happen, for example, when users from profiles 1 and 2 connect to the same network in public places or at work.

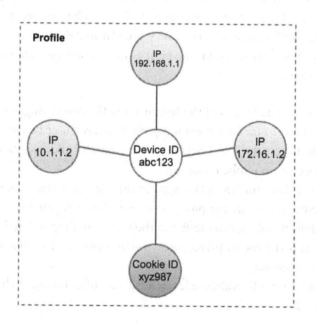

Figure 4.18　A simple identity graph profile

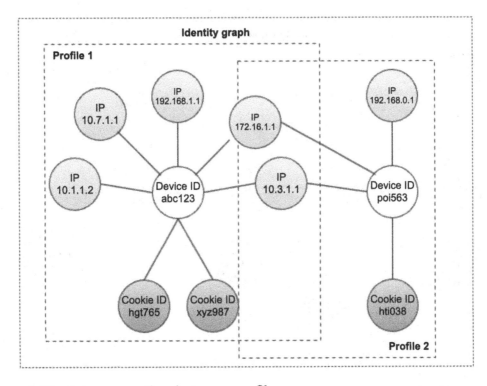

Figure 4.19   Interconnection between profiles

Figure 4.20 shows more advanced profiles with an additional generic identifier, such as the country the requests typically come from, or the username (often an email address) used when logging in. The country will significantly increase the interconnection of profiles within the graph.

The preceding picture can be a lot more complex if you imagine hundreds of users potentially sharing the same IP address and dozens of them sharing the same device ID. Identity graphs are designed to recognize recurring site visitors and prevent their accounts from being taken over and identities from getting stolen. Over time, the identity graph will learn about the devices and software users use when connecting to the site. We may all own several devices, but we also own a finite number of devices and are creatures of habit. The site will look up the identity graph at each visit to see if the device is known. A full match may be considered a factor of trust. A partial match may increase the risk factor. A site owner can then decide to take further action to identify the user if a significant deviation is found between the current request fingerprint and the known identities.

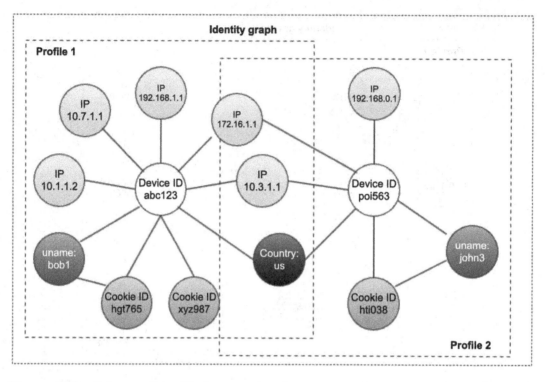

Figure 4.20 Advanced profile interconnection

Detecting Abnormal Behaviors   Once the means of identifying users is established, their behavior can be evaluated over time. This may include how long they spend on the site, the number and type of pages visited, the path used to access various resources, and where users connect from. These interactions will establish a reference point for normal behaviors to detect anomalous behavior better.

Each request with individual users is an opportunity to learn about them (establish or update a profile) and evaluate their behavior. The user should be allowed to interact with the site undisturbed if their behavior fits their profile and the norm:

- The user is using a previously seen device from a known location.
- The user is not formerly known for bad behavior.
- The user request pattern does not exceed typical behavior.

We live in a mobile world, and people travel with their devices. So, they may end up connecting from different locations. Users buy new devices or install new software regularly, which may change their fingerprints and, in turn, their identifiers. Privacy-conscious users also clear their cookies or browse websites using incognito mode. Also, new users start interacting with a website daily based on the success of marketing campaigns. Therefore, seeing requests coming from users without an established profile is expected.

Each anomaly found in user behavior may not be deterministic enough to classify a request as fraudulent, so most user-behavior anomaly detection methods use a risk score model (discussed later in this chapter). A single anomaly found when comparing the current request with the known user profile will not significantly affect the risk score. However, the risk score will be significantly affected if several anomalies are found. Beyond deviation from the known profile, excessive requests, unusual browsing patterns, or requests from unusual locations may further increase the risk score. What "excessive number of requests" or "unusual browsing patterns" means depends on the context of the request and the site:

- For an e-commerce site, a user browsing hundreds of product pages within a few minutes would be considered abnormal.
- For e-commerce sites, if the first user interaction is to access the login endpoint, it could be a sign of account takeover since users would typically browse product pages before logging in. However, such interaction is expected at a banking site.
- For all websites, a user sending dozens of login requests within a few minutes is a sign of a credential stuffing attack.
- A user creating dozens of accounts on a site within minutes is also anomalous and a sign of account opening abuse.

Email Intelligence

An advanced approach to detection is to evaluate the data the user inputs in specific workflows. As we've seen before, most websites use the email address as an identifier. Assessing the email address when users open an account on the site helps detect account opening abuses, and running the same evaluation on the login endpoint can prevent the usage of fake accounts and, subsequently, prevent the fraud scheme they were intended to be used for. The email address consists of the email local-part or handle and the email domain, separated by the @ sign: *local-part@domain*. For example, *john_doe@example.com*, where *john_doe* is the email local-part, and *example.com* is the email domain.

As noted previously, fraudsters create thousands of fake accounts. Each account created requires a unique email address. Considering the sheer volume of emails required, fraudsters often develop email address generators, which, depending on their sophistication, may present some apparent anomalies compared to legitimate accounts. The following table includes a few concrete examples of legitimate email addresses:

Pattern	Email address	Structure
1	John.doe@example.com	First + last name
2	jdoe@example.com	First name initial + last name
3	jd0130@example.com	First and last name initials + month/day birthday
4	j.doe013099@example.com	First name initial + last name + month/day/ year birthday
5	therock@example.com	nickname

In contrast, fraudsters who want to create fake accounts don't always follow this model. The randomization techniques they use for the email address local-part may include the following patterns:

Pattern	Email address	Structure
1	Eft5327qavp12@example.com Odp4228fntp94@example.com	Random letter and number combination (three letters + four numbers + four letters + two numbers)
2	John_doe01@example.com John_doe02@example.com	Email versioning First and last name + version
3	j.o.h.n.doe@example.com jo.h.n.d.oe@example.com joh.n.d.o.e@example.com	Email aliasing First and last name with each letter separated with special characters
4	Johndoe+123da@example.com Johndoe+23sdfe@example.com	First and last name with random value in the plus/sub addressing part
5	nkslhjpqs@example.com	Email address with no vowels making it unpronounceable
6	8798o34r978@example.com	Email address with a high number of digits

Once again, privacy features blur the line between malicious and legitimate traffic. Legitimate users may sometimes have the previous anomalies in their email addresses, especially when they use disposable email services like `Temp-mail.org` or Apple's email privacy feature to preserve their anonymity on the Internet or protect their accounts against credential stuffing while opening accounts on multiple websites.

RFC Compliance   One detection strategy to detect the most extreme offenders is to validate that the email address provided follows the RFCs that define the email address structure (Wikipedia, 2024a). Common anomalies found in the local-part that make the email address invalid include:

- The local part is empty.
- The local part is longer than 64 characters.
- The local part starts or ends with a . (dot).
- The local part has two or more consecutive dots (..).
- The local part contains an unescaped space; this anomaly is sometimes caused by typos when the user types their email address, and the user interface doesn't automatically validate or sanitize the input.
- The special characters (),;:<>@[]\ are not used within quotes. Although these characters, when used within quotes, are technically valid, most email system administrators only allow the use of the hyphen (-), underscore (_), dot (.), and plus (+). All other special characters are very uncommon and may be considered invalid.
- The local part has more than one @ special character.

Other anomalies may be found in the email domain, including the following:

- The domain doesn't conform to the requirements of a DNS domain.
- The domain part is empty.
- At least one part of the domain separated by a dot is longer than 63 characters.
- The email domain only consists of numerical values.
- The domain includes unauthorized special characters; the only special characters allowed for the domain are dot (.) and hyphen (-).

The following table shows a few examples of invalid email addresses:

Email address	Anomalies
domain.com; @domain.com	Missing local part
johndoe; johndoe@	Missing domain
john doe@example.com	Unauthorized unescaped space
john@doe@example.com	Unauthorized use of special characters in the local part

(continued)

(continues)

Email address	Anomalies
john..doe@example.com	Unauthorized consecutive special characters in the local part
johndoe@example_site.com	Unauthorized use of special characters in the domain
.john.doe@example.com	Unauthorized dot at the start of the local part

Detecting Randomization Patterns   However, most fraudsters follow the RFC's email structure, so additional syntax validation methods are required. Based on the anomalous patterns previously discussed, the assessment of the email local part helps detect attempts to create fake accounts:

- A high number of special characters, which includes the dot (.), underscore (_), and dash (-)
- Use of plus/sub addressing method
- Low alpha-to-digits ratio
- Low vowel-to-consonant ratio
- Excessive number of consecutive vowels or consonants
- Unusual alpha and digit pattern

Fraudsters who develop more advanced email generators may not show the preceding anomalies. Instead, the email generator inputs thousands of common first and last names and generates a million unique, perfectly structured email addresses. The easiest way for attackers to create email addresses is to run their own email systems. As we've seen in the section discussing account opening abuses in Chapter 2, attackers may register hundreds of domains with registrars offering services for as low as $1 per month per domain. Once they own the domain, fraudsters can create as many email accounts as they need; they will later be used to create fake accounts on various targeted websites.

Since most legitimate users use one of the major email services such as Yahoo!, Gmail, Outlook, or similar to create accounts on a website, disposable domains stand out when one pays attention to the email domain used to create an account. There are two main methods to detect disposable email domains.

The Whois Method   Whois is a query and response protocol used for querying databases that store an Internet resource's registered users or assignees. Whois is available as a command line on all Unix/Linux operating systems. When comparing the output of the Whois query for legitimate email domains to the disposable ones, there are two striking differences:

- **The registration date:** For legitimate domains, the domain was registered decades ago when the Internet became a thing, whereas, for disposable domains, it was registered within the last three years or less. Some disposable domains on some websites were registered within a month.
- **The registrar name:** Fraudsters gravitate toward registrars that offer domain registration at low cost, while corporations use more established registrars that offer full brand protection.

Figure 4.21 shows the output of the `whois` command on a disposable domain.

```
Domain name: onetpoczta.xyz
Registry Domain ID: D389607234-CNIC
Registrar WHOIS Server: whois.namecheap.com
Registrar URL: http://www.namecheap.com
Updated Date: 0001-01-01T00:00:00.00Z
Creation Date: 2023-08-22T08:09:55.00Z
Registrar Registration Expiration Date: 2024-08-22T08:09:55.00Z
Registrar: NAMECHEAP INC
Registrar IANA ID: 1068
Registrar Abuse Contact Email: abuse@namecheap.com
Registrar Abuse Contact Phone: +1.9854014545
Reseller: NAMECHEAP INC
Domain Status: serverTransferProhibited https://icann.org/epp#serverTransferProhibited
Domain Status: clientTransferProhibited https://icann.org/epp#clientTransferProhibited
Domain Status: addPeriod https://icann.org/epp#addPeriod
Registry Registrant ID:
Registrant Name: Redacted for Privacy
Registrant Organization: Privacy service provided by Withheld for Privacy ehf
Registrant Street: Kalkofnsvegur 2
Registrant City: Reykjavik
Registrant State/Province: Capital Region
Registrant Postal Code: 101
Registrant Country: IS
Registrant Phone: +354.4212434
Registrant Phone Ext:
Registrant Fax:
Registrant Fax Ext:
Registrant Email: c24573df02754bdc87cdefd24eac805b.protect@withheldforprivacy.com
```

Figure 4.21   Output of the `whois` command on a disposable domain

The Email Domain Behavior Method   Email creation activity from disposable domains is typically sporadic, with a surge of activity within a few minutes. In other scenarios, the activity is continuous, with a new account created every few minutes, day and night. This is a dramatically different pattern compared to registrations from legitimate users following the daily circadian pattern.

(continues)

Service	Enriched data
Social media presence (based on the email and phone number)	Evaluate if the email address or phone number is used as an identifier on social media or messaging platforms like LinkedIn, Facebook, X (Twitter), Yahoo!, Instagram, Telegram, WhatsApp, Quora, etc. Legitimate users are very likely to have a social presence on at least one of the platforms. No presence on any of the platforms is suspicious.
Data breach	Identifies if the email address was part of any known data breaches. This can help in two ways: • An email address that has been involved in multiple data breaches, especially some that took place years ago, can help assert the maturity and legitimacy of the email when a user attempts to create a new account. • When protecting login, an email address involved in a recent breach can be used as an indicator to prevent account takeover.

Advanced KYC solutions can challenge users based on their Social Security number, driver's license, or credit history.

Risk Scoring

By now, you should have a better understanding of the threat landscape and how detection works. Managing bad traffic through many detection methods can sometimes be challenging and confusing. The various detection methods are designed to detect multiple threats. When they are well-tuned, they can be very deterministic and accurate on their own. But combining multiple signals to detect nonlegitimate activity with high accuracy may be necessary to detect more sophisticated attacks.

Risk score algorithms are designed to obfuscate the complexity of individual detection methods and combine multiple signals to detect advanced threats better. The exact algorithm used to build a risk score can vary. Some vendors may use machine learning models. Others use statistical models or simple formulas. The simpler the model, the easier it is to explain, maintain, and tune. The ability to develop a complex ML model largely depends on the availability of labeled data, which is very hard to come by considering how fast the threat landscape and

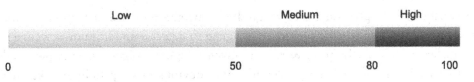

Figure 4.22   Risk score band and risk classification

digital ecosystem evolve. I've always gravitated to simpler models that combine the best of each detection method and are centered around a quantifiable risk associated with specific types of anomalies detected and their known false positive risks.

The outcome of a risk score model is to produce a value typically between 0 and 100, where 0 represents the lowest risk, and 100 is the highest. Having a good risk score model is challenging because website owners are usually more inclined only to mitigate traffic flagged as high risk, and anything that falls under a lower classification is only monitored or ignored. What score range is considered high risk depends on a company's security strategy. Companies with a more aggressive security strategy and more tolerance for false positives would consider any session scored at 70 and above high risk. In contrast, companies with a more conservative security strategy and less tolerance for false positives would consider any sessions scored at 90 and above high risk. As a product architect, I typically target 80 and above as high risk, as shown in Figure 4.22. Low risk generally refers to any session scored 50 and below, and anything in between is medium risk.

Ultimately, the risk score model should be tuned as much as possible to be deterministic. This means limiting the activity that falls into the "medium" risk band, which represents the detection's gray area and is difficult to act on. Good traffic must fall into the low-risk band, while truly malicious traffic must fall into the high-risk score range for an effective web security strategy.

Formula

Bot and fraud detection products consist of several detection methods. Generally, each detection method produces a contributing score used to generate a risk score. How the contributing score of the individual detection method is generated varies from a static model where a default weight is applied to a more dynamic method where the weight may vary depending on various factors, like the volume of requests.

In the simplest model, the risk score represents the sum of the contributing scores of individual detection methods triggered during the assessment. In the following formula, $score_n$ represents the detection method n contribution score. The value is capped at 100.

$$Risk_{score} = \text{Min}\left(\sum_{1}^{n} score_n, 100\right)$$

A variation of the preceding is to weigh the contribution of each detection method based on how critical the anomaly the method is designed to detect is and its known accuracy. Critical anomalies with low false positive risk are given a higher weight. An example would be a client that sends an invalid fingerprint with some obvious incompatibilities, like an iPhone running the Windows operating system. In contrast, a method designed to detect a common anomaly found in attack traffic and occasionally in legitimate traffic should have a much lower weight. An example in this category would be traffic from proxy servers, which is very common with attack traffic but also frequent with legitimate traffic.

$$Risk_{score} = Min\left(\left(\frac{1}{a} score_1 + \frac{1}{b} score_2 + \ldots + \frac{1}{c} score_n\right), 100\right)$$

A machine learning model trained on site-specific traffic may be used to modulate each detection method's weight or contributing score to take into account variations that can exist for the site ecosystem.

The quality of a risk score model is not defined by the complexity of the formula used but rather by its accuracy at classifying traffic. I've seen complex risk models that can take a significant amount of resources to train and maintain that, in the end, offer a marginal performance improvement compared to more straightforward, easy-to-maintain models.

Consuming the Risk Score

For web security services running on top of a content delivery network, website owners can take action on the medium and high-risk traffic at the edge and offload that traffic off the origin web server. Security products with advanced detection methods usually provide a deterministic and actionable signal.

Some website owners adopt a multi-vendor strategy to protect their web properties. Each vendor offers a unique perspective on the traffic. Combining multiple signals may help reduce the chance of malicious traffic slipping through the net cast by the various web security methods. It may specifically help with the traffic categorized as medium risk. If more than one product is used to protect the site, the second vendor may help reinforce the signal of the first vendor, classifying the traffic as high risk. A possible way to combine the risk score from two web security products may be to take the highest risk score from both products and use the lowest to boost the overall risk score. The formula may look as follows:

$$Risk_{score} = Min\left(\left(MAX\left(Risk_{vendor1}, Risk_{vendor2}\right) + \frac{1}{3} MIN\left(Risk_{vendor1}, Risk_{vendor2}\right)\right), 100\right)$$

The following table represents a simulation of how combining the score of multiple products can make the traffic categorized by one of the products as a medium be boosted and upgraded to high risk:

Risk Score 1	Class 1	Risk Score 2	Class 2	Combined Risk Score	Combined Class
20	Low	50	Medium	$50 + 20/3 = 57$	Medium
70	Medium	40	Low	$70 + 40/3 = 83$	High
30	Low	40	Low	$40 + 30/3 = 50$	Medium
60	Medium	70	Medium	$70 + 60/3 = 90$	High

Building an efficient model that combines the output of multiple web security products may be challenging. For such systems to be truly efficient, all products must be tuned to contribute meaningfully.

Summary

As the bot management space matures, vendors combine the interactive and transparent detection strategy in their product definition to achieve the highest accuracy and best user experience. A successful product requires several detection layers with varying levels of complexity that consume different types of data collected on the client and server side to match the botnet's sophistication. The complexity of the detection methods is best consolidated into a risk score to make it more actionable and straightforward to consume and integrate with third-party web security products that may complement the web security system to achieve the strongest security posture. With an understanding of how detection works, let's look into how to interpret the detection outcome and evaluate its accuracy.

5 | Assessing Detection Accuracy

Bot detection is about classifying web traffic as human or bot. Regular assessment of the traffic is necessary to ensure optimal user experience and prevent bot traffic from accessing the web resource. This chapter provides a methodology on how to assess the accuracy of the detection visually.

Prerequisites

Detecting bots, fraud, and abuse online is not a perfect science. Despite every effort vendors make to create products that are as accurate as possible, results may vary due to the ever-changing threat landscape and evolution of the Internet digital ecosystem. To ensure the optimal performance of the solution to keep the malicious traffic at bay while providing legitimate users with the best experience possible, regular assessment of the traffic is necessary to adjust the detection methods when necessary.

This chapter describes a proven method for assessing any detection method. It assumes you know and understand the OSI model and the TCP/IP, TLS, and HTTP protocols. A strong knowledge of the HTTP protocol and, in particular, the meaning of the various headers, as described in the "HTTP Headers 101" section in Chapter 3, "The Evolution of Botnet Attacks," is essential. You must also have an adequate understanding of how websites are structured and a good understanding of JavaScript and how it may trigger API calls or Ajax requests to retrieve data and render a page. This is especially important when dealing with a single-page application where most content navigation is achieved with API/Ajax calls. It also assumes you have access to an interface that allows you to analyze the relevant data. At a minimum, this means having visibility into the statistics and trending information relative to the following:

- **What content is requested:** URL, HTTP method
- **Who requested the content:** IP address and any information inferred from it, such as the AS number, the company that owns it, the type of connection (mobile, residential, corporate, cloud services)
- **How the content was requested (in other words, the device or application used):** User-Agent or the Sec-ch-ua header, any information inferred from it, and information relative to the settings used when establishing the TCP, TLS, and HTTP connections

If the product collects a fingerprint from the client using JavaScript, having access to that information can be a significant plus. However, it will require some level of understanding of the meaning of the data, how it is collected, and some proficiency in identifying inconsistencies.

The methodology requires a high-level assessment to understand the context of the site and its digital ecosystem, followed by a low-level assessment to look at the data from several angles to make an informed decision and confirm accuracy. As shown in the following table, several metrics define the accuracy:

Metric	Description
True positive (TP)	The number of requests coming from a botnet where the detection engine found anomalies and correctly identified them as nonlegitimate
False positive (FN)	The number of requests coming from a botnet where the detection engine did not find any anomalies and incorrectly identified them as legitimate
True negative (TN)	The number of requests coming from legitimate users where the detection engine did not find any anomalies and correctly identified them as legitimate
False negative (FP)	The number of requests coming from legitimate users where the detection engine found anomalies and incorrectly identified them as nonlegitimate

The two metrics in the following table can be derived from the preceding metrics and are generally the most closely monitored to assess accuracy:

Metric	Description
False positive rate (FPR)	The false positive rate, also called the missed rate, equals the total number of false positives divided by the sum of the false positives and true negatives. $$FPR = \frac{FP}{FP + TN}$$
False negative rate (FNR)	The false negative rate equals the total number of false negatives divided by the sum of false negatives and true positives. $$FNR = \frac{FN}{FN + TP}$$

High-Level Assessment

To start the assessment, it's essential to understand the environment you are assessing. This means understanding the website's structure, the typical audience, and the type of client susceptible to making requests.

Website Structure

Context is everything. The first step in evaluating detection accuracy is having a high-level understanding of the website's structure. For each of the following use cases, determine the URL path, the methods used (GET or POST), and the type of request (HTML or Ajax) for the relevant resource. Knowing the website structure will help better identify the resources that are more likely to be abused.

Web Scraper   For e-commerce sites, the most abused resources are the product detail pages or APIs that provide inventory and pricing information. It may be the property/accommodation detail pages and the API used to search for availability for travel and hospitality sites. For social media sites, it may be user profiles.

Credential Stuffing and Account Takeover   Be sure to identify all login APIs. Some sites use a unified API for all their applications or brands across devices. In contrast, others have different APIs depending on whether the user logs in to manage their account or logs in as part of the checkout workflow. Different APIs may also be used to handle native and web traffic. Some sites have an API to validate that a username exists. The "account verification" API can be utilized for credential stuffing for a targeted account takeover attack.

Account Opening Abuse   Some sites ask for minimal information (email address and password) from the users through a single-step workflow, while others require more information like first and last names and phone numbers and involve multiple steps. The most advanced account creation workflow may also require users to validate their email address and phone number through a one-time token process.

Gift Card Fraud, Coupon Abuse, Payment Fraud, Promotion Abuse   The steps required and their corresponding URLs to complete the checkout process, adding an item to the cart, adding payment methods, entering coupons, gift cards, and shipping addresses, and, finally, submitting the order. The steps included in a checkout flow may depend on the website.

When assessing the detection accuracy, doing a separate analysis for each use case is preferable to avoid a high volume of activity on specific endpoints (like traffic on product pages) as it may mask potential inaccuracies on endpoints with lower traffic (like the account creation endpoint). Attack patterns and sophistication may also vary depending on the use case. Understanding these patterns helps you to understand the threat the site is under, which can help you adjust the defense strategy to get the best results.

Modern website architectures leverage APIs queried by the client through Ajax requests. Single-page applications may load only a single HTML page. The rest of the navigation and rendering are handled by Ajax requests. Most websites combine HTML and Ajax requests. When the web security product collects a fingerprint through JavaScript, it's essential to identify when an HTML page is loaded and ensure the JavaScript is added to the page to guarantee effective fingerprint and telemetry collection.

Website Audience

Another essential point to understand is the website's audience: is it a business-to-consumer (B2C) website or a business-to-business (B2B) one? This distinction will impact the variety of clients requesting the content and the spread from where the traffic is coming. In the former, the activity is expected to come from hundreds of thousands of clients. In the latter case, the activity may be coming only from thousands of clients and become a solid indicator to detect anomalies in the traffic pattern. Also, B2B sites may see a higher ratio of their traffic coming from corporate proxies, VPNs, or Internet gateways since companies sometimes enforce using these services for security reasons or to limit congestion with their Internet traffic. Such elements must be considered to avoid misinterpreting these signals on B2B websites that could otherwise be considered suspicious with B2C websites.

Also, websites supporting globally well-known brands expect traffic from multiple countries. In contrast, a site that supports a brand that mainly operates in a specific market like the United States is expected to see traffic only from that region. Of course, patterns may change over time as companies expand their market internationally. Also, consumers travel internationally with their mobile devices and may choose to interact with the protected site on the go. Therefore, seeing some requests from unusual locations should be considered abnormal only once the traffic pattern exceeds a certain volume.

Types of Clients

Different websites or applications may also have different types of clients connecting to them. Some sites are exclusively designed to be consumed from a mobile application, so seeing traffic from web browsers may be considered unusual and even suspicious if the traffic volume is abnormally high. Other websites are designed to handle a mix of browser and mobile app traffic. Knowing the typical split between mobile and regular browser traffic can help evaluate whether the pattern is abnormal.

Gaming platforms may also expect a large part of their traffic to come from game consoles, which would be considered highly unusual on an e-commerce or banking site but normal for gaming.

Sites that offer streaming services may have an even more complex variety of devices connecting to the service, including smart TVs, mobile apps, game consoles, and regular browsers. Each of these types of clients can usually be easily identified by looking at the `User-Agent` header value.

Assessing the Shape of the Traffic

Assessing detection accuracy doesn't mean poring over hundreds of thousands of log lines. In fact, this is the last thing you should do. You should always start with a visual analysis of the traffic pattern. The product you are working with should have good reports or dashboards that allow you to review the traffic patterns for the last few days or weeks. Ideally, the product should allow for reviewing the previous 90 days of traffic. One report should clearly show the activity trend for the bot/fraud (high-risk) and human (low-risk) traffic. When looking at a week's worth of traffic, the plot may resemble the one shown in Figure 5.1, with the more abundant high-risk attack traffic trend line at the top and the less volumetric legitimate low-risk traffic trend line at the bottom.

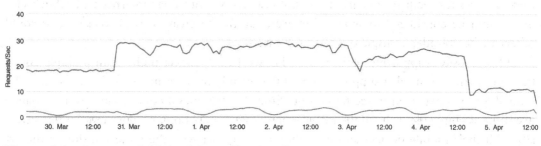

Figure 5.1   Low- and high-risk traffic timeline

Recognizing the Typical Human and Bot Pattern   There are a few behaviors to understand when interpreting the traffic pattern. Humans mostly visit websites during the day when they are awake. This means that when looking at the traffic over 24 hours, the volume of activity will increase during the early hours of the morning to a peak in the mid-to-late afternoon and decrease during the evening. As shown in Figure 5.2, the pattern looks circadian or like a sinusoid. Some website activity also varies depending on the day of the week. Banking or B2B

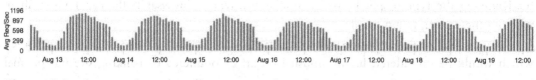

Figure 5.2   A repeating circadian pattern based on a seven-day time frame

Figure 5.3   A circadian pattern with lower amplitude

websites typically see more activity during the week, while the activity is significantly lower during the weekend. In contrast, e-commerce websites may see the opposite pattern, with higher weekend activity than weekdays.

With a lower traffic volume, the circadian patterns may be slightly more subtle, with a lower amplitude between the peak and valleys (Figure 5.3).

Unlike humans, bots do not sleep, and their activity does not follow the human-like circadian pattern. Figure 5.1 shows a strong illustration of this. Depending on the type of attack and the botnet sophistication, their request pattern may vary. As shown in Figure 5.4, some bots will send traffic for days at a consistent rate.

In other cases, the traffic may sometimes be interrupted, as shown in Figure 5.5. Bots are designed to collect certain types of data or perform specific tasks. Once they are done, the activity will stop. It may resume after a few days.

Other times, the activity can appear sporadic, as shown in Figure 5.6.

Figure 5.4   A continuous and persistent bot activity pattern

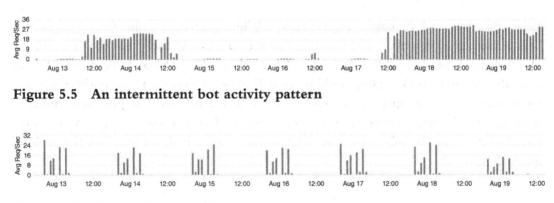

Figure 5.5   An intermittent bot activity pattern

Figure 5.6   A sporadic bot activity pattern

Or, activity can spike with sudden bursts (Figure 5.7). Those sharp traffic increases can cause website stability issues when in high volume.

Other patterns are more subtle, like the one shown in Figure 5.8, where the botnet attempts to simulate a circadian pattern. Note, however, that it is the 12-hour cycle instead of the typical human 24-hour cycle.

The wave pattern shown in Figure 5.9 also attempts to reproduce a human-like pattern, although it fails to produce the "dome" of an actual circadian pattern.

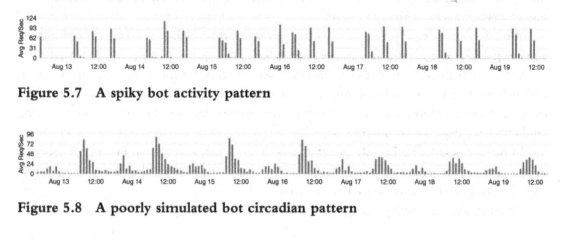

Figure 5.7   A spiky bot activity pattern

Figure 5.8   A poorly simulated bot circadian pattern

Figure 5.9   A wave bot activity pattern

False Positive and Negative Assessment   When analyzing traffic for false positives, look at the high-risk traffic over several days (at least one week) and check the overall shape of the activity over time: a noticeable circadian pattern with peaks of traffic during the day and valleys at night, on the plot, would be an indication of a possible false positive, whereas inconsistent, regular, or spiky traffic would indicate a true positive. The process is similar to assessing for false negatives but instead focuses on the low-risk traffic and looks for non-circadian patterns. The following table summarizes what to look for based on the angle of the analysis:

Analysis Angle	Traffic Pattern Characteristics
True positive	Focus: High-risk traffic
	Pattern to look for: Irregular, continuous, or sporadic activity (i.e., noncircadian)
False positive	Focus: High-risk traffic
	Pattern to look for: Circadian
True negative	Focus: Low-risk traffic
	Pattern to look for: Circadian
False negative	Focus: Low-risk traffic
	Pattern to look for: Irregular, continuous, or sporadic activity (i.e., noncircadian)

Quantitative Assessment (Volume)

When you look at the traffic volume from one day to the next, you will notice that patterns repeat. The daily high is almost the same as on the same day a week ago. Traffic patterns can vary from one day to the next. For example, e-commerce sites generally see the highest volume on weekends. This is why comparing a day's traffic pattern with the same day a week before is preferable. Sales events like Black Friday can also influence traffic volume.

Figure 5.10 shows a seven-day traffic trend (Saturday to Friday) on a banking website. The first two days (Saturday and Sunday) show the lowest volume, while from Monday to Friday, the traffic doubles compared to the weekend. The Wednesday (corresponding to the 5th "bump" in the graph) was the first of the month (payday) and showed the highest volume.

When comparing traffic volume, look for abnormal spikes or lows. The example in Figure 5.11 shows abnormal traffic spikes happening on four out of seven days around the same time. Note the higher-than-usual valley on the second day. All these anomalies must be closely investigated and are generally strong evidence of bot activity.

Figure 5.10   Traffic volume variation throughout the week for a banking site

that is not mitigated, a high correlation between the high-risk traffic and the high authentication failure rate in that segment will provide strong evidence of true positives. Just like for the challenge action, there is at least one caveat to consider: the authentication failure and high-risk traffic will not completely match since the attacker will likely be able to authenticate successfully for 10% to 15% of the credentials tested.

Response Strategy Assessment

Detecting the activity is one thing, but an adequate response strategy must be applied to eliminate the threat effectively. Various products offer different options, from the crude deny, where a 403 (Deny) HTTP status code will be served to the client, to the more nuanced tarpit, which will not send a reply, simulating as if the server is hanging. These two response strategies are the most effective as they block the attack traffic. However, they can be applied only to the most accurate detection methods since denying legitimate users (false positive) translates to the worst user experience and may lead to complaints, site abandonment, and revenue loss. Other response strategies offer the possibility to challenge a user. The challenge represents a way to detect legitimacy through alternate detection methods.

It is essential to consistently apply an adequate response strategy to the right threat type to mitigate the activity and ultimately force the bot operator to stop their operation and move on to a different, less protected target. Understandably, most website owners do not want to take any risk, apply a conservative response strategy, and mitigate only the highest-risk traffic (say 90 or greater). Other potentially equally malicious traffic (for example, with a risk score between 70 and 89) is left unmitigated. This lack of aggressive response strategy is usually unnecessary, and the website owner will perceive that the defense in place has a high false negative rate since, after all, the bad traffic was allowed to access the protected resource. Assessing the traffic as broadly as possible will help clearly define and adjust the boundaries of low, medium, and high risks and apply the mitigation strategy based on these risk segments to define the most effective defense posture. If applying mitigation to the high-risk traffic segment is not possible due to a high false positive rate, perform a low-level assessment as described in the following section to identify the root cause of the false positive and solve the problem to make the high-risk segment actionable.

Low-Level Assessment

This section presents the data points that should be considered for the low-level assessment to help classify the traffic. The availability and fidelity of these data points may vary from one bot management product to another. Bot operators often make small mistakes when sending traffic that does not fit the typical context of the site or the current Internet ecosystem. These small mistakes can be found in the low-level assessment and are very helpful in helping confirm the nature of the traffic.

IP Intelligence

All good bot management products include information derived from the client's IP address. Looking at the country, AS number, and type of connection can help assess low- and high-risk traffic. The type of information included may vary depending on the vendor. The IP intelligence assessment helps understand the botnet's load distribution strategy and scale.

Top Countries   Looking at which country the traffic from different risk categories comes from can help with the accuracy assessment. Based on the expected audience, consider the following scenarios:

Scenario	Suggested Classification	Caveats
High-risk traffic originating from unusual markets/countries in high volume	True positive	A low volume of traffic is acceptable as regular visitors may travel.
Low-risk traffic originating from unusual markets/countries at high volume	False negative	A successful marketing campaign designed for international expansion could generate a lot of traffic.
High-risk traffic originating from usual markets/countries	True positive	Attackers commonly send traffic from the same market expected by the website.
Low-risk traffic originating from usual markets/countries at a high volume	True negative	Attackers may try to blend in with the legitimate traffic.

Evaluating the shape of traffic from individual countries is key. Figure 5.14 shows what legitimate traffic from various countries may look like for a site with a global audience. Each sparkline represents seven days of traffic, and each bar represents three hours. You can recognize the characteristic circadian pattern from legitimate users. If this activity is classified as low risk, this is a sign of a true negative.

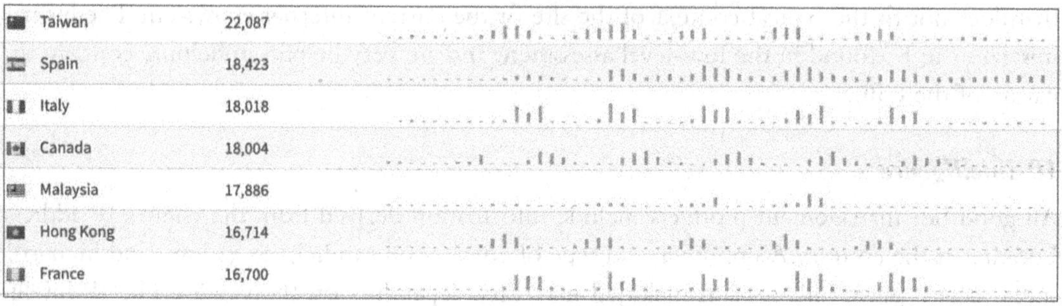

Taiwan	22,087	
Spain	18,423	
Italy	18,018	
Canada	18,004	
Malaysia	17,886	
Hong Kong	16,714	
France	16,700	

Figure 5.14   Legitimate traffic pattern by country

South Africa	28,513	
Portugal	25,210	
Bangladesh	5,994	

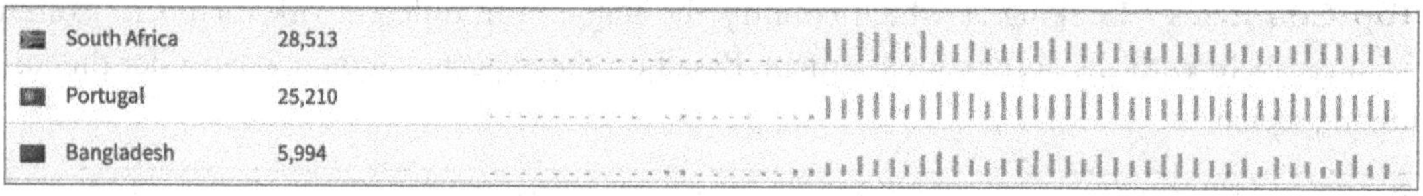

Figure 5.15   Bot traffic pattern by country

In contrast, in Figure 5.15, the shape of this traffic from various countries does not have the typical circadian pattern. If such traffic is classified as low risk, this would be a sign of false negatives.

Top AS Number and ISP   The AS number identifies networks on the Internet. Large Internet service providers (ISPs) and cloud service providers typically have their own ASN. Your web security product may provide the company's name associated with the ASN. It is common to see company names that offer cloud services associated with high-risk traffic, just like in Figure 5.16. Notice the continuous or sporadic traffic pattern indicative of bot activity.

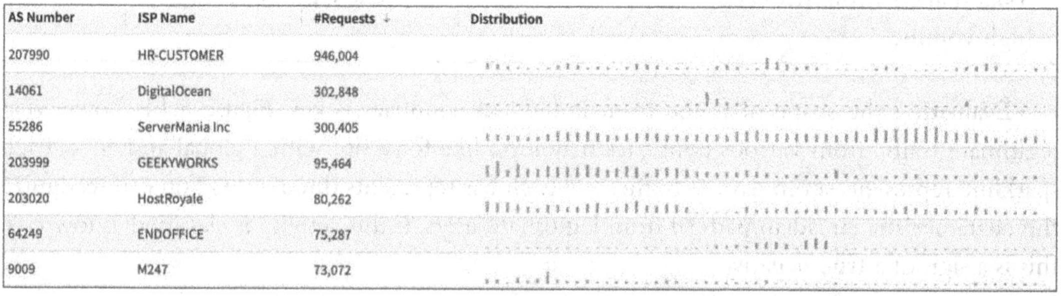

AS Number	ISP Name	#Requests	Distribution
207990	HR-CUSTOMER	946,004	
14061	DigitalOcean	302,848	
55286	ServerMania Inc	300,405	
203999	GEEKYWORKS	95,464	
203020	HostRoyale	80,262	
64249	ENDOFFICE	75,287	
9009	M247	73,072	

Figure 5.16   Traffic pattern from cloud services' AS number

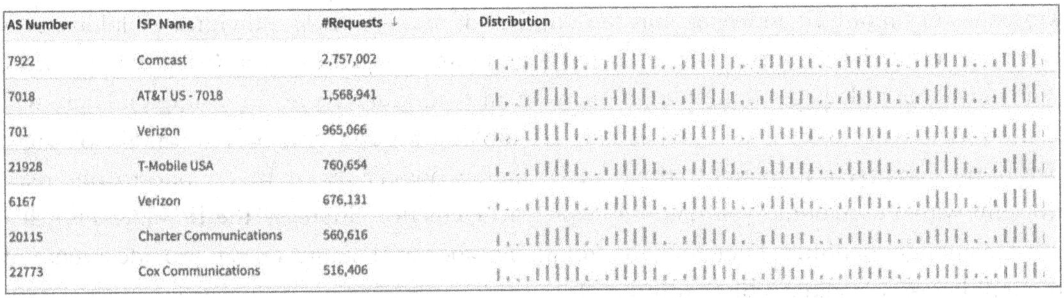

AS Number	ISP Name	#Requests ↓	Distribution
7922	Comcast	2,757,002	.ı..ıllll..ıllll..ıllll..ıllll...ıllll...ıllll...ıllll
7018	AT&T US - 7018	1,568,941	.ı..ıllll..ıllll..ıllll..ıllll...ıllll...ıllll..ıllll
701	Verizon	965,066	.ı..ıllll..ıllll..ıllll..ıllll...ıllll...ıllll..ıllll
21928	T-Mobile USA	760,654	.ı..ıllll..ıllll..ıllll..ıllll...ıllll...ıllll..ıllll
6167	Verizon	676,131	.ı...ıllll..ıllll..ıllll..ıllll...ıllll...ıllll..ıllll
20115	Charter Communications	560,616	.ı..ıllll..ıllll..ıllll..ıllll...ıllll...ıllll..ıllll
22773	Cox Communications	516,406	.ı...ıllll..ıllll..ıllll..ıllll...ıllll...ıllll..ıllll

Figure 5.17 Traffic pattern from residential and mobile ISPs

In contrast, you can expect to mostly see mobile and residential ISPs for traffic classified as low risk. Figure 5.17 shows what the pattern may look like when originating from North America. Also, note the circadian pattern.

The scenarios described in the following table must be considered for properly assessing the traffic coming from the cloud providers, residential ISPs, or mobile networks.

Scenario	Suggested Classification	Rationale
High-risk traffic originating from cloud providers at high volume	True positive	Botnets are commonly running on virtual machines running from cloud providers.
Low-risk traffic originating from cloud providers with a circadian pattern	True negative	Legitimate end users use proxy or VPN services for privacy reasons and remain anonymous on the Internet.
High-risk traffic originating from residential and mobile ISPs	True positive	Advanced botnet operators commonly load balance their traffic through proxy relays hosted on mobile devices, desktops, or laptops.
Low-risk traffic originating from residential and mobile ISPs	True negative	Legitimate users primarily come from residential and mobile ISPs.

Top IP Addresses Going one level deeper from the AS number, it helps to look at the distribution of IP addresses and the number of requests from individual IPs to get a sense of the spread of the traffic. From the low-risk traffic point of view, you would see hundreds of thousands of unique IP addresses, and the number of requests from individual IP addresses is evenly distributed. Of course, there will always be more engaged users on the site than others, who check multiple pages (multiple products on an e-commerce site, for example). There will also be users who know exactly what they are looking for and visit only a handful of pages before they complete their transaction. An IP address doesn't always have a one-to-one relationship with a user, but as you saw in Chapter 4, "Detection Strategy," the IP address is still a reliable enough identifier. Therefore, the unique number of IP addresses can provide a sense of the number of users interacting with the site.

Similar behavior can be seen regarding high-risk traffic if the attacker has built an advanced botnet and evenly load balanced the traffic through many IP addresses (generally facilitated by proxy services). However, in the case of high-risk traffic, it is also common to see a small set of IP addresses sending a very high number of requests. Looking up the company that owns the IP addresses that is making excessive requests will also help you understand the nature of that traffic. Once again, seeing cloud providers associated with these IP addresses is prevalent. Looking at the unique number of IP addresses will provide a sense of the size of the botnet and its sophistication. The bigger the number, the higher the sophistication and the higher the risk that the attack will persist.

Figure 5.18 shows an example of a few IP addresses that belong to the same botnet. Note how the number of requests for each is evenly distributed, and the activity is synchronized between each IP address. The full IP address was masked for privacy reasons.

In contrast, for low-risk traffic, Figure 5.19 shows activity from individual IP addresses that is sporadic and uncoordinated.

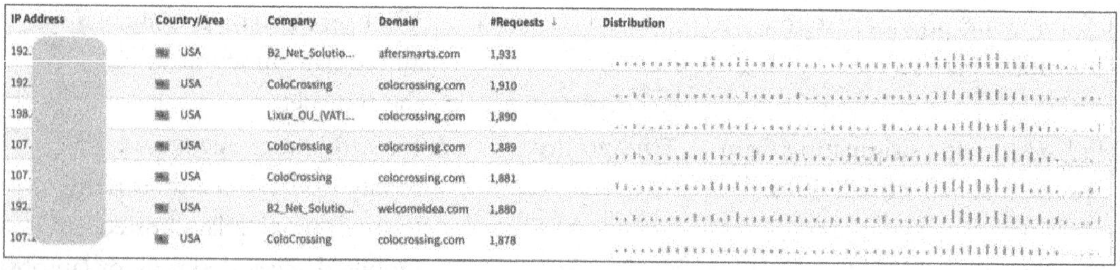

IP Address	Country/Area	Company	Domain	#Requests ↓	Distribution
192.	USA	B2_Net_Solutio...	aftersmarts.com	1,931	
192.	USA	ColoCrossing	colocrossing.com	1,910	
198.	USA	Linux_OU_[VATL...	colocrossing.com	1,890	
107.	USA	ColoCrossing	colocrossing.com	1,889	
107.	USA	ColoCrossing	colocrossing.com	1,881	
192.	USA	B2_Net_Solutio...	welcomeidea.com	1,880	
107.	USA	ColoCrossing	colocrossing.com	1,878	

Figure 5.18   Evenly distributed synchronized bot activity on several IP addresses

Proxy and VPN Service Usage   Your web security product may provide insight into proxy usage, VPN, and TOR (The Onion Router) services. These services are increasingly more popular with legitimate users as a means to improve their anonymity on the Internet. Currently, 10% to 15% of legitimate users use proxy or VPN services.

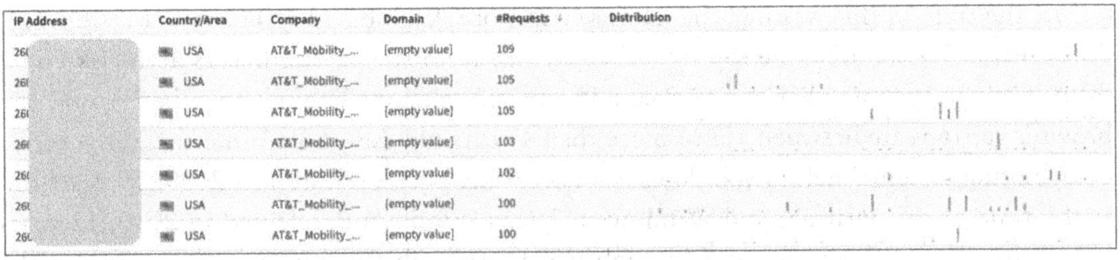

IP Address	Country/Area	Company	Domain	#Requests ↓	Distribution
26	USA	AT&T_Mobility_...	[empty value]	109	
26	USA	AT&T_Mobility_...	[empty value]	105	
26	USA	AT&T_Mobility_...	[empty value]	105	
26	USA	AT&T_Mobility_...	[empty value]	103	
26	USA	AT&T_Mobility_...	[empty value]	102	
26	USA	AT&T_Mobility_...	[empty value]	100	
26	USA	AT&T_Mobility_...	[empty value]	100	

Figure 5.19   Sporadic activity from legitimate users

However, platforms built by companies like Zyte, Oxylabs, Smartproxy, and Bright Data are explicitly designed to facilitate the scraping of websites. Bot operators can choose from the cheapest options that will give them access to thousands of IP addresses hosted in data centers to more advanced options that allow access to residential and mobile IP addresses.

Device Intelligence

When assessing bot traffic, the device intelligence assessment helps evaluate the sophistication of the botnet's fingerprint. It will also help identify false positives. Some bot management solutions are more generous than others regarding the diversity of dimensions available to evaluate. At the minimum, they should all offer the User-Agent header from which the browser and operating system names and versions can be derived. Additional HTTP headers like the Accept-Language header, secure client hints (Sec-CH-UA), and, in some cases, the full set of HTTP header names received from the client may also be available. This section provides guidance on how best to use the different data points.

Top Browsers and Operating Systems   Because of the common operating systems (OSs) and browser randomization patterns included in most scripted botnet logic, bot traffic (true positive) is more likely to come from older browser and OS versions. At the same time, considering all modern browsers auto-update as soon as a new version is available, good traffic will show more recent browser and OS versions (within three releases).

Depending on the vendor, new browser versions are released every four to six weeks. New OS versions are released less regularly. There is typically a new iOS version every two months, a new macOS version every three months, and a new Windows version once a year. While investigating false positives, knowing the current version for the top five browser brands (Chrome, Firefox, Safari, Edge, and Opera) is helpful to put the versions you may observe into perspective.

At the time of this writing, the latest version of Chrome and Firefox was version 121. As shown in Figure 5.20, the top five User-Agents from traffic classified as high risk come from browser versions that are between 15 and 43 versions behind. In other words, the browser versions are between 1.5 to more than 4 years old. Also note some ancient versions of operating systems such as Windows 6.1 (aka Windows 7, released in 2009, 15 years old at the time of this writing) and Windows 6.2 (aka Windows 8, released in 2012, 12 years old at the time of this writing). Although it is possible that a legitimate user could make requests from a system running outdated software, it is not expected to see such a high volume of traffic.

In contrast, as shown in Figure 5.21, low-risk traffic from legitimate users is expected to come from the latest operating systems and browser versions. In this case, Chrome versions 120 and 121, Edge version 121, and Safari 17.2. Seeing a high volume of low-risk traffic coming from outdated browser versions may indicate false negatives.

User-Agent	#Requests ↓
Mozilla/5.0 (Windows NT 6.2; WOW64) AppleWebKit/537.36 (KHTML, like Gecko) Chrome/78.0.3904.108 Safari/537.36	345,950
Mozilla/5.0 (Windows NT 6.1; Win64; x64; rv:95.0) Gecko/20100101 Firefox/95.0	187,254
Mozilla/5.0 (Windows NT 10.0; Win64; x64) AppleWebKit/537.36 (KHTML, like Gecko) Chrome/96.0.4664.110 Safari/537.36	181,167
Mozilla/5.0 (Macintosh; Intel Mac OS X 12_1) AppleWebKit/537.36 (KHTML, like Gecko) Chrome/96.0.4664.110 Safari/537.36	138,779
Mozilla/5.0 (Windows NT 10.0; Win64; x64) AppleWebKit/537.36 (KHTML, like Gecko) Chrome/106.0.0.0 Safari/537.36	64,808

Figure 5.20   Top five User-Agent for high-risk traffic

User-Agent	#Requests ↓
Mozilla/5.0 (iPhone; CPU iPhone OS 17_2_1 like Mac OS X) AppleWebKit/605.1.15 (KHTML, like Gecko) Version/17.2 Mobile/15E148 Safari/604.1	432,639
Mozilla/5.0 (Linux; Android 10; K) AppleWebKit/537.36 (KHTML, like Gecko) Chrome/121.0.0.0 Mobile Safari/537.36	285,476
Mozilla/5.0 (Windows NT 10.0; Win64; x64) AppleWebKit/537.36 (KHTML, like Gecko) Chrome/121.0.0.0 Safari/537.36	187,134
Mozilla/5.0 (Windows NT 10.0; Win64; x64) AppleWebKit/537.36 (KHTML, like Gecko) Chrome/120.0.0.0 Safari/537.36	186,398
Mozilla/5.0 (Windows NT 10.0; Win64; x64) AppleWebKit/537.36 (KHTML, like Gecko) Chrome/121.0.0.0 Safari/537.36 Edg/121.0.0.0	129,695

Figure 5.21   Top five User-Agents for low-risk traffic

The following table summarizes the various aspects to consider when evaluating the User-Agent. As usual, looking at the shape of the traffic patterns for each User-Agent will help classify the traffic.

Scenario	Classification	Caveats
High-risk traffic coming from outdated `User-Agent` in high volume	True positive	Some legitimate users may send requests from a system running outdated software.
Low-risk traffic coming from outdated `User-Agent` at a high volume	False negative	Some applications require custom clients that may be based on outdated versions of Chrome.
High-risk traffic coming from recent `User-Agents`	False positive	Attackers may send traffic using the latest `User-Agent` version to blend in with legitimate traffic.
Low-risk traffic coming from recent `User-Agent` at a high volume	True negative	

HTTP Headers   Your bot management solution may provide visibility into the HTTP header sent by the client. As described in Chapter 3, having a good understanding of the HTTP protocol and the set of headers a browser brand is expected to send is key. While doing an accuracy assessment, check the following indicators:

HTTP Version   All browsers, most web servers, and CDNs support at least HTTP/2. Most browsers also support HTTP/3, but the adoption is slow on the server side. HTTP/3 will be used only if the web server or CDN distributing the traffic supports the version and the protocol is configured. HTTP/2 and HTTP/3 enforce the use of HTTPS. Seeing secure traffic coming over HTTP/1.1 is highly unexpected. Most of the time, HTTP/1.1 traffic can be correlated to bot activity unless the traffic requested is not secure, which is becoming very rare since all website owners upgraded to serve traffic over HTTPS by default a few years ago. Secure traffic over HTTP/1.1 is also possible when the traffic is proxied through legacy Internet gateways or corporate proxies that don't support HTTP/2 or greater.

Secure Client Hint Headers   The secure client hint headers—`Sec-CH-UA` (MDN Web Docs, 2024b), `Sec-CH-Mobile` (MDN Web Docs, 2024c), and `Sec-CH-Platform` (MDN Web Docs, 2024d)—were launched several years ago at the initiative of Google Chrome to reduce the opportunity for uniquely identifying users and are eventually supposed to replace the `User-Agent` header. All Chromium-based browsers support the client hint. Knowing which brands and versions support the client hint can help reveal botnets, as most of them are very good at sending a `User-Agent` with the latest browser and OS version but may fail at sending the expected set of client hint headers. In contrast, seeing the client hint header set on browser versions and brands that do not support it is also unexpected and a strong indicator of bots.

User-Agent Header   In parallel to rolling out the client hint, Google Chrome has been working on reducing the entropy of the `User-Agent` string (Chromium Projects, 2024). For example, the minor Chrome version has been zeroed out since v101. The phone model is replaced with the value K from version 110 for a mobile device. Here's what the reduced `User-Agent` looks like for Google Chrome running on an Android device:

```
Mozilla/5.0 (Linux; Android 10; K) AppleWebKit/537.36 (KHTML, like
Gecko) Chrome/93.0.0.0 Safari/537.36
```

The `User-Agent` reduction and its impact on bot detection will be discussed further in Chapter 7, "Internet User Privacy." Once more, bots that continue randomizing the `User-Agent` send a value that doesn't align with the new `User-Agent` format, making them easier to recognize.

***Sec-Fetch* Headers**   The `Sec-Fetch` header set was introduced several years ago and is supported by most browser brands (Chromium, Mozilla, and Apple products). Knowing which brands and versions support the `Sec-Fetch` headers can help expose bots.

Accept-Language   This header describes the user's preferred languages configured on the client machine. Depending on the typical website audience, this information can reveal bot activity, especially when the audience is restricted to a specific region. For example, let's take the website of a low-cost airline that serves various cities in Europe. In this case, we expect most of the traffic to come from all the countries the airline is flying to, with the `Accept-Language` header showing the language spoken in those countries. Seeing excessive traffic advertising languages not widely spoken in those countries (for example, Chinese, Thai, or Vietnamese) can help confirm the activity is coming from bots.

Here's an example of the expected `Accept-Language` header for the preceding example with the Spanish and English (Great Britain) languages advertised:

```
Accept-Language: es-ES,es;q=0.9
Accept-Language : en-GB,en;q=0.9
```

Compared to an excessive amount of traffic advertising the Chinese language, this at least helps bring some context to the origin of the bot traffic.

```
Accept-Language: zh-CN,zh;q=0.8,zh-TW;q=0.7,zh-HK;q=0.5,en-US;
q=0.3,en;q=0.2
```

Header Set   Most basic botnets are not good at reproducing the set of headers expected from various browser brands. In most extreme cases, the botnet will send the bare minimum number of headers (three or hour headers in total compared to at least 11 headers expected from Chromium products, as shown in the following example):

```
Host: www.example.com
Sec-CH-UA: "Google Chrome";v="123", "Not:A-Brand";v="8",
"Chromium";v="123"
sec-ch-ua-mobile: ?0
User-Agent: Mozilla/5.0 (Windows NT 10.0; Win64; x64) AppleWebKit/
537.36 (KHTML, like Gecko) Chrome/123.0.0.0 Safari/537.36
sec-ch-ua-platform: "Windows"
Accept: */*
sec-fetch-site: same-site
sec-fetch-mode: cors
sec-fetch-dest: empty
Accept-Encoding: gzip, deflate, br, zstd
Accept-Language: en-US,en;q=0.9
```

On the other hand, Safari does not yet support the client hint headers; the set of headers included in this case will be restricted and look as follows. Note how the position of the headers changes when compared to Chrome.

```
Host: www.example.com
Accept: application/json, text/plain, */*
sec-fetch-site: same-site
Accept-Language: en-CA,en-US;q=0.9,en;q=0.8
Accept-Encoding: gzip, deflate, br
sec-fetch-mode: cors
```

(*continued*)

(continues)

```
User-Agent: Mozilla/5.0 (iPhone; CPU iPhone OS 17_3 like Mac OS X)
AppleWebKit/605.1.15 (KHTML, like Gecko) Version/17.3 Mobile/15E148
Safari/604.1
sec-fetch-dest: empty
```

Assessment Guidelines

Most of the time, none of the preceding indicators is deterministic enough to classify the traffic as low or high risk. However, combining some of them will help tip the balance in one way or another. Remember that some of the signals will seem normal due to the complexity of some attacks. When evaluating the accuracy of detection methods, you must assess the good traffic (low risk), questionable traffic (medium risk), and bad traffic (high risk) separately. Please review Chapter 4 for more details on the risk score boundaries between each classification.

For high-risk traffic, look at false versus true positives. Figure 5.22 shows the different dimensions to evaluate and how to classify the traffic based on the outcome. Note that the traffic's shape and volume should be assessed for each dimension whenever possible.

There are two essential facts to keep in mind while doing a false positive assessment:

- **The traffic looks clean except for the pattern:** The most advanced botnets are designed to mimic legitimate traffic as best as possible. In this case, little indicators will point toward "true positive." Sometimes, the traffic shape is the only indicator that seems wrong and points toward "true positive." In contrast, for the other indicators, the traffic will seem "clean" (recent browser and OS, residential or mobile ISP, extensive spread of IP address, acceptable velocity per IP address).
- **Visible circadian pattern:** No detection is ever 100% accurate. During the assessment, you may find some "pockets" of false positive traffic. Identify the signature as best as possible and tune the detection to eliminate the false positive without significantly affecting the true negative rate.

When evaluating low-risk traffic, look at false versus true negatives. As shown in Figure 5.23, the same methodology applies.

When looking for false negatives, some caveats also apply. Seeing the following indicators typical of high-risk traffic can be expected in low volume:

- **VPN, proxy:** Legitimate users may leverage proxy and VPN services to preserve their anonymity on the Internet. Most of these cheap proxy services are generally hosted on cloud providers.

- **Spikes in traffic:** Sales events such as Black Friday may cause an abnormal increase in traffic, causing unusual activity spikes.
- **Outdated software versions:** Less tech-savvy users may use older devices running outdated versions.

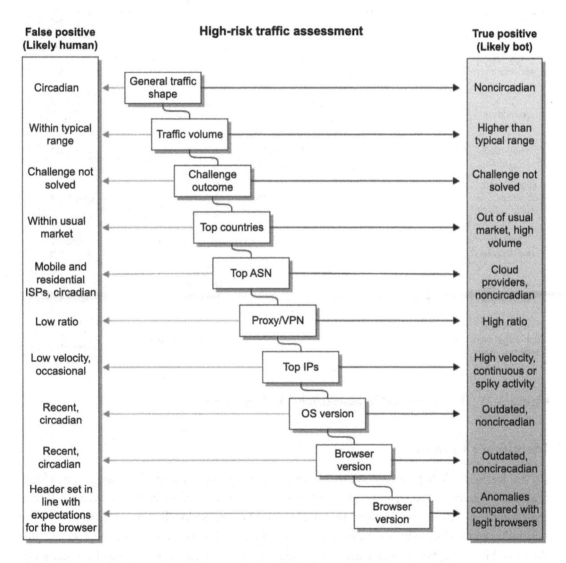

Figure 5.22 High-risk traffic assessment decision tree

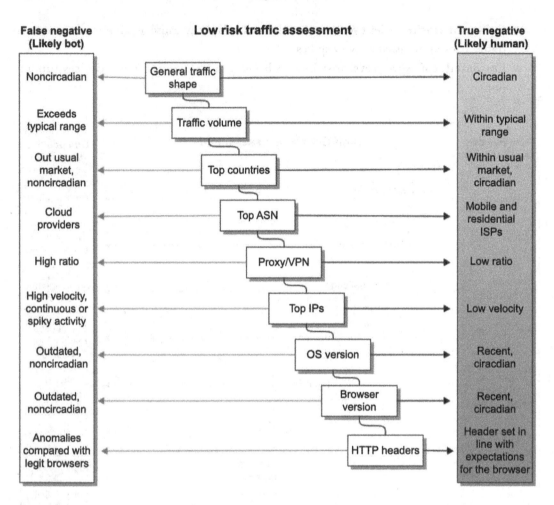

Figure 5.23   Low-risk traffic assessment decision tree

Identifying Botnets

As you learned in Chapter 1, "A Short History of the Internet," a *botnet* is a group of machines that run the same software, and a *command-and-control center* coordinates their activity. A botnet may consist of tens of thousands of nodes. Because the nodes run the same software, they can generally be identifiable by a common signature. The fact that they are coordinated means that they exhibit similar behavior, are active simultaneously and send requests toward the same target. Visually, botnets can typically be identified based on a noncircadian traffic pattern. This rule may have some exceptions, with the most advanced botnets trying to mimic "human" traffic patterns. It is helpful to know how to identify botnets to streamline the analysis and better understand the threat the site is under. This also helps with assessing the effectiveness of the bot management strategy. This section describes how to identify botnets.

Because of the sophistication of today's botnets, identifying them can be challenging. It requires finding a set of characteristics whose values are stable, or, in other words, not part of the botnet randomization strategy if one is applied. Ideally, the attributes selected to craft the botnet signature must also be consistently available with all requests. The characteristics from the various protocol layers (TCP, TLS, HTTP) used to establish the connection between the client and the server and transport the data are ideal candidates. The following table shows examples of usable data:

Data Type	Example of Usable Protocol Characteristics
TCP hash	Settings the client sends when first establishing the TCP connection with the server. The way the TCP connection is established is a function of the browser and operating system running on the client side. The information is available only with HTTP/1.1 and HTTP/2, which leverage the TCP protocol at the transport layer. HTTP/3 uses the UDP protocol at the transport layer, which does not require a connection to be established before data can be exchanged. The TCP connection settings the client advertises include the following and can be combined in a hash value and used as part of the botnet identifier: • Initial packet size • Initial TTL • Window size
TLS hash	Settings the client sends during the TLS handshake when establishing the secure connection (DataDome, 2022). The way the TLS connection is established is a function of the browser and operating system running on the client side. The following settings can be used to compute a hash value and used as part of the botnet identifier: • Algorithm order • Cipher order • TLS extensions Each type of client (web browsers, mobile applications, botnets) uses specific values when connecting to a web server. These settings depend on the technology stack on the client side.

(continued)

The following are a few examples of web scraping botnets on an e-commerce website. Most sites get traffic from various botnets that vary in sophistication. Some show sophistication in their behavior, the fingerprint their use, or their load distribution strategy. Botnets rarely excel in the three categories simultaneously, which helps to find them.

The Evening Crawler

As its name implies (and as shown in Figure 5.24), the Evening Crawler botnet is active only for a few hours during the late evening hours, making it more visible. When active, it sends almost a million requests, increasing the risk of overwhelming the website infrastructure. This botnet lacks sophistication when it comes to its behavior, but the sophistication of its fingerprint and load distribution strategy makes up for it. The traffic is distributed through close to 200,000 unique IP addresses that belong to residential and mobile ISPs. The number of requests per IP address is very low, and there is little reuse of an IP address from one day to the next. The botnet HTTP and TLS signatures closely match requests from legitimate browsers, indicating that headless technology is likely used. All these factors combined make detection more challenging.

Characteristic	Description
Behavior	Sophistication: Low The botnet is active in the evening sending 900,000 to 1 million requests within one to two hours with a very high request rate.
Traffic load balancing strategy	Sophistication: High - Leverage advanced proxy services that offer residential and mobile ISP IP addresses, which represent 95% of the activity. - Around 150,000 IP addresses used per event. - Little to no IP reuse day after day. - More than 874,000 unique IP addresses within seven days. - All traffic comes from the typical market of the website.
Fingerprint	Sophistication: Medium - More than 1.1 million unique `User-Agents`. - Recent version of Google Chrome (within four versions). - HTTP protocol: v2. The very high number of unique `User-Agent` values means that some are invalid, which is the reason for the downgrade to medium sophistication.
Type of bot	Likely a headless browser botnet.

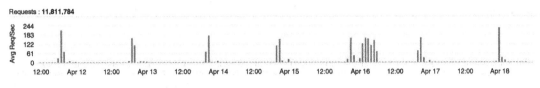

Figure 5.24   Daily recurring and intense bot activity

The Sprint Scraper

As shown in Figure 5.25, the Sprint Scraper botnet is primarily active during the day to mimic real user traffic patterns, which is its main strength. Overall, this botnet presents a low sophistication level since the number of unique IP addresses used is limited to a few hundred per day, most of them belonging to the Sprint network. This botnet's fingerprint is very basic. It uses unique User-Agents with an outdated Chrome version more than two years old. Unlike modern browsers, which send traffic over the more efficient HTTP/2 protocol, this botnet sends the traffic using the outdated version 1.1 of the HTTP protocol. These characteristics make this botnet easy to detect.

Characteristics	Description
Behavior	Sophistication: High
	Active during the day; follows a circadian pattern to mimic legitimate traffic with a moderate to high request rate.
Traffic load balancing strategy	Sophistication: Low
	- Limited number of unique IP addresses.
	- Around 400 IP addresses per event.
	- Little to no IP reuse day after day.
	- More than 180,000 unique IP addresses within seven days.
	- All traffic comes from the typical market of the website.
	- Traffic mostly coming from the Sprint network.
Fingerprint	Sophistication: Low
	- Unique and outdated `User-Agent`: *Mozilla/5.0 (Windows NT 10.0; Win64; x64) AppleWebKit/537.36 (KHTML, like Gecko) Chrome/90.0.4430.93 Safari/537.36.*
	- HTTP protocol: v1.1.
Type of bot	Likely a script.

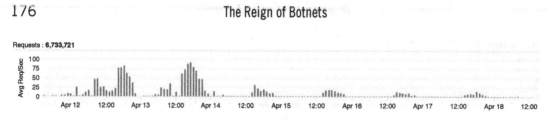

Figure 5.25   Daily bot activity with a circadian pattern

The Night Crawler

The Night Crawler botnet is active from late afternoon until the middle of the night. The "square shape" pattern shown in Figure 5.26 during the late hours makes it noticeable. The botnet shows a sophisticated traffic load balancing strategy with requests from nearly 200,000 unique IP addresses during each scraping session. However, the fingerprint sent is of low quality. Despite sending requests with more than 4,000 unique User-Agents, the browser versions advertised are one to two years old, and all requests are made using the obsolete HTTP/1.1. Overall, the characteristics of the fingerprint make this botnet easy to detect.

Characteristics	Description
Behavior	Sophistication: Low Active from late afternoon to early hours of the morning following a "square" pattern with a low request rate.
Traffic load balancing strategy	Sophistication: High - Leverage advanced proxy services that offer residential and mobile ISP IP addresses, which represent 98% of the bot traffic. - ~195,000 IP addresses (on average) within the botnet per event. - Little to no IP reuse day after day. - ~631,000 unique IP addresses in the U.S. within seven days.
Fingerprint	Sophistication: Low - About 4,000 unique outdated User-Agents (12 to 27 versions behind, Chrome and Firefox). - HTTP protocol: v1.1.
Type of bot	Likely a script.

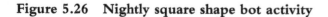

Figure 5.26   Nightly square shape bot activity

The Cloud Scraper

Figure 5.27 shows a botnet that scrapes the website only occasionally. However, it is very active during rare appearances and sends requests at a moderate to high rate. During the scraping session, the traffic is load balanced through more than 7,000 unique IP addresses that belong to cloud providers. The Cloud Scraper botnet also sends requests using 400 unique `User-Agent` values advertising recent Chrome versions within four releases (less than six months old). However, all requests are sent using the obsolete HTTP protocol version 1.1. Overall, the characteristics of the fingerprint make this botnet easy to detect.

Characteristics	Description
Behavior	Sophistication: Low – Sporadic activity with excessive request rate.

Traffic load balancing strategy	Sophistication: Low
	  – More than 7,000 IP addresses per event.
	  – All IP addresses belong to cloud providers.

Fingerprint	Sophistication: Medium
	  – More than 400 unique `User-Agents` with recent versions of Chrome (within four versions).
	  – HTTP protocol: v1.1.

Type of bot	Likely a script.

Figure 5.27   Occasional but intense bot activity

Summary

Despite their efforts, bot operators continuously make mistakes in their load balancing strategy, fingerprint, or behavior. This helps web security teams differentiate the bot activity when visually assessing the traffic. Assessing the bot activity and validating its accuracy requires visibility on key dimensions like HTTP headers, TCP parameters, and TLS parameters. It also requires some visibility on the IP address and information inferred from it, like the country it is in and the company that owns it. The tool used for the analysis should allow the user to visualize the traffic pattern over several days. But before diving into the analysis, one must understand website structures, communication protocols, and what a request from legitimate browsers should look like. Also, having a good understanding of the website being assessed and its typical audience is a plus for spotting anomalies. Once the assessment is completed and potential false positives are addressed, the next step to start truly managing bots is to apply a mitigation strategy to the activity detected.

6 | Defense and Response Strategy

Effective detection methods must be tightly coupled with adequate response strategies. This chapter provides best practices for efficiently handling bot and fraud activity.

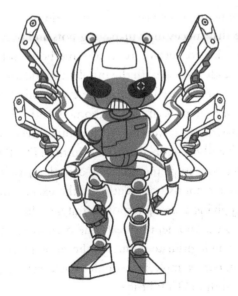

Developing a Defense Strategy

The detection methods (IP intelligence, device intelligence, proof of work, email intelligence, headless browser detection, etc.) must be adapted to the use case (credential stuffing, account opening abuse, web scraping, etc.). However, the detection methods must be coupled with strong response strategies to efficiently mitigate the activity detected. Procedures must also be in place to operationalize the solution, analyze the activity regularly using the methodology described in Chapter 5, "Assessing Detection Accuracy," and adjust the detection and mitigation strategy to obtain the best result. A good detection and mitigation strategy and strong operational procedures that explain what is to be protected, for what purpose, and how often the bot activity and setup should be assessed define your defense strategy.

The strength of the defense strategy and the discipline of the web security team executing it is key to the endeavor's success. This is not a race. This is a marathon, so be prepared to consistently follow the defense strategy in the long run and never let your guard down. The adversary will always exploit any possible weaknesses of the system. In this chapter, we'll review the components required in the detection and mitigation strategy and the various options to build an efficient bot management system.

Do-It-Yourself

If you're reading this, you're better armed than ever to tackle your company's bot problems, and by now, you should realize that successfully managing bots and preventing fraud is not an easy proposition. Sure, you'll be able to develop detection methods and score victories against the adversary, but you must be ready to deal with the problem in the long run. This means continuously developing new detections to keep up with the evolution of threats.

As we've seen, you need to expect all sorts of botnets with various levels of sophistication to hit the critical workflows of your website. All too often, security teams tend to focus on simple detection methods based on anomalies found in the HTTP request headers, which are visible to all web servers, without implementing any complex JavaScript-based data collection. This negative security approach consists of identifying the exact signature of the current attack vectors on live traffic and applying a strong response strategy. This leads to developing detection methods or rules tailored to the moment's threat. The definition of the detection rule is very specific to avoid any impact on legitimate traffic. But because it is so specific, it is relatively easy for the adversary to defeat it. For example, in a simple attack scenario, the security analyst might notice very unusual values in the HTTP header:

- An outdated operating system or browser version is advertised in the `User-Agent` or `Sec-CH-UA` header.
- Some headers, like the `Sec-Fetch` of `Sec-CH` headers expected on certain browser types or versions, are missing or incorrect.

- Some unexpected headers are included in the request. For example, seeing `Content-Length` or `Content-Type` headers on a GET request is unexpected but can be seen regularly on poorly defined botnets when the operator programs them to send the same set of headers for all requests, no matter the method (GET or POST).
- Requests are coming from a specific set of IP addresses.

Developing detection methods to block these anomalies is a valid approach to provide immediate relief. When well-defined and maintained, these methods can prevent similar issues from coming back in the long term if other botnets with similar anomalies poke at the site in the future.

However, such a strategy can take you only so far. Sometimes, adversaries only need to change a value in the HTTP headers or send requests from different locations or IP addresses to defeat the defense strategy. This results in a never-ending analysis, detection rule development, deployment, and validation cycle, commonly called a *whac-a-mole cycle*. This cycle, shown in Figure 6.1, can be automated using a machine learning model, providing some accurately labeled data is available to the system. A very sophisticated model may be able to achieve good results. Still, the system will constantly need to learn new signatures, resulting in inconsistency in the detection while the system is learning and discovering the new signature after the adversary evolves the botnet attack strategy.

This method has its limitations, too. It can help with simpler botnets but is inadequate to defend against more advanced threats, especially those from botnets that closely mimic real browser signatures or botnets based on headless browsers.

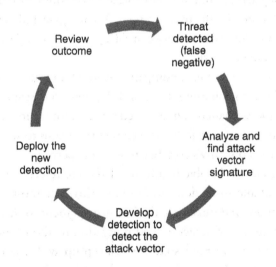

Figure 6.1   Bot detection life cycle

Therefore, a strong holistic detection engine that includes the set of detection methods described in Chapter 4, "Detection Strategy," must complement the simpler whac-a-mole approach.

Whether the detection engine is updated manually, automatically, or a combination of both, care must be taken to ensure that introducing new rules or detections will not negatively affect the detection accuracy by introducing false positives.

On the surface, the whac-a-mole cycle sounds very simple to implement. In practice and the long term, however, it's difficult to operationalize, costly to maintain, and, overall, relatively inefficient:

- Maintaining and evolving the detection and mitigation strategy requires a data science and engineering team to research and develop new methods, deploy the latest detection, analyze the effect once live, and adjust the methods to deal with inaccuracies.
- The infrastructure hosting the detection and mitigation engine must be able to scale up to handle unpredictable botnet attacks that can start at any time and scale down when the attack is over.
- Fighting a botnet requires rare, specific, and expensive skill sets.
- Attacks can happen anytime, day and night, or over the weekend. New attacks starting at 6 p.m. on Friday night are very common, so the team supporting the system must be ready to act 24/7.

Buying a Bot Management Product from a Vendor

Efficiently defending against all sorts of botnet attacks requires having a comprehensive defense strategy that includes several detection layers that look at the traffic from various points of view and reduce the false negatives as much as possible. It also requires an adapted response strategy to ensure the high-risk traffic is effectively mitigated while gracefully handling the possible and occasional false positives. The balance between false positives and false negatives is difficult to maintain and requires some expertise.

The core business for e-commerce companies is to sell products online; they are experts in showcasing their products, maintaining stock, and shipping to customers. Online banking is all about managing customers' finances. Digital media is all about informing or selling entertainment. Each company in various verticals has web security teams to secure the website, but web security is not part of the company's core business and expertise.

Larger corporations might be able to afford a dedicated research and development team to build a bot management and fraud detection system. However, most corporations will partner with a web security vendor and outsource the bot management to them. The vendor's product should come with the necessary detection and mitigation methods out of the box, and it's the vendor's responsibility to evolve their solution to keep up with the evolution of threats and maintain detection accuracy. All the web security team has to do is operate and adjust the vendor's solution as needed. Forrester, a research and advisory firm, regularly reviews the various bot management products on the market and provides their ranking. Figure 6.2 shows the

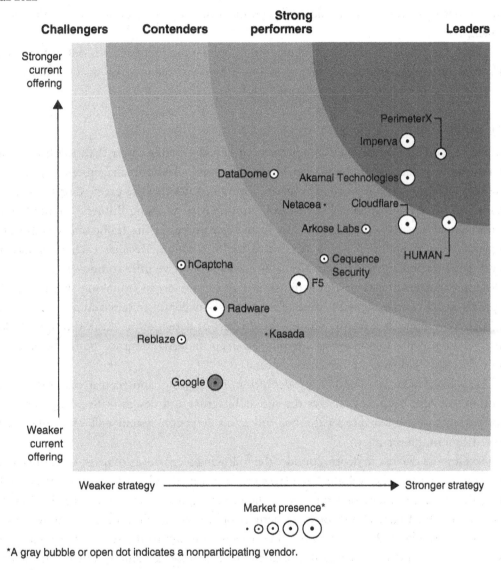

THE FORRESTER WAVE™
Bot Management
Q2 2022

Figure 6.2   The Forrester Wave, Bot Management, Q2 2022

ranking of various solutions available on the market in 2022. Products are ranked based on the strength and efficacy of their offering, innovation, and overall strategy. Solutions highlighted in the top-right corner have the most robust offering and strategy. They are considered leaders, while other up-and-coming vendors may be identified as strong performers, contenders, or challengers.

Note that providing any recommendation on which product to buy is out of the scope of this book. Web security teams looking to buy a bot management product should do their research and due diligence.

Defense in Depth

As you've seen, bot operators' strategies evolve quickly—often faster than the bot management solutions available on the market. Layering commercial bot management solutions with internal detection logic may be appropriate for companies that are prime targets for various attacks discussed in Chapter 2, "The Most Common Attacks Using Botnets." Figure 6.3 illustrates this defense-in-depth architecture. Each layer processes the traffic and weeds out the high-risk activity while allowing legitimate traffic through. Because each layer has been developed independently, the detection approach should have little to no overlap. Each layer still aims to detect the same thing (bots), but the layers do so by taking slightly different approaches. This is an essential feature of the defense-in-depth strategy and makes the attackers' task more difficult since they have several layers of detection to break through. Building such a system can be complex and requires a deep understanding of the bot problem and tuning each layer to achieve the best outcome.

Each layer requires careful scope definition, monitoring, and regular maintenance. The solution may also need to evolve as the site architecture and design evolve. Skipping regular monitoring and maintenance of the bot and fraud detection system will, over time, cause a degradation in the accuracy.

To illustrate defense in depth, consider the following scenario: a company with three detection layers to protect the website. Each layer has been tuned to limit false positives, and robust mitigation strategies (deny or tarpit) are applied to all high-risk bot traffic. The first detection layer may be able to detect 80% of attack activity but cannot catch some of the more advanced activity. This results in 20% of the bot traffic passing through to the second layer. The second layer runs different detection algorithms, catching 75% of the remaining activity. This results in 5% of the initial bot activity being passed to the third layer. While the first two layers typically detect anomalous traffic based on device and browser characteristics or user behavior, the third and last layer runs focused detection that takes advantage of the user context that none of the

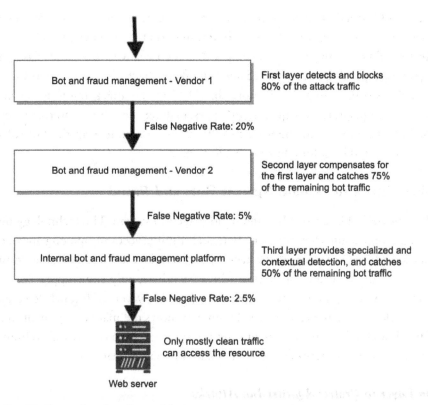

Figure 6.3 Defense-in-depth architecture

first two layers can access. For example, the last layer may consider the users' past purchase history, location, or other behavioral attributes specific to the site. The custom logic from the last layer may cut the remaining bot activity by another 50%, which means that only 2.5% of the bot activity can access the protected resource.

The preceding example is used only for illustration purposes. The result and efficacy of each layer may vary over time. The following three factors can cause variation in the solution performance:

- The sophistication of the product used at the different layers
- How well each layer is maintained
- The persistence and sophistication of the attack

Also, 2.5% of bot activity gaining access to protected resources may seem like a lot. Still, bot management always requires some level of compromise on the false negative rate to not significantly affect the false positive rate. Achieving a 0% false negative with a 10% false positive rate does not provide a good user experience and will likely affect the revenue generated from the website. It's also worth noting that if more than 97% of the attack traffic is blocked in most scenarios, the bot operators' cost quickly increases, making the whole enterprise very ineffective. If the bot operator cannot increase its efficacy by re-architecting the bot software, they eventually give up and look for a less protected target.

Technology Stack to Defend Against Bots and Fraud

Let's look at the logical layers of a bot and fraud detection system. The technology needed may vary depending on the use case. Scraper, credential stuffing, account opening abuse, carding, or similar attacks have in common that attackers commonly use botnets. Some companies are affected by all of the preceding scenarios, while for others, only some apply. So, a strong bot management layer is required in the defense strategy. However, additional detection may be needed to handle specific use cases better. Figure 6.4 shows the main components that must be included in a bot and fraud management system to protect the most critical website resources. Each of these components was described in detail in previous chapters.

Detection Layer to Protect Against Bot Attacks

A solid bot management layer is required to defend against the most common bot attacks and help prevent fraud. As shown in Chapter 5, a botnet's sophistication can be defined based on its fingerprint accuracy compared to legitimate browser traffic, load distribution strategy, and behavior. Also, when the incentive for the adversary is high, one can expect the most sophisticated botnet with broad load distribution through residential and mobile ISPs, well-defined fingerprints, and traffic blending with the legitimate traffic pattern.

All websites will typically see a broad spectrum of botnet sophistication. To consistently defend against all kinds of botnets, the bot detection layer must be able to evaluate the traffic from different points of view.

- **Detecting good (known) bots:** The good bot activity can be tied to specific companies, and their intent can be inferred. Most good bots are critical to the business's success and serve many purposes, including helping with supporting a company's SEO and social media strategy and ensuring the site is easy to find through search engines. Bots are also used to monitor the site availability and performance. The bot management solution must be able to recognize these common bots with high accuracy to ensure content is served promptly to them.

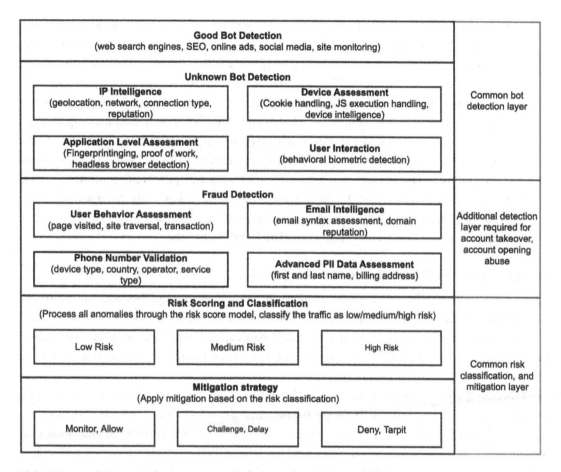

Figure 6.4   Bot and fraud management component architecture

- **Detecting unknown bots:** Unknown bots can be detected through the methods described in Chapter 4 but don't identify themselves in the HTTP header. Also, their activity cannot be tied to a particular entity, and their intent is unclear or may negatively affect the business. Unknown bots are detected by assessing various aspects of the request.
  - *IP intelligence*: Get the geolocation, network, and connection type associated with the IP address. Based on the protected website's context, requests from a specific location or network can represent a higher risk. Although not mentioned in Chapter 4 as a major detection method, detection systems handling significant Internet traffic can also infer the reputation of the IP address based on past behavior seen on multiple websites, which can help detect botnets in some cases.

- *Device assessment*: Evaluate how the client establishes the connection with the server at the different layers of the OSI model: TCP, TLS, and HTTP. Verify that the parameters negotiated align with the ones expected from the most common web browsers and mobile applications. Validate the client supports cookies and JavaScript.
- *Application-level assessment*: The device and browser characteristics and user preferences are collected when the client runs JavaScript. The fingerprint data is compared and cross-checked against the protocol-level data to verify consistency. Evaluate the client's ability to execute complex cryptographic operations with the proof of work method. This layer should also be able to detect more complex headless browser botnets.
- *User interaction assessment*: Evaluate how a human interacts with the device through standard peripherals like a touch screen, keyboard, and mouse. Lack of interaction or abnormal interaction is typically associated with bot traffic.

Detection Layer to Protect Against Online Fraud

Account takeover (ATO) and payment fraud can be automated through botnets but can sometimes involve manual labor. Bot management solutions are not designed to detect manual fraud. An additional detection layer is required to detect fraud attempts by evaluating the user behavior over time. Several identifiers are used to monitor user activity when creating and using an account.

Preventing account opening abuse and using fake accounts during sales events, for example, requires additional detection technology beyond bot detection. When creating an account, most websites use the customer's email address as the identifier. Users must provide additional personally identifiable information (PII) data, such as their first and last names and billing address, during checkout. The following additional detection layers leverage PII data, help reinforce the bot management layer, and reduce the attack surface:

- **Email intelligence:** This method is designed to analyze the syntax of the email address local-part and detect patterns typical of attack traffic, such as repeating characters and excessively using special characters, digits, or aliases. The email domain is also evaluated for abnormal traffic patterns from major, disposable, or uncommon email services.
- **User behavior assessment:**
  - *Page visited and site path traversal*: This detection method aims to monitor the user journey through the website. Legitimate users usually have a more diverse and richer browsing journey than botnets, which typically go after specific content, resulting in significant differences.
  - *Behavior analysis*: The current request pattern is evaluated against previous request patterns to detect deviations in the behavior, such as an excessive number of new accounts

created from a single identifier or the email address being used an excessive number of times within a short period.

- **Advanced PII data assessment:** This can help detect synthetic identities.
  - *First and last name validation*: Most legitimate users will format their email local part using part of their first and last names. Not finding even a partial match when validating the first and last names against the email address handle can be a sign of attack.
  - *Billing address validation*: Subscription-based services require users to enter their credit card information and billing addresses. Attackers may use a virtual or stolen credit card to open the account and provide a fake billing address. The billing address can be evaluated in the context of the request and all the other information provided to detect apparent discrepancies.
- **Phone number validation:** Phone numbers are also considered PII. Although not mentioned in Chapter 4 as a common bot detection method, a lot can be inferred from the phone number, such as the country or the type of number, whether mobile, landline, or burner. This information can be assessed in the overall context of the session to weigh into the risk assessment.

Defending against various types of fraud is complex and requires looking at the traffic and the data submitted by the user from multiple angles. The use of PII data is becoming more common to help detect more advanced botnets and human fraud.

Response Strategies

Detecting bots and fraudulent activity is half the battle. Ensuring that high-risk activity is mitigated correctly is just as important. The technology of an efficient web security system must include a solid set of response strategies to apply to various situations.

One key element of deciding on the most appropriate response strategy is understanding the threat, the detection accuracy, and, more specifically, the false positive rate. When the detection layer's false positive rate is low, one can apply the simplest and bluntest response strategy like deny. The ideal false positive rate should be as close as possible to 0, but that's not only hard to achieve, it's also hard to sustain over time. Chapter 5 discussed analyzing the traffic, identifying false positives, and calculating the false positive rate. A false positive rate of 0.1% is achievable but may be considered high on a highly trafficked website. For an e-commerce site that handles 100,000 transactions per day, this still represents 100 transactions impacted, which, if we consider an average basket value between $50 and $100, means $5,000 to $10,000 in possible revenue loss per day, which can result in 1.8 to 3.2 millions of dollars per year. On the other hand, not adequately mitigating bot activity can result in worse damage, including site stability issues, reputation damage, and customer churn, ultimately also resulting in loss of revenue. The exact annual revenue loss may be hard to measure and vary depending on the severity of the attack, its duration, and the rate of occurrence.

At a minimum, the web security system must provide the ability to monitor or deny high-risk traffic. Monitoring the traffic is initially useful when rolling out a new detection method to see how it behaves, assess its accuracy, and tweak its settings to reduce false positives. Once that's done, it's time to start mitigating the activity. This section describes the various response strategies available on most bot management products and their benefits.

Simple Response Strategies

A response strategy is considered simple when it requires no specific configuration or customization. These strategies also provide the most obvious signals to bot operators that they have been detected, which will typically cause them to react and attempt to evade detection.

Deny

Denying the traffic is a common and popular option, but it assumes a detection layer with a very low false positive rate to avoid impacting the user experience. Denying can come in slightly varied forms:

- On logins, you may serve an HTTP 401 – Unauthorized to match the typical response when the credentials provided are incorrect. Bot operators expect a high failure rate when executing a credential stuffing attack. This strategy will make it more challenging for them to detect the protection in place.
- On other endpoints, serve an HTTP 403 – Forbidden response.

Tarpit

This action is like denying, except in this case, no response is returned to the client. The server keeps the connection open but never sends a response, giving the impression that the site is not responsive. This is a great strategy for dealing with bots and a better alternative to the deny action since it will instill some doubt into the adversary, wondering whether their activity was too aggressive. They may be led to believe that they unintentionally DoSed the site they tried to extract data from, which is never a good thing from an attacker's point of view. This option should be used only with accurate detection methods.

Delay

In this case, the server will add 5 to 10 seconds of delay before responding to the client. This strategy helps throttle the bot traffic. The good thing is that users in the false positive category can still access the resource, with the only drawback being that the site will appear slow. For attackers, this will significantly slow their attack rate, frustrating them and ideally pushing them to abandon their attacks. Consider an added delay of 10 seconds per request; if a typical attack campaign consists of 1 million requests sent at a rate of 50 requests per second, this reduces the capacity of the botnet forced to wait for each response, increasing the time it takes to complete the attack from about six hours to more than two days.

Advanced Response Strategies

Advanced response strategies require configuration, customization, and maintenance over time to achieve the best result. They offer a better experience for legitimate users falling into the false positive category and a more subtle and sometimes misleading response to botnets, which can help slow their evolution.

Serve Alternate Content

Instead of simply denying the request, consider serving a custom message indicating why the user cannot access the requested resource. The message may include basic self-help recommendations on updating their software or using alternate browsers or devices to avoid falling victim to false positives. You may provide a number for a technical support center to get additional help. The feedback from the user may help adjust the detection to further reduce the risk of false positives. With the serve alternate content strategy, users impacted by false positives still cannot access the web resources they wanted to use but at least have a more user-friendly explanation of what happened and a possible way forward by contacting a technical support team that can help remedy the situation.

From the botnet standpoint, the alternate content resulting in a positive HTTP response (200 – OK) may lead them to believe the attack is successful at first, that is, until they verify the content received.

Serve Stale/Static Content

This strategy mainly applies to the web scraping use case. It serves cached or static content to high-risk traffic from bots while still servicing legitimate users through the regular website infrastructure. This strategy not only helps offload the critical e-commerce infrastructure from all the bot activity but also makes it harder for bot operators to detect that they are being fed static or stale content, keeping their evolution to a minimum. This strategy is easy to implement if the website infrastructure includes a content delivery network (CDN) and the bulk of the bot detection is done at the CDN layer. For high-risk traffic, the CDN layer can either serve cached content to bots or forward the traffic to a dedicated "honeypot" infrastructure.

Random Failure

This response strategy is a variation of the "deny" or "tarpit" strategies. As its name implies, it consists of randomly denying or tarpitting a percentage of the high-risk activity. In a false positive scenario, legitimate users may experience intermittent failures, making it difficult for them to use the site.

In my experience, this strategy is very effective against bot traffic but is not used often enough. From the attacker's point of view, they get the impression that some of their requests are succeeding and don't suspect as much that most of their requests are being blocked on purpose. I used this strategy to prevent airfare scraping on an airline, randomly denying 80% of the bot activity. This strategy helped extend the usefulness of even basic detection methods. It confuses the bot operator, and they end up not adjusting their attack strategy as often.

Challenge

As discussed in Chapter 3, "The Evolution of Botnet Attacks," a challenge can be used as a primary or secondary detection layer. When used as a response strategy, a challenge is, in effect, a secondary detection layer looking at the traffic from a different point of view and allowing legitimate users who are unfortunate enough to fall into the false positive category to get a second chance at proving their humanness and access the protected resource.

There are different types of challenges:

- **Crypto challenges** test the ability of the client to execute complex cryptographic operations. The client must run custom software in a JavaScript or mobile SDK integrated into the application as part of the web security solution. This is similar to the proof of work detection method described in Chapter 4.
- **Behavioral challenges** test whether a human controls the client and requires the user to do a simple operation like clicking a button. While the user performs this operation, behavioral telemetry (mouse events, keystrokes, and touch events) is collected from the client and assessed by the web security solution.
- **CAPTCHA challenges** may include aspects of behavioral challenges and require the user to solve a simple puzzle or select the images that correspond to a description. CAPTCHA challenges are effective to deal with false positives, but they add some friction to the user experience.
- **Multifactor authentication** evaluates the user's ownership of an email address or a phone number. In the first type, an email with a one-time token will be sent to the user's email. In the second case, the one-time token will be sent to the user's phone as an SMS message.

As you saw in Chapter 3, botnets can be enhanced to solve challenges. However, this significantly increases the operation's complexity and cost, helping weed out the least sophisticated botnet and least motivated botnet operators.

Operationalization

Having a strong detection layer associated with a strong response strategy in the infrastructure is critical, but ensuring that all these components are used effectively with an optimal configuration and process to maintain it over time is what glues it together and will ensure long-term success.

I often see a strong detection strategy combined with a weak response strategy or a weak detection strategy combined with a strong response strategy. The effect of the first scenario will be perceived as a false negative, and the second strategy will provide a false sense of security while still letting through a lot of bot traffic (false negative).

Mapping a Response Strategy to a Risk Category

Not all bot detection methods are deterministic enough to categorize bot or fraudulent traffic as high risk. Some traffic will inevitably fall into the medium-risk category, representing a gray area. Advanced attackers understand how bot management solutions work. Their job is to send as much traffic as possible into the gray area. The defender's job is to adjust the bot management policy to ensure the gray area is as small as possible. Unfortunately, keeping the gray area small is a continuous battle due to the ever-changing Internet, digital ecosystem, and the attackers' ability to adapt and evolve their attack strategy.

Depending on how well the bot management solution is tuned and the sophistication of the attacker at any given time, the size of the human, undesired bots, desired bots, and the gray area may vary. Figure 6.5 represents a situation where:

- The topmost band represents the high-risk, undesirable bot traffic.
- The second band represents tolerated good bot traffic, for example, web search engines, SEO bots, and online ad bots.
- The third band represents the medium-risk questionable traffic, including anomalies common to legitimate traffic and undesirable bot traffic.
- The bottom band represents the "premium," low-risk, legitimate end-user traffic.

The size of the bands is proportional to the volume of traffic they each represent and may vary over time depending on the threat and the efficacy of the protection in place.

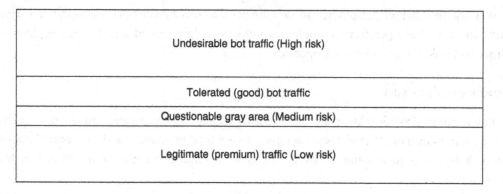

Figure 6.5 Traffic distribution by risk category

The medium-risk band must be monitored and kept at a minimum at all times. An increase in the size of this band indicates a degradation of the detection strategy.

To efficiently deal with the various traffic categories, it is necessary to adopt a strong response strategy to mitigate the bot activity. The response strategies fall into different categories, as shown in the following table:

Type	Strategy	Where to Apply It
Block	Deny, tarpit, serve alternate content, random failure.	High-risk traffic.
Allow/throttle	Monitor or delay.	Monitor all business-critical good bot categories (web search engines, social media, online ads, site monitoring) while applying a stricter response strategy (delay) to nonessential categories of good bots like RSS feed readers or web archivers.
		When under duress (an attack) or during a sales event (Black Friday), some essential good bot traffic like social media, SEO, or online ads may be throttled (delay) to free up some needed resources to serve legitimate users. To avoid any SEO ranking downgrades, always allow web search engine traffic.
Challenge	Crypto challenge, CAPTCHA.	The medium-risk traffic, especially if it appears to include a high ratio of bot traffic.
Allow	Monitor.	The low risk category, which corresponds to legitimate traffic.

Preparing for Special Events

Online sales events can draw large crowds. Like any major sales event at a regular store, online events must be adequately prepared. If the event were to occur in a traditional store, the manager would typically increase the sales and security staff to ensure there is no trouble and every consumer gets a fair chance at buying the item on sale. The line may form in an orderly fashion in front of the store before it opens. Extra security staff or police may also watch the line in front of the store. Online events should be managed the same, although the tools and methods differ:

- **Ensure your web infrastructure can support the load:** The traffic these events generate can overwhelm the web infrastructure. Add enough capacity to your web infrastructure to support the additional load. If the content is served through a CDN, it may be worthwhile to review the caching strategy to offload as much of the traffic to the edge and preserve the web server for essential and dynamic traffic.

- **Work with your vendor's professional services team:** Get in touch ahead of the event to ensure your bot manager configuration is tuned to get the best detection accuracy and adequate response strategies are in place to defeat the bot activity. The more bot activity is mitigated at the web security layer, the less load the web server will have to handle. Someone should also watch the activity during the event and analyze it once it's over to assess the effectiveness of the solution in place. Bot attack methods and bot detection evolve continuously. The lessons learned from previous events can help tune the setup to improve the defense strategy and ensure the success of future events.

- **Protect each step of the workflow:** This should include at least the endpoints that handle account creation, login, password reset, add to cart, and checkout. The page where the item for sale will be announced should also be protected. Bot operators may create multiple new accounts ahead of time and use them during the event. Protecting the account creation endpoint is especially important if the event is available only to exclusive club members. Preventing the mass creation of new accounts will reduce the risk of attackers infiltrating your premium user channel.

- **Adopt the challenge response strategy:** A crypto, behavioral, or CAPTCHA challenge will alter the workflow for suspicious traffic and provide a second opportunity to detect bots on traffic that appears suspicious. Enforcing a CAPTCHA in one of the workflow steps will break the automation and require the user to be present to complete the transaction. Because some of the bot solutions support the ability to offload the puzzle solving to a third party, you may also consider applying the crypto challenge to one of the steps of the workflow for diversity. Even if bots can solve one type of challenge, they are unlikely to be able to complete both, thus significantly affecting the effectiveness of the botnet. It is preferable to enable the challenge only minutes before the event starts to catch the bot operators off guard and turn it off after the event to deny them the opportunity to learn and update their bot. Remember that only bots will be challenged. Legitimate users will not be affected.

- **Implement a waiting room:** Some technical solutions offer a virtual waiting room. The waiting room should be positioned after the bot management solution. Only legitimate traffic will be added to the waiting room queue. This is also a way to enforce consumer fairness and offer a front-of-the-line position to the most loyal customers who showed up early for the event, just like in real life.

Defending Against CAPTCHA Farms

CAPTCHA vendors claim resilience against CAPTCHA-solving services, but as you learned in Chapter 3, the offerings for solving the CAPTCHAs are extensive, and the practice of integrating with these services for sophisticated botnet operators is well developed. There are telling signs that help identify requests coming from CAPTCHA farms:

- The workers tend to be located in developing countries (refer to Figure 3.7, Chapter 3).
- They own cheap, low-end devices exclusively running Windows or Android.
- Each client will send more requests than usual.

Also, looking back at the workflow from Figure 3.8, Chapter 3, the client connecting to the CAPTCHA service (step 3) differs from the one connecting to the targeted website (step 5). Suppose the CAPTCHA provider shares some of the basic characteristics of the client from step 3, such as geolocation, browser, and operating system name and version, when the targeted website verifies the token at step 6. In that case, it is possible to confirm that the machine that requested the protected endpoint is the same one that solved the challenge.

Carefully evaluating all the preceding characteristics will help differentiate between the legitimate users that were challenged and should be granted access to the protected resource and the botnet traffic that should be denied access.

When the CAPTCHA provider suspects the request comes from a CAPTCHA farm, it should serve an adapted challenge. Some providers have complex puzzles designed to force the CAPTCHA solver to spend more time resolving a challenge: they will be served challenges that require more attention and play multiple rounds, potentially within a limited time. With this frustrating and time-consuming experience, the goal is to discourage the CAPTCHA farm workers and push them only to accept easier CAPTCHAs.

The CAPTCHA provider should also include some features designed to defeat computer vision. One of the known methods is to generate the challenge images with some noise to force the attacker to continuously label and retrain their models. This is known as the *adversarial image method*. The added noise will not affect legitimate users. In the worst-case scenario, they may notice a slight discoloration. However, this will significantly impact the computer vision model's ability to accurately identify the image's content. In the example shown in Figure 6.6, the computer vision model will classify a picture of a panda that includes an adversarial image as a gibbon. In contrast, it is still very much a panda to the human eye.

Other methods to defeat computer vision include developing puzzles requiring continuous content labeling. The model will also have to be retrained regularly. Imagine a set of images consisting of a large catalog of objects that may or may not be relevant depending on the question asked in the challenge. In this case, the attacker will have to collect a large set of puzzle challenges that include enough variety in terms of items in the image and label each image accordingly. Moreover, if these items are custom-designed and not easily recognizable by pre-trained models like ResNet, the task is much more labor intensive. If, on top of this, the CAPTCHA provider has a large bank of challenges that it can change regularly, the attacker's task will be a lot more difficult.

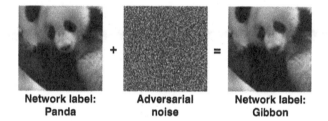

Network label: **Adversarial**   **Network label:**
Panda   **noise**   **Gibbon**

Figure 6.6   Traffic distribution by risk category

Summary

A sound response strategy associated with an advanced detection strategy adapted to the use cases is key to a successful defense strategy and efficiently protecting a website. However, it also requires adequately staffing the team responsible for maintaining and supporting the solution to ensure consistent performance over time and limit any significant impact on the user experience. The complex evolution of attack strategies combined with an increasingly dynamic digital ecosystem can make the task arduous. What makes the task even more complex is the continuous evolution of privacy laws worldwide that influence what data can be collected and how it must be stored. To top this off, browser vendors (Google, Mozilla, Opera, Microsoft, Apple, and myriad others) regularly introduce new privacy features that change the fidelity of certain data points and potentially impact detection accuracy. In the final chapter, I'll discuss the recent focus on user privacy on the Internet and its effect on the effectiveness of bot management.

7 | Internet User Privacy

This chapter discusses the privacy conundrum when dealing with fraud and bot detection and the evolving impact on the effectiveness of bot and fraud management products.

The Privacy vs. Security Conundrum

Developing accurate bot detection in a world where threats and the Internet ecosystem constantly evolve is complex. But what adds even more complexity into the mix is the evolution of privacy standards and regulations and the introduction of features developed by browser vendors or independent focus groups that, over time, reduce the quality of the data collected from the client and consequently impact the accuracy of fraud and bot detection products.

For years, online advertisers, marketers, social media, and large tech companies have collected massive amounts of data about their users to understand what system they run, where they are, and what they like. With all that data, one can figure out who they are, which is a significant intrusion into their privacy. This data is used for several purposes, from recommending content to users to increasing the time they spend on the site and increasing ad revenue or enticing them to buy products. In the worst-case scenario, the data can be used to send users targeted content and influence their opinions on various matters. Because of the historical lack of guidance or regulation on how the data should be handled, some companies, especially the ones offering their services for free, took the liberty of using the data to generate more revenue by sometimes selling it to third parties. When the practice was revealed, it caused an outcry, and consumers demanded more privacy.

Governments worldwide took the problem seriously and started developing and enforcing new regulations, such as General Data Protection Regulation (GDPR) in Europe, which came into effect in May 2018, and the California Consumer Privacy Act (CCPA) in California, which came into effect a month later. Other U.S. states and countries have also developed their privacy laws. Standardization bodies such as the W3C (World Wide Web Consortium, 2024) went further by setting new standards and guidelines for fingerprinting that are to be implemented by browser vendors and website owners to limit data collection further or reduce data granularity. Some privacy focus groups like EasyPrivacy or companies like `Disconnect.me` also chip in by developing software to further restrict data collection from domains or URLs associated with online advertising and marketing or simply because it looks like a lot of data is transferred through a URL. Lastly, browser vendors top it off by developing new privacy-preserving features such as Safari's Intelligent Tracking Prevention (ITP), Firefox's Enhanced Tracking Protection (ETP), or Google's Privacy Sandbox. For vendors that build privacy-preserving features, it comes down to preventing any entity from uniquely identifying a user through the combination of the identifiers discussed in Chapter 5, "Assessing Detection Accuracy": the IP address, session cookies, and fingerprinting.

Privacy on the Internet is an important issue. No one likes their data being misused or sold without their consent. Having ads following us around the Internet for days after visiting a website can also make one feel uneasy about being watched. The data set that marketers and online advertisers use to identify users overlaps with the data that web security solutions use to protect websites and their users against fraud and abuses. It's important to recognize the need for data collection to secure the user experience online. Web security companies collect, process, and store data responsibly and only use it to build security products. They also work hard to comply with regulations like GDPR and CCPA and adapt to additional restrictions enforced by privacy-focused groups and vendors that don't always consider why the data is collected and how it's used. They acknowledge that privacy features may cause compatibility issues with sites protected by fraud or bot detection products (the site may not work correctly). But in the end, most of the time, they leave it up to the user to assess the risk associated with adding an exception to the tools' privacy policy. Unfortunately, most Internet users don't understand the Internet ecosystem, the threat landscape, and web security in general enough to make an informed decision. They will most likely choose to trust the tool by default and move on to a different site if it is not responding properly. This could have an impact on the revenue of an e-commerce site. Ultimately, users must choose between adopting the best privacy experience while visiting websites by not sharing their data and helping web security teams ensure a consistent and safe experience when they visit their sites. Ironically, the impact of fingerprinting restrictions from privacy features can lead to less accurate detection and an increase in the occurrence of accounts taken over, which, in itself, is a huge privacy violation for the victims.

The State of Privacy and Its Effect on Web Security

Privacy protection features aim to prevent user tracking through their IP address, cookies, or fingerprinting techniques. But can users truly be tracked using these three classes of identifiers? This section reviews how the Internet truly sees individual users, the various methods available to users to protect their privacy online, and their effect on web security.

IP Privacy

The most basic identifier that has existed since the creation of the Internet is the IP address. When connecting to the network, this address is usually dynamically assigned to the user through the Dynamic Host Configuration Protocol (DHCP). Users who connect to a private network at home or in a corporate office are given an IP address from the reserved private IP range, typically 10.0.0.0/8 or 192.168.0.0/16 for IPv4. The router that connects the network to the Internet will be assigned a public IP address by the Internet service provider (ISP). A web server that processes a client request only sees the ISP's public IP. Requests from all users connected to the same network—for example, the family members of a household or the employees of a company—will come from the same IP address. This configuration means there is generally a one-to-many relationship between IP address and end users, an equation that can be even more complex considering that most users own more than one device and may connect on different networks throughout the day (home, office, coffee shops, and mobile network while in transit).

Figure 7.1 shows an example of a user with three different devices connecting to four networks (four public IP addresses) throughout the day while interacting with a website. The user uses a laptop to connect to the website from home and the office. On the way to the office, they stop at a coffee shop where they use a cell phone connected to the coffee shop's network to resume browsing on the same website while sipping their coffee. They use a tablet to browse the same website while in transit and finally resume using their laptop in the office. In a post-pandemic world, however, working from home has become more common, potentially reducing the diversity of the IP address a user's traffic may come from throughout the day.

In theory, such configuration doesn't allow using the IP address to identify a user uniquely, but in practice, it's close enough, and one can at least uniquely identify the activity from a household or corporate network.

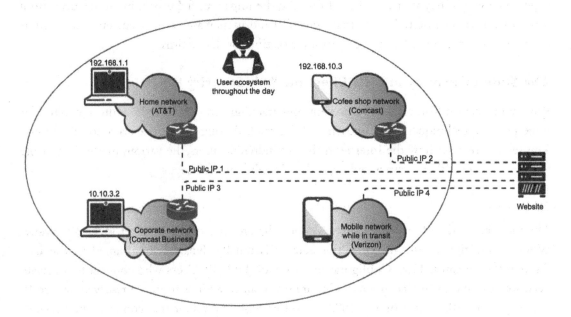

Figure 7.1   IP address diversity throughout the day

Users keen to preserve their anonymity on the Internet frequently use proxy or VPN services. The Onion Router, for example, was one of the first of its kind and was designed for this purpose. When connected to the service, the user's requests will go through different paths to reach the web server. For the web server, the requests will appear as coming from multiple IP addresses, making it impossible to track the user based on that identifier. The Opera browser offers a built-in VPN feature that a single click can enable. Many other browser extensions offering VPN and proxy services exist on the market. Figure 7.2 illustrates the communication path between a user and a web server through a proxy service. The web server will only see the

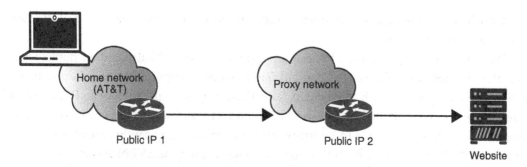

Figure 7.2 Communication through a proxy service or VPN

IP address from the proxy service forwarding the request and cannot see the end user's true IP address. Proxy servers are supposed to share the end user's IP address with the web service through the X-Forwarded-For header, but proxy services designed to offer privacy do not follow this rule.

The preceding configuration offers only partial privacy. The proxy and VPN services provide users anonymity from the point of view of the website they visit but not from the proxy or VPN service they use. The proxy or VPN services can access the end user's IP address and the hostname requested. Proxy services also have access to the HTTP header set, which includes the full URL visited and session cookies. New emerging private relay technologies like the iCloud Private Relay, launched in 2021 and available on Safari and iOS devices, can further bridge that gap. When the private relay is enabled, requests are sent through two separate secure Internet relays, as shown in Figure 7.3.

- The user IP address is visible to the network provider and to the first relay, which Apple operates. The DNS records are encrypted, so the first relay cannot see the website address the user tries to visit.
- The second relay, operated by a third-party CDN, generates a temporary IP address, decrypts the website name requested, and connects to the site. The second relay or the website cannot see the end user's IP address.

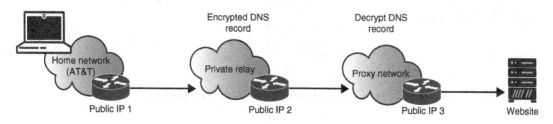

Figure 7.3 Communication through a private relay

Google is working on a similar initiative called *IP Protection* to hide the user's real IP address from third-party domains.

Bot operators use proxy and VPN services extensively to load balance their traffic. Therefore, the IP intelligence method of bot and fraud detection engines has traditionally flagged traffic from these services with a higher risk level. Evaluating the reputation of an IP address and detecting whether it is part of a proxy service has always been complex and prone to false positives. However, this signal used to be trustworthy enough to significantly contribute to a risk score model. But with more legitimate users turning to proxy and VPN services to preserve their anonymity increased by their ease of adoption, the value of this signal has degraded. To prevent false positives, this signal has become a minor contributor to the risk score.

Cookie Tracking Prevention

For the reason previously discussed, user mobility, tracking user behavior through IP address has never been enough. Online advertisers and marketers have also used long-lasting third-party cookies to silently collect user activity on websites for years. Figure 7.4 illustrates how tracking through third-party cookies works. Consider the situation where a user first browses a website to catch up on the news and later visits an e-commerce site to shop. If both sites are integrated with the same tracking technology that loads a pixel image from `tracker-example.com` and the domain has a cookie stored in the user's browser, then the company that runs the tracking technology will know the user activity on both sites.

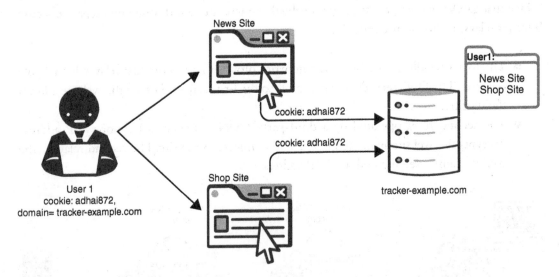

Figure 7.4   User activity tracking through third-party cookies

The website itself does not generate these cookies, and from the point of view of privacy laws, these cookies are considered nonessential. Websites with an audience in the European Union must get the user's consent on the type of cookies they want to allow.

Browser vendors, however, are on a mission to prevent third-party cookies as much as possible. They all take different approaches to reach that goal:

- Mozilla takes the blocklist approach for Firefox. They partner with the company `Disconnect.me`, which continuously evaluates web activity in search of Internet domains or cookies used to track user activity. The technology is directly integrated into Firefox and updated regularly.
- Apple takes a machine learning approach with its WebKit by collecting statistics on resource loads and user interaction, such as taps, clicks, and text entries for each domain. A machine learning model embedded in the browser uses the statistics to determine which domains can track users across sites. Cookies for domains a user has not interacted with for 30 days will be purged, thus preventing long-term user tracking. Cookies of domains interacted with during the last 30 days but not the last 24 hours will be partitioned. The partitioning will ensure the cookies are not deleted but cannot be used for third-party tracking.
- Google takes a more aggressive approach with its Chrome and Chromium products and plans to phase out third-party cookies completely by the end of 2024. The Cookies Having Independent Partitioned State (CHIPS) alternative will only allow third-party cookies through partitioning.

With Google leading the charge on making third-party cookies a thing of the past, one can expect Mozilla and Apple to eventually follow in Google's footsteps.

Bot and fraud solution vendors must also identify users uniquely and leverage cookies. CDN-based solutions that protect the site and distribute the content can set first-party cookies and are not impacted by third-party cookie restrictions. However, stand-alone security solutions may not have the same flexibility. These solutions have historically collected data and identified users leveraging a dedicated third-party hostname. The changes Google plans to enforce will force the web security vendors to adapt their products and collect their data using a subdomain of the site they protect. This brings in some complexity related to managing certificates to transport the traffic securely. Web security companies that continue to leverage third-party cookies will ultimately see their detection quality degrade significantly as the new restriction is rolled out.

Anti-fingerprinting Technology

Cookies help identify users uniquely, but they cannot always be relied on consistently: users may clear their cookies at any time or use a private browsing session, also known as *incognito mode*. Also, as browser vendors continuously work on eliminating third-party cookies, there has been a notable shift toward JavaScript-based fingerprint technology. As we've seen before, fingerprinting consists of collecting device characteristics (screen size, model, number of CPU cores, amount of memory, operating system, canvas fingerprint), browser characteristics (browser brand, plug-ins, extensions), and user preferences (fonts installed, preferred languages, time zone, screen orientation, display mode). Similar data can be collected from native mobile applications with a custom SDK. Individually, these data points can, at best, identify large groups of users who share the same software and hardware configuration. However, when combined in a signature, the minute differences between each user configuration can at least help uniquely identify a smaller group of users. For example, two users may have the same software (the latest version of Google Chrome and the current version of macOS) running on the same hardware (a 16" MacBook Pro with 16 GB of memory and 10 CPU cores). But if one user located in California (PST time zone) added "French" as an additional supported language and used the dark display mode, their fingerprint would be different enough from a user in New York with the preferred language set to English and using the light mode. Now, there may be hundreds of French speakers in California with this exact configuration, but this small population would stand out.

To preserve user privacy, browser vendors or browser extension developers use several strategies to prevent fingerprinting. Some prevent the information from being sent; others try to make the fingerprint look the same for all users, and others adopt a data randomization approach.

Blocking Fingerprinting   Preventing the data from being sent (for example, the canvas or audio fingerprint) might seem like a logical response to prevent fingerprinting, but it can have unexpected consequences on the usability of some websites. Indeed, the data is used not only for fingerprinting and tracking users on the Internet but may also be legitimately used by websites to optimize the user experience or monitor the site's performance.

Again, Mozilla Firefox takes the blocking approach through its partnership with Disconnect.me, which curates a list of domains known to collect data for fingerprinting and user tracking. The content blocking feature is available in the strict and advanced settings, but at the time of this writing, it is still disabled by default with the standard settings. Figure 7.5 shows the domains blocked from the Firefox web developer tool with the strict settings.

🚫	GET	dpm.demdex.net	id?d_visid_ver=2.5.0&d_fieldgroup=MC&d_rtbd=json&d_ver=2&d_org
🚫	POST	collect.tealiumiq.com	i.gif
200	GET	🔒 sanalytics.autozone.com	id?d_visid_ver=2.5.0&d_fieldgroup=A&mcorgid=0E3334FA53DA8C98(
🚫	GET	dpm.demdex.net	id?d_visid_ver=2.5.0&d_fieldgroup=MC&d_rtbd=json&d_ver=2&d_org
🚫	GET	login-ds.dotomi.com	ws?dtm_cid=62261&dtm_cmagic=eda7ed&dtmc_tms=1&dtm_fid=1018

Figure 7.5   **Requests blocked by `Disconnect.me` in Firefox strict privacy mode**

In contrast, when the standard mode is used, Figure 7.6 shows the list of URL-collecting data, which could have been blocked in strict mode.

The developers of the browser extension uBlock Origin follow the same model, except the list of tracking domains is curated through an open-source community. The tool supports multiple blocklist, the most popular of which is known as the *EasyList*. The AdBlock extension and the Brave browser also consume the EasyList.

The community approach to curating the list of domains or URLs to block sometimes leads to legitimate web security solutions being included in the blocklist, which leads to degraded user experience on the site these solutions protect. Consider a bot management solution used to protect a financial institution login API. If the URL used by the bot management solution to collect data on the client side gets included in the EasyPrivacy or `Disconnect.me` list, this could lead to the user being locked out of their banking account. To solve the problem, users can add an exception to their strict settings, but they may not always realize that the

200	GET	🔒 🚫 td.yieldify.com	main-web-worker.js
200	POST	🔒 🚫 siteintercept.qualtrics....	Targeting.php?Q_ZoneID=ZN_enhmrspG8idZYMd&Q_CLIENTVERSION
302	GET	🔒 🚫 tr.snapchat.com	s?bt=1d53c387&pnid=140&cb=1714363945387&u_scsid=093d21ef-7(
302	GET	🔒 🚫 pixel.tapad.com	push?partner_id=2884&partner_url=https://tr.snapchat.com/cm/p?ran(
204	POST	🔒 🚫 bat.bing.com	t
302	GET	🔒 🚫 pixel.tapad.com	check?partner_id=2884&partner_url=https://tr.snapchat.com/cm/p?rar
200	GET	🔒 🚫 tr.snapchat.com	p?rand=1713914744687&pnid=140&pcid=bb061e23-2012-419a-94e7-
200	GET	🔒 🚫 v2.dc.yieldify.com	i?e=ue&tv=2-3.8.0&aid=101102&yuid=f2d2667c-d9aa-460e-addc-23c
200	GET	🔒 🚫 v2.dc.yieldify.com	i?e=ue&tv=2-3.8.0&aid=101102&yuid=f2d2667c-d9aa-460e-addc-23c
200	POST	🔒 🚫 v2.dc.yieldify.com	p

Figure 7.6   **Requests flagged by `Disconnect.me` in Firefox standard privacy mode**

problem is caused by their strict privacy settings and instead turn to their banker for support. Web security solution vendors must continuously monitor these lists to ensure the custom URLs used for data collection are not blocklist. Once added, getting removed from the list can be challenging. To prevent being blocked, web security vendors must resort to developing complex schemes to obfuscate their URLs. This is a cat-and-mouse game they would rather not play with the privacy vendors and instead concentrate their energy on protecting websites. After all, protecting users from fraud and abuse also helps preserve their privacy.

Uniform Fingerprint   Making all users look the same may appear like a complex proposition since, at first glance, it requires cross-vendor coordination. However, this is happening at some level due to the browser software market consolidation and a few vendors' overwhelming dominance.

Let's first take a look at the browser software market. Figure 7.7 shows the browser market share for 2023 (Statcounter, 2024). Note the dominance of Google Chrome, with close to 64% of the market share, followed far behind by Safari, with close to 20% of the market share.

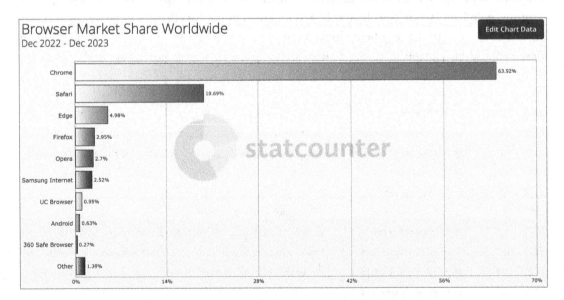

Figure 7.7   The global browser software market share in 2023

Now, if the dominance of Google Chrome was not enough, we've also observed a consolidation with the browser engines over the last 10 years. Indeed, in the past, each browser vendor had their own engine, but a lot of them are now using Chromium open source as the foundation of their product—for example:

- Opera switched from the Presto engine to Chromium and the Blink engine in 2013.
- Tencent's QQ browser, popular in China, adopted Chromium in 2015.
- Microsoft Edge switched from the EdgeHTML engine (a branch from Internet Explorer's Trident) to the Chromium Blink engine in 2019.

Emerging browser vendors in various parts of the world predominantly use Chromium open source as the basis for their software. This is true, for example, for the Russian Yandex or the Korean Naver Whale browser.

Regarding hardware, the technology giants Samsung and Apple owned between them 39.5% of the smartphone market share in 2023 (International Data Corporation, 2024). According to the forum AppleInsider, Lenovo, HP, Dell, and Apple cover more than 74% of the desktop and laptop market (AppleInsider, 2023).

The way the data points used for fingerprinting are generated is, to some extent, a function of the software and the hardware it's running on. However, because of the consolidation in the browser software market and the dominance of some tech giants, the uniqueness of a fingerprint is continuously decreasing, and the population that each fingerprint identifies is growing.

Beyond the software and hardware market consolidation, some data points' entropy, like the `User-Agent`, has been reduced. The `User-Agent` was once a good differentiator for fingerprinting. One could see not only the browser name and its version but also the OS and its version installed, the type of platform, and, for mobile devices, its model and the manufacturer. However, all that changed with Google Chrome's plan to reduce the `User-Agent` HTTP header value as part of the broader Privacy Sandbox project. The transition took several carefully orchestrated steps to ensure no significant adverse effect on website usability and was completed in 2023. Here's what changed:

- The browser minor version is no longer available and now shows a series of zeros, for example, Chrome/120.0.0.0.
- The OS version number for Windows and Android is set to the static value of 10.
- The mobile device model is now obfuscated and set to the static value K.

Here's an example of `User-Agent` values for a desktop and mobile device before and after the reduction, with the reduced values highlighted in bold:

Desktops

Old User-Agent	Mozilla/5.0 (Windows NT **6.3**; Win64; x64) AppleWebKit/537.36 (KHTML, like Gecko) Chrome/93.**0.1234.56** Safari/537.36
New User-Agent	Mozilla/5.0 (Windows NT **10**; Win64; x64) AppleWebKit/537.36 (KHTML, like Gecko) Chrome/93.**0.0.0** Safari/537.36

Mobile Devices

Old User-Agent	Mozilla/5.0 (Linux; Android **9; SM-A205U**) AppleWebKit/537.36 (KHTML, like Gecko) Chrome/93.**0.1234.56** Mobile Safari/537.36
New User-Agent	Mozilla/5.0 (Linux; Android **10; K**) AppleWebKit/537.36 (KHTML, like Gecko) Chrome/93.**0.0.0** Safari/537.36

The following table shows that Google offers an alternative to collect some of the obfuscated data through the client hint interface (`Sec-CH-UA` headers). The information is sent only on secure connections over TLS. Once the secure connection is established, the client will send the reduced `User-Agent` and equivalent information in a set of client hint headers.

Header Name	Example Value
Sec-CH-UA	"Not_A Brand";v="8", "Chromium";v="120", "Google Chrome";v="120"
Sec-CH-UA-Mobile	?0
Sec-CH-UA-Platform	"Windows"

If the server wants additional information, it must ask for it using the `Accept-CH` header. The following table provides examples of additional headers for which the server can ask the client. Whether the browser will send the information may depend on browser settings.

Accept-CH Value	Sec-CH-UA Header Value
Sec-CH-UA-Platform-Version	10.0.0
Sec-CH-UA-Model	Pixel 2
Sec-CH-UA-Full-Version-List	" Not A;Brand";v="99.0.0.0", "Chromium";v="98.0.4750.0", "Google Chrome";v="98.0.4750.0"

At this time, the `Sec-CH-UA` header and the reduced User-Agent are available only on browsers based on Chromium. Safari and Firefox have not yet adopted the new client hint headers. Firefox did, however, implement the reduced `User-Agent`.

Data Randomization   The preceding phenomenon contributes to the increasing difficulty of crafting a fingerprint that uniquely identifies a user, but this is not the only factor. Mozilla, Apple, Google, Brave, and other members of the W3C organization are continuously working on adding more restrictions to reduce the usefulness of some APIs traditionally used for fingerprinting. The following are two examples of data points that were previously strong contributors to a fingerprinting recipe that have recently lost a lot of their value:

- Canvas fingerprinting
- TLS fingerprinting

The Canvas API is designed to draw graphics using JavaScript and HTML. The fingerprinting technique exploits the HTML5 canvas element. It relies on variations in how canvas images are rendered on different web browsers and platforms to create a personalized digital fingerprint of a user's browser. The fingerprint value is a function of the screen resolution, fonts installed, GPU capabilities, and the web browser engine. Brave Software started randomizing the value a few years ago using a technique they call *farbling*, which consists of making the fingerprint unique to a session, thus preventing fingerprinting over time and across websites (Brave, 2020).

So far, I've mainly discussed active fingerprinting techniques based on JavaScript data collection, but fingerprints usually also include passive fingerprint data points. Passive fingerprinting data points consist of information collected at the protocol level (TCP, HTTP, and TLS). TLS fingerprinting has been used extensively and successfully over the years to help differentiate between botnet and legitimate browsers. TLS fingerprinting relies on the settings the client advertises when the secure TLS connection is established with the web server. This includes the protocols, ciphers, and extensions the client supports, among other parameters. The TLS fingerprint reflects the settings from the TLS library the client uses. Mozilla, Microsoft, Apple, and Google each use different TLS libraries. Purpose-built botnets may also use different TLS libraries that come with their favorite programming language. Each library is optimized differently and presents different settings (ciphers and extension supported), which results in a different TLS fingerprint. Web security products use the TLS fingerprint to validate that a client that advertises, say, Google Chrome in the `User-Agent`, is indeed Google Chrome by cross-checking its TLS fingerprint. Now, Google has always been concerned with websites or web security vendors leveraging the TLS fingerprint too much, which could limit their ability to extend the TLS protocol in the future. To limit the usage of the TLS fingerprint, Google implemented the GREASE protocol (Generate Random Extensions And Sustain Extensibility). This technique added entropy to the list of extensions, making each TLS hash appear unique. Some web security vendors reacted by implementing an antidote and de-GREASEd the TLS extensions. This worked for a few years until Google went further by randomizing the order of the list of extensions. Web security vendors reacted by sorting the list of TLS extensions. TLS fingerprinting is still useful today, but sorting the extensions makes the resulting fingerprint more uniform and has lost some of its original value.

Google Privacy Budget   Google has talked about the privacy budget for a few years. At the high level, it consists of limiting the amount of data one site may be able to collect from the client. The details on how Google plans to implement the privacy budget are scarce, but web security vendors are closely monitoring this proposal. Based on the information available at the time of this writing (2024), it seems like the full implementation of the privacy budget will be challenging. Although there is a need to bring some sanity to how much data is collected, one must look at the reality of the set of products integrated into a website.

- In an ideal world, a site would require only a single security vendor to protect the site with a single JavaScript collecting data to be used by the detection engine. In reality, several products from the same or different vendors may protect the site for different use cases. Each product may have its own JavaScript collecting data.
- The website owner may collect data for various purposes, including passwordless support or an in-house fraud prevention product.
- Most websites are integrated with marketing and advertisement solutions that may also do their own data collection.

This could result in at least half a dozen JavaScript running on a web page collecting data for different purposes. The website owner pays for these services, so it's fair to assume that they consider them essential for the good operation of their business. Now, in an ideal world, we'd have a single universal and trusted JavaScript that collects and distributes the data to service providers that need it. But in reality, this cannot be done since it would require close collaboration between companies that don't have the same needs and may be direct competitors. Or maybe the data collection could be done through a trusted third-party data broker. Since a universal data collection model does not exist today, how can one decide which service should get the budget to collect the essential data? Who decides what to prioritize? Should it be centered around the business needs and use the budget for marketing/advertising to increase revenue, or should the budget be assigned to security solutions that protect the website against fraud and abuse?

The Impact on Web Security   All these initiatives have a valid purpose to preserve user privacy. The purpose of this discussion is not to negate the need for privacy but to acknowledge the effect these changes have on the efficiency of web security products. Features limiting data collection or fidelity represent a challenge for web security vendors that require it to feed their detection models or research new ones. They need to stay informed on the evolution of standards and feature updates in various web browsers to anticipate the changes and adapt their detection methods. This takes away some of the focus from the ever-increasing threats and can lead to a temporary degradation of detection accuracy, which can have damaging effects on the protected website, impact their revenue, or affect their users' security.

The Private Access Token Approach

Private Access Tokens (PAT) is an Internet Engineering Task Force (IETF) standard proposal aiming to provide an alternative to help identify HTTP requests from legitimate devices and people without compromising their identity or personal information. Apple announced support for PAT in 2022 with the release of iOS 16 and macOS Ventura. Google, Microsoft, and Mozilla are also participating in defining the IETF standard for PAT and are working on updating their Internet browser products to support the initiative. CDN vendors like Cloudflare and Fastly have also announced support for the protocol. The PAT concept stems from the earlier Privacy Pass standard initially developed by hCaptcha and Cloudflare. The original goal of the Privacy Pass initiative was twofold:

- To reduce the amount of data collected on the client side to make the browsing experience more private.
- To reduce the number of times a legitimate user is challenged with a CAPTCHA when incorrectly identified as a bot. Such events may be more common with less accurate detection methods. Both PAT and Privacy Pass work more or less the same way, except the Privacy Pass seems to allow several tokens to be issued..

The High-Level Architecture

The PAT architecture includes four different key roles that work together to validate a user request and preserve user privacy.

Client   The client represents the software, typically a web browser, used to request content from a web server, also identified as the origin in the PAT protocol. When instructed by the origin, the client requests tokens from the issuer through the mediator and redeems them with the origin to access a resource.

Mediator   The mediator's role is to assess the validity of the client. The standard keeps the methodology the mediator should use to assess the client very open. Some companies, like Apple, may use a method that authenticates the user and identifies the device, and bot management products may assert that the device is legitimate (not a bot). Fraud detection solutions may verify the user does not behave abnormally.

Issuer   This entity generates and issues the PAT to the client on behalf of the origin. The issuer knows about the origin but should also anonymize the origin to the mediator. The client's identity is obfuscated before the mediator forwards the request to the issuer. The data the client may have shared with the mediator is not shared with the issuer. CDN vendors are well-positioned to play the role of issuers.

Origin   The website, application, or API that receives the request from the client. The origin will initiate the token request to the client to access a protected resource. It is also responsible for redeeming the tokens. To preserve privacy, the origin doesn't have direct visibility of the data the client may have shared with the mediator.

The PAT Workflow

Figure 7.8 shows the interaction between the different entities/roles when the user has no tokens to redeem.

1. The client requests access to a protected web resource, for example, an attempt to log in.
2. If the type of client and resource qualifies for access through PAT, it will return a set of headers to the client requesting one. The origin will also direct the client to a mediator if no tokens are left.
3. If the client has no token, it will request one from the issuer through the mediator.

4. The mediator will authenticate the client. The authentication method will vary depending on the provider: some may validate that the request comes from a legitimate user, not a bot. In contrast, others will authenticate the device and its owner. If the authentication or validation process is successful, the mediator will forward the client's anonymized request to the mediator to issue tokens.

5. The issuer will evaluate the origin policy and issue tokens. The number of tokens issued will depend on the policy. Note that the Privacy Pass standard allows for issuing multiple tokens, but the PAT standard suggests only issuing a single token every time.

6. The mediator forwards the token to the client.

7. The client redeems the token with the origin to access the web resource. The origin web server is responsible for verifying that the token is valid and that it has not already been redeemed.

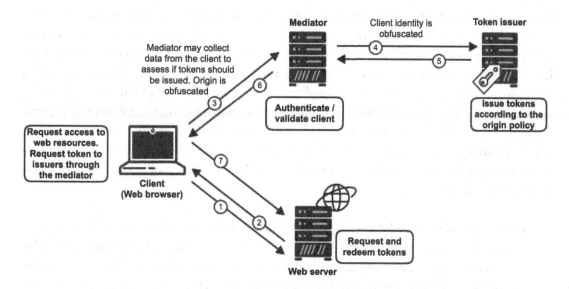

Figure 7.8 The PAT workflow when the user has no tokens to redeem

Figure 7.9 shows the workflow when several tokens were issued to the client. On subsequent requests, steps 1 and 2 are identical. If the client has some PAT left in its local storage, it will redeem one to access the resource without contacting the mediator/issuer. The origin web server will go through the steps described to validate the token.

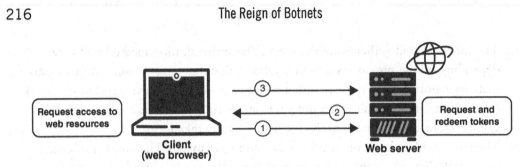

Figure 7.9   The PAT workflow when the user has tokens to redeem

PAT Adoption

PAT can reduce data collection, and the positive effect on user privacy is a plus. However, at the time of this writing, outside the Apple implementation, adoption of the new protocol by other vendors is slow. Web security vendors typically define their roadmap based on customer requirements, and so far, despite occasional inquiries, the demand for PAT support has been anecdotal. Website owners continuously demand more accurate detection from web security vendors. However, the need for privacy mostly comes in the context of compliance with local laws like GDPR in Europe, which can be achieved by abiding by specific standards and going through a certification process. New technologies or standards can take a while to see meaningful adoption. The fact that guidelines on adopting PAT are hard to find is not helping. It seems the only way to get some guidance on adopting the new protocol is to talk to the author of the standard directly, which is not scalable. As an influencer in technology adoption for my company, here are a few issues that remain unanswered and prevent me from making a strong case to adopt the standard:

- **PAT is a new standard:** Like with any new technology, additional revisions may be required to mature the concept. Major internet companies have already announced their participation in some of the key roles of the PAT ecosystem, but considering the significant paradigm shift the standard introduces for protecting web resources, it may take some time before we see a meaningful adoption.
- **Tracking redeemed tokens:** Bot operators have mastered the art of replaying cookies or fingerprints used by web security products. Assuming bot operators find a way to harvest enough private access tokens, they represent another opportunity to leverage the "replay strategy". Website owners must track the token they have already redeemed to prevent an easy exploit of the PAT standard and defeat their defense. Tracking

redeemed tokens requires a responsive infrastructure. The standard offers little guidance on the best way to implement this function, which may lead to inadequate implementation.

- **Limited built-in protection:** To prevent token abuses, the standard recommends using rate limiting, linking the token to an IP subnet, and limiting the token time to live (TTL). Bot operators know how to work around rate limiting. As mentioned in Chapter 6, it's very common for attackers to load balance their attack traffic through thousands of unique IP addresses. If the token usage is limited to a subnet, legitimate users who leverage proxies to preserve their anonymity may run into issues redeeming their tokens if their IP address subnet is inconsistent throughout the session. Limiting the token TTL may not be practical in some workflows.

- **Impact on page load time:** When users have no token to redeem, they must go through the validation process to be issued some. This process requires communication with several entities and takes time. The token redeeming process is lightweight but may also incur a delay in processing the request. Most website administrator of major brands carefully monitor their page load time. In extreme cases, an increment of 10ms in page load time may be unacceptable. The impact of performance worldwide depends on the distance between the client and the nearest mediator/issuer to get tokens or the origin to redeem tokens. The potential impact on page load time is not trivial.

- **Blind trust in the mediators' decision:** When a legitimate client is denied access, the web security team must investigate the problem, which requires access to the data that led to the decision not to issue the token. Similarly, investigating the cause of the false negative will be almost impossible if a bot operator can get tokens. The PAT protocol doesn't allow the web security team responsible for the origin to access any useful information to help with their investigation.

Based on the above caveats, using PAT may not be practical for some use cases. Assuming PAT only allows a single token to be issued per request, its usage to protect product pages of an e-commerce site is out of the question since it would significantly increase the latency to serve the content. For more e-commerce sites, any latency increase beyond 50ms is considered excessive. The privacy pass standard that suggests issuing multiple tokens may be more acceptable in this case. PAT seems more appropriate for protecting transaction endpoints like log-in or account creation. But will the web security team blindly trust the decision of the mediator? For web security teams who wish to protect their entire website content and not just specific endpoints, having inconsistency in the protection method doesn't make sense since it would break the privacy aspect, which is PAT's main value proposition.

Summary

There is a need for more constructive collaboration between web security and privacy practitioners. Both parties have noble and legitimate goals to protect the user's life online, prevent fraud, and protect their privacy. All these are very important goals. Web security products aim to protect major websites that generate, in some cases, millions of dollars in revenue per day. Because of inadequate collaboration, privacy products become usable only to elite power users who understand the Web well enough to use them efficiently and adjust their settings when they become too aggressive for a website. The rest are just left guessing and must choose between privacy and the quality of their online experience.

Better collaboration between both worlds would help develop better compromises to ensure user privacy and safety online and reduce the constant friction that web attackers take advantage of and Internet users become the ultimate victims of.

References

AppleInsider (2023) *Duelling Analysts Offer Differing Takes on Mac in the PC Market.* Available at: `https://forums.appleinsider.com/discussion/233895/duelling-analysts-offer-differing-takes-on-mac-in-the-pc-market` (Accessed 11 April, 2024).

BBC (2013) *Adobe Hack: At Least 38 Million Accounts Breached.* BBC News. Available at: `www.bbc.com/news/technology-24740873` (Accessed 12 March, 2024).

Brave (2020) *Fingerprinting Defenses 2.0.* Available at: `https://brave.com/privacy-updates/4-fingerprinting-defenses-2.0` (Accessed 11 April, 2024).

DataDome (2022) *How TLS Fingerprinting Reinforces DataDome's Protection.* Available at: `https://datadome.co/engineering/how-tls-fingerprinting-reinforces-datadomes-protection` (Accessed 26 March, 2024).

Chromium Projects (2024) *User-Agent Reduction.* Available at: `www.chromium.org/updates/ua-reduction` (Accessed 26 March, 2024).

Cubrilovic, N. (2009) *RockYou Hack: From Bad to Worse.* TechCrunch. Available at: `https://techcrunch.com/2009/12/14/rockyou-hack-security-myspace-facebook-passwords` (Accessed 12 March, 2024).

Guardian (2021) *PlayStation Network Hackers Access Data of 77 Million Users.* Available at: `www.theguardian.com/technology/2011/apr/26/playstation-network-hackers-data` (Accessed 12 March, 2024).

International Data Corporation (2024) *Apple Grabs the Top Spot in the Smartphone Market in 2023 along with Record High Market Share Despite the Overall Market Dropping 3.2%, According to IDC Tracker.* Available at: `www.idc.com/getdoc.jsp?containerId=prUS51776424` (Accessed 11 April, 2024).

Luck Stork (2022) *Behavioral Biometrics: Raising the Bar for Attackers*. Available at `https://securityboulevard.com/2022/01/behavioral-biometrics-raising-the-bar-for-attackers`.

McLean, R. (2019) *A Hacker Gained Access to 100 Million Capital One Credit Card Applications and Accounts*. CNN Business. Available at: `www.cnn.com/2019/07/29/business/capital-one-data-breach/index.html` (Accessed 12 March, 2024).

MDN Web Docs (2024a) *Fetch Metadata Request Header*. Available at: `https://developer.mozilla.org/en-US/docs/Glossary/Fetch_metadata_request_header` (Accessed 15 March, 2024).

MDN Web Docs (2024b) *Sec-CH-AU*. Available at: `https://developer.mozilla.org/en-US/docs/Web/HTTP/Headers/Sec-CH-UA` (Accessed 28 March, 2024).

MDN Web Docs (2024c) *Sec-CH-AU-Mobile*. Available at: `https://developer.mozilla.org/en-US/docs/Web/HTTP/Headers/Sec-CH-UA-Mobile` (Accessed 28 March, 2024).

MDN Web Docs (2024d) *Sec-CH-AU-Platform*. Available at: `https://developer.mozilla.org/en-US/docs/Web/HTTP/Headers/Sec-CH-UA-Platform` (Accessed 28 March, 2024).

Norton (2018) *New Report Says Zynga Breach in September Affected 172 Million Accounts*. Available at: `https://us.norton.com/blog/emerging-threats/new-report-says-zynga-breach-in-september-affected-172-million-a` (Accessed 12 March, 2024).

OWASP (2021) *OWASP 2021 Top Ten – Identification and Authentication Failures*. Available at: `https://owasp.org/Top10/A07_2021-Identification_and_Authentication_Failures` (Accessed 12 March, 2024).

Perlroth, P. (2017) *All 3 Billion Yahoo Accounts Were Affected by 2013 Attack*. New York Times. Available at: `www.nytimes.com/2017/10/03/technology/yahoo-hack-3-billion-users.html` (Accessed 12 March, 2024).

ProWebScraper (2023) *Top 10 Captcha Solving Services Compared*. Available at: `https://prowebscraper.com/blog/top-10-captcha-solving-services-compared` (Accessed 15 March, 2024).

Reals, T. and Picchi, A. (2018) *Quora Data Breach Exposes 100 Million Users' Personal Info*. CBS News. Available at: `www.cbsnews.com/news/quora-data-breach-exposes-100-million-users-personal-info-2018-12-04` (Accessed 12 March, 2024).

Shaban, H. (2018) *Under Armour Announces Data Breach Affecting 150 Million MyFitnessPal App Accounts*. Washington Post. Available at: `www.washingtonpost.com/news/the-switch/wp/2018/03/29/under-armour-announces-data-breach-`

affecting-150-million-myfitnesspal-app-accounts (Accessed 12 March, 2024).

Shuster, Elad (2017) *Passive Fingerprinting of HTTPv2 Clients*. Available at: `www.blackhat.com/docs/eu-17/materials/eu-17-Shuster-Passive-Fingerprinting-Of-HTTP2-Clients.pdf` (Accessed 26 March, 2024).

Statcounter (2024) *Browser Market Share Worldwide*. Available at: `https://gs.statcounter.com/browser-market-share#monthly-202212-202312-bar` (Accessed 11 April, 2024).

Usenix.org conference (2020) *An Object Detection Based Solver for Google's Image reCAPTCHA v2*. Available at: `www.usenix.org/conference/raid2020/presentation/hossen` (Accessed 30 March, 2024).

Vijayan, J. (2020) *Twitter Breach Highlights Privileged Account Security*. Dark Reading. Available at: `www.darkreading.com/attacks-breaches/twitter-breach-highlights-privileged-account-security-issue` (Accessed 12 March, 2024).

Wikipedia (2024a) *Email Address*. Available at: `https://en.wikipedia.org/wiki/Email_address` (Accessed 25 March, 2024).

Wikipedia (2024b) *robots.txt*. Available at: `https://en.wikipedia.org/wiki/Robots.txt` (Accessed 25 March, 2024).

Winder, D. (2020) *Zoom Gets Stuffed: Here's How Hackers Got Ahold of 500,000 Passwords*. Forbes. Available at: `www.forbes.com/sites/daveywinder/2020/04/28/zoom-gets-stuffed-heres-how-hackers-got-hold-of-500000-passwords/?sh=4c86f335cdc4` (Accessed 12 March, 2024).

World Wide Web Consortium (2024) *Mitigating Browser Fingerprinting in Web Specifications*. Available at: `https://w3c.github.io/fingerprinting-guidance` (Accessed 11 April, 2024).

Index